DOMINE SALVAM FAC REGINAM NOSTRAM VICTORIAM PRIMA

CITIES

This edition published by Parragon Books Ltd 2014

Parragon
Chartist House
15–17 Trim Street
Bath BA1 1HA, UK
www.parragon.com

Original edition: Natalie Blei/Petra Hammerschmidt, Alex Media, Gierstorfer, Ferstl & Reichert GbR, Augsburg.

Concept: Michaela Mohr/Gerhard Klimmer/Michael Kraft
Illustrations: Evgen Lutskevych
Picture research: Michaela Mohr/Stephan Kraft

Cover design by five-twentyfive.com

English edition produced by APE Int'l, Richmond, VA
Translation from the German: Linda Marianiello
Editing of English edition: Dr. Maureen Basedow and Tammi Reichel for APE Int'l

ISBN 978-1-4723-3205-9
Printed in China

CITIES

Explore 100 Fascinating and Iconic Cities

FALKO BRENNER

Parragon

Bath • New York • Cologne • Melbourne • Delhi
Hong Kong • Shenzhen • Singapore • Amsterdam

Contents

Cities are arranged within each continent according to their latitude, from north to south.

Introduction

In the pages of this book readers will find more than just the great cities of the world. Naturally, New York, Paris, London, Moscow, Tokyo and many other cities of global importance are presented and put into proper perspective. But how familiar are you with St. Louis, Quito or Algiers? Their names may be familiar, but when it comes to the finer details, many people simply shrug their shoulders. These cities also have an allure, and continue to play a leading role in the history of their respective countries. Did you know that St. Louis was the main point of departure for the settlement of the Wild West, or that the centuries-long search for the legendary riches of El Dorado was launched from Quito?

Yet many of the cities described in this book are true global cities: Rome must be counted as the first, indisputable prototype. At one time, practically the entire known world (from a European perspective) was ruled from Rome – and the lasting impact of the Roman Empire has been felt around the world.

But what is it that distinguishes a global city from a metropolis? In general, global cities are considered to have major, worldwide significance. The word metropolis, by contrast, often used synonymously, applies to regional centres of political, commercial, cultural and social importance.

In terms of economics, global cities are first and foremost the centres of international finance and banking. The three most important economic regions have each produced a leading metropolis: Tokyo, London and New York. Hong Kong, Shanghai, Sydney, Milan, Madrid and Chicago are complementary financial hubs that also have international significance.

Trying to define major international cultural centres is a far more difficult enterprise. Cultural metropolises are places where the universal language of art is promulgated. Cultural meccas attract artists and creativity, are home to important institutions such as museums and theatres, and are leaders in cultural innovation. There is a simple litmus test for all of these factors: a global city is one whose name is immediately recognizable to almost everyone.

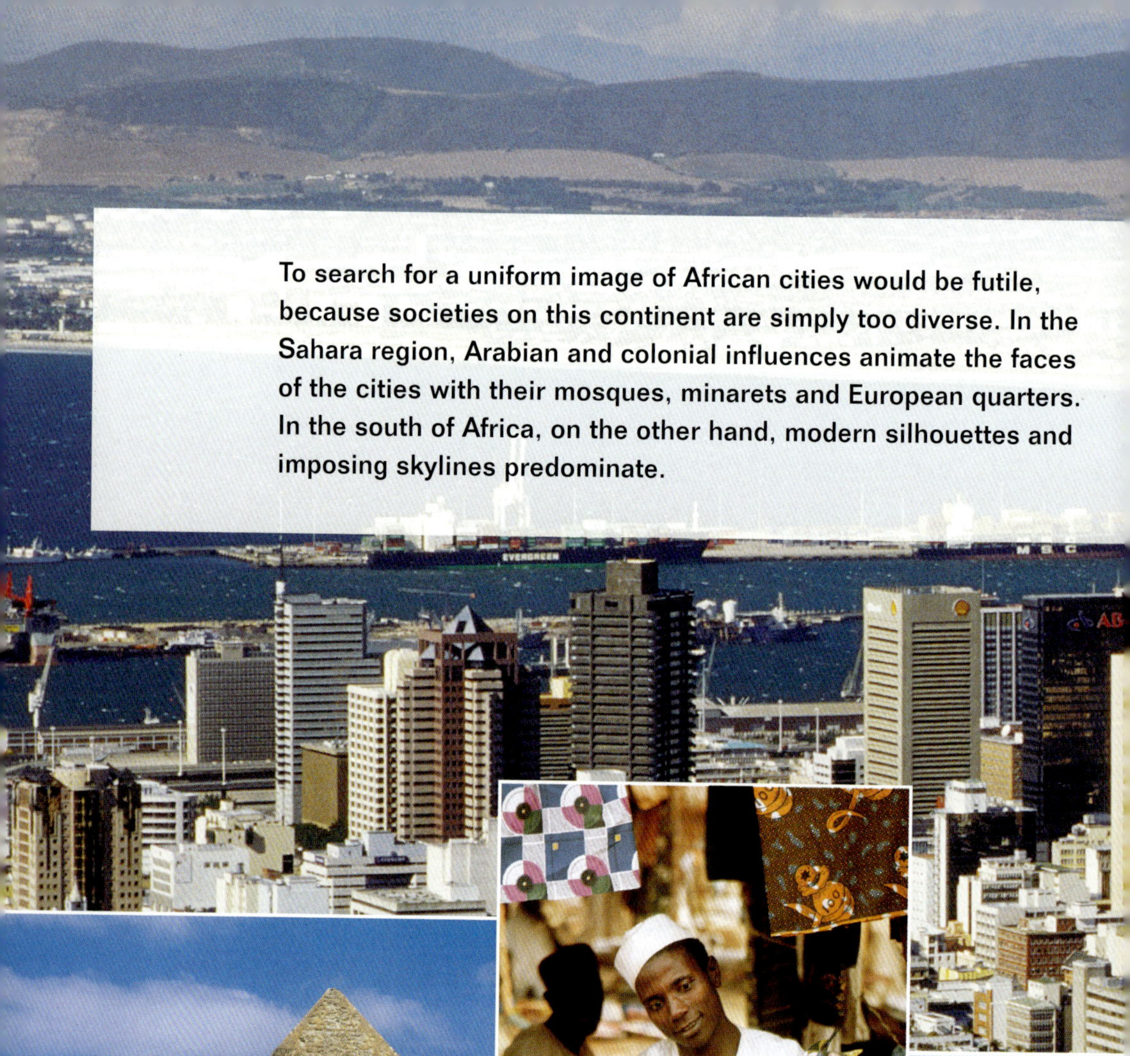

To search for a uniform image of African cities would be futile, because societies on this continent are simply too diverse. In the Sahara region, Arabian and colonial influences animate the faces of the cities with their mosques, minarets and European quarters. In the south of Africa, on the other hand, modern silhouettes and imposing skylines predominate.

AFRICA

ALGERIA

Algiers

A WONDROUS MIXTURE OF FRENCH ELEGANCE, MOORISH PRIDE AND AFRICAN CASUALNESS PREVAILS, TOGETHER WITH THE GRIME OF A BUSTLING HARBOUR METROPOLIS – ALL OF THAT IS ALGIERS.

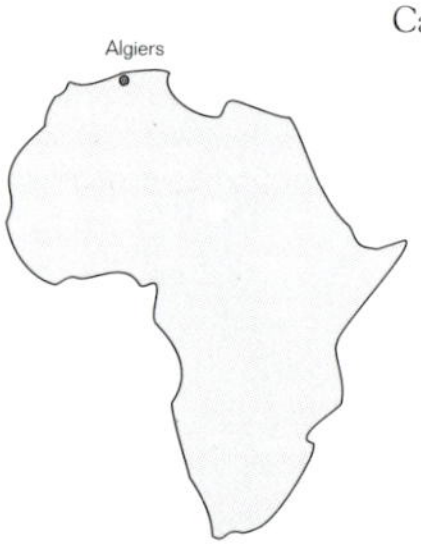

Algiers is located on a series of terraces that clamber up the hillsides from the sea, towered over by the ramparts of the medieval Casbah, the Old City. Full of flowers, beautiful villas and luxuriously green gardens, the geography of this Mediterranean city is best understood as a huge triangle. The seaside European quarter is its wide base, which narrows as it ascends the close winding lanes to the Moorish quarter, eventually coming to a point at the city's old fortress high above.

Island of the Gull. The first settlers on the coast of Algiers, aside from the native Berber tribes, arrived around 400 BCE. These were Carthaginian merchants in search of a convenient harbour in the western Mediterranean. During the Punic Wars between Rome and Carthage, this settlement, known as Ikosim ("Island of the Gulls") fell to the Roman Empire. The most significant moment in the city's history came with the conquest of the Late Roman Numidian Kingdom by the Muslim Arabs around 700 CE. The official founding of the city did not take place until 935 CE, when the Berber tribes (by then converted to Islam) named their harbour Al-Jazir ("White Island"). The city extended no further than what is today the Old City of Algiers, the Casbah.

Right: Algiers has the second-largest Mediterranean harbour in Africa.

Below: In the Casbah. Algiers' Old City was declared a UNESCO World Heritage Site in 1992.

A bastion for pirates. After the Moors were driven out of Spain in the fifteenth century, Algiers was the launching point for numerous military expeditions to the Iberian Peninsula, but the Moors were never able to regain control of Spain. In fact, the Catholic Spaniards conquered Algiers instead, taking control of the city in 1509. The city suffered under Christian oppression for ten years before Ottoman Khaireddin Barbarossa recaptured Algiers in 1519 in a daring naval assault. The city and country would henceforth be part of the Ottoman Empire.

In the following years, Khaireddin Barbarossa built Algiers into one of the most powerful bastions on the Mediterranean. Up until his death in 1546, he used it as the base for countless raids along the Mediterranean coast, besieging Spanish as well as Moorish cities, and bringing all of Algeria under his control. In Europe, the name Algiers became synonymous with a pirate's den. In France, however, this was not the case. The French had long been in league with Khaireddin.

From allies to conquerors. Although European nations tried again and again to recapture the city, all attempts failed miserably. Then, in the nineteenth century, the French gave it another try. Their conquest of Algeria began with the landing in 1830 at Sidi Fredj near Algiers. The final subjugation took over fifty years. After Algiers became a French colony in 1882, a huge influx of French companies and workers arrived and the city grew exponentially. The European residential areas built at that time still shape the cityscape of contemporary Algiers, particularly at the base of the "triangle" along the 2-km-long boulevard along the harbour.

In the Casbah. The interplay between Berber pride, Ottoman organization and French sophistication lends Algiers a special charm. Visitors climbing from the French-influenced harbour district up to the Old City of the Casbah experience the city's different cultures as well as its history. Built around 1500 CE and declared a UNESCO World Heritage Site in 1992, the Casbah is the old citadel of the Ottoman governors of Algiers. The higher one climbs, the more narrow and twisting the lanes become. The houses are crammed so close together that they nearly touch, and balconies are connected to one another above street level. Several important mosques are located in the midst of this confusion, including the Grand Mosque, the New Mosque and the Ketchaoua Mosque. All are renowned for their antiquity and architectural diversity.

FACTS

*** Population of Algiers:** *circa* 1.52 million

*** Population of the metropolitan area:** *circa* 2.6 million

*** Places of interest:** Army Museum, Bardo Museum, New Mosque, Ketchaoua Mosque, Casbah, Grand Mosque, Citadel

FAMOUS CITIZENS

*** Albert Camus** (1913–1960), French author (1957 Nobel Prize)

*** Alain Savary** (1918–1988), French Minister of Education

*** Jacques Derrida** (1930–2004), philosopher

*** Jacques Attali** (b. 1943), French economist, political advisor

*** Hassiba Boulmerka** (b. 1968), Olympic and World Champion runner

TUNISIA

Tunis

TUNIS IS ONE OF THE MOST ANCIENT CITIES ON THE MEDITERRANEAN, IN EXISTENCE LONG BEFORE THE PHOENICIANS' ARRIVAL IN THE NINTH CENTURY. IT WAS NORTH AFRICA'S MOST IMPORTANT CITY PRIOR TO THE FOUNDING OF CARTHAGE, ARCH-RIVAL OF ROME.

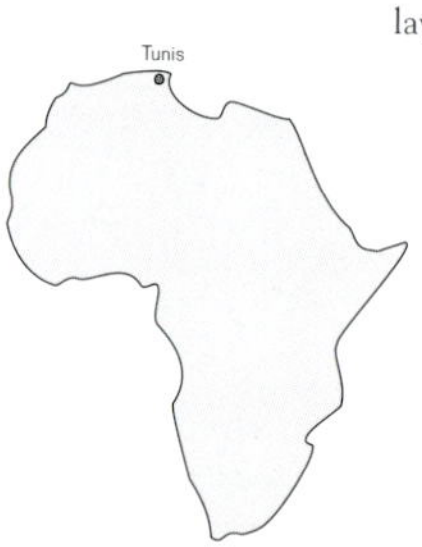

The Romans rebuilt Carthage after the Punic Wars (third and second centuries BCE), and for many centuries the nearby town of Tunis lay in its shadow. Tunis only began to come into its own after the final destruction of Carthage in the seventh century. Though it was often beleaguered and besieged by Algerian pirates, Tunis remained independent until well into the sixteenth century, when it was finally conquered by the Ottoman Turks. Like its neighbour, Algeria, Tunisia fell under French colonial rule in the nineteenth century and did not regain its independence until 1956.

The centre of the North African world. Tunis was, and remains, a melting pot of North African and Islamic cultures. Berbers, Arabs, Turks and Moors all lived and worked together in the ancient city on the Mediterranean. Christian mariners and Jewish merchants have also left traces of their legacy in its streets. There are perhaps 700 monuments – including palaces, mosques, mausoleums, dwellings and markets – that attest to the city's magnificent and glorious past. During its heyday from the twelfth to the sixteenth centuries, it was one of the greatest and richest Islamic cities in the world, the seat of the powerful Hafsid caliphs and the centre of North African culture.

Ez-Zitouna, or the Olive Tree Mosque, stands in the heart of the Old City.

FACTS

* **Population of Tunis:** *circa* 728,400
* **Population of the metropolitan area:** *circa* 2 million
* **Places of interest:** Dougga, Ez-Zitouna Mosque, Hammamet, Carthage, National Museum in Bardo, Medina, Sidi Youssef Mosque, St. Vincent de Paul, Tourbet el-Bey Mausoleum

FAMOUS CITIZENS

* **Loris Azzaro** (1933–2003), Italian fashion designer and parfumier
* **Roberto Blanco** (b. 1937), German pop singer
* **Claudia Cardinale** (b. 1938), Italian actress
* **Azzedine Alaia** (b. 1940), fashion designer

The Medina. The Medina is the heart of old Tunis, and in 1981 it was added to the UNESCO World Heritage List. Souks, open-air bazaars filling streets and alleyways, are everywhere to be seen. Just about everything is for sale in the Medina. At the Souk el-Berka, Arab traders once sold slaves. Winding lanes lead to the centre of the Old City, where the Ez-Zitouna Mosque, built in 732 CE, is located. Also known as the Olive Tree Mosque, it serves as the symbol of the city. Here the faithful gather in prayer halls whose columns were salvaged from nearby Ancient Carthage.

Almost like Paris. The "other" Tunis came into being during the period of French rule. The modern portions of the city are a mixture of Middle Eastern tradition, French flair, modern skyscrapers and grimy industrial districts. Slums have sprung up on the outskirts of the city. Habib Bourguiba Avenue dominates the distinctly French centre of Tunis, the Ville Nouvelle. Based on the Champs-Elysées in Paris, the broad thoroughfare is lined with luxury hotels and office blocks. Open-air cafés and pastry shops contribute to the European atmosphere. The main attraction is the Cathedral of St. Vincent de Paul.

The Bardo Museum is yet another must-see for visitors to Tunis. It is located in the erstwhile Bardo Palace, built in the fifteenth century. Once the official residence of the Hussein Beys, it is today the meeting place of the Tunisian Parliament. The museum is only about 4 km west of the city centre, easily accessible by taxi or tram.

Ancient Carthage. A visit to the excavation site of Ancient Carthage should be part of every visit to the Tunisian metropolis. Located just 15 km outside the city in what is now a posh residential district bearing the ancient name, its stunning ruins, mostly dating to the Roman period, should not be missed. Byrsa Hill provides the best view of the ancient city. The Roman villas above the amphitheatre provide a spectacular panorama of the Gulf of Tunis. The seaside baths of the Roman emperor Antonius Pius (131–161 CE), second in size only to the Baths of Caracalla in Rome, are particularly well preserved.

Centre: The Cathedral of St. Vincent de Paul defines the centre of European Tunis.

Bottom: A visit to the ruins of Carthage is a must for visitors to Tunis. These are the thermal springs of Emperor Antonius.

MOROCCO

Casablanca

HISTORY WAS MADE IN CASABLANCA. IN 1943, AT THE HEIGHT OF WORLD WAR II, BRITISH PRIME MINISTER WINSTON CHURCHILL AND US PRESIDENT FRANKLIN D. ROOSEVELT MET HERE TO AGREE ON A PLAN FOR JOINT MILITARY OPERATIONS AGAINST THE THIRD REICH.

Mention Casablanca in a Western country, and most likely the film starring Humphrey Bogart and Ingrid Bergman is what first comes to mind. Casablanca, however, is much more than just a backdrop for the 1942 Hollywood classic. Contemporary Casablanca is a modern metropolis on the Atlantic at the western end of Islamic North Africa. It is the largest city in Morocco and its business and economic centre, if not its political capital (that title belongs to Rabat), as well as home to the busiest port in North Africa. Decades of French colonial rule in the twentieth century left behind a number of buildings and a lingering atmosphere of mystery and intrigue in its streets.

Archaeological traces. Settlement in this region goes way back in time. About 11 km outside of the city, in the quarry of Sidi Ahmed er Rahman, archaeologists and palaeontologists discovered fossil skull fragments from the Palaeolithic Age dating to before 8000 BCE. The first permanent settlements, however, came about much later, beginning only in the eighth century with the Berber city of Anfa.

The city of Anfa. The city's growth began with the conquest of Anfa by the Muslim Almohads in the twelfth century. The new Anfa developed into an important trade centre and, more importantly, a base

Right: A view over the rooftops of Casablanca.

Below: The illuminated Mosque of Hassan II.

for pirates raiding the Iberian Peninsula. Portugal sent one expedition after another to smoke out the pirates' nests. In the end, after a century of conflict, Portugal occupied the city in 1575 and took over control of the government. They renamed it Casa Blanca.

Sidi Mohammed Ben Abdallah. The oldest core of Casablanca dates back only to the eighteenth and nineteenth centuries. Everything that existed here prior to that was destroyed in a devestating earthquake in 1755. The Portuguese had no interest in spending a lot of money to rebuild, and chose to abandon the city instead. Now under the reign of the Alauoite prince Sidi Mohammed Ben Abdallah, the city flourished. Buildings sprang up everywhere, including houses, the *medersa* (Koran school), mosques and public baths. To honor Sidi Mohammed, one of these mosques bears his name today.

Casablanca becomes French. Attracted by the Alauoite reconstruction, European merchants from Spain began to set up business in the city, and it is they who gave it its present name. The French, always at home in North Africa, were one of many groups of European merchants. Europeans and Muslims lived in peace together for half a century, but in 1906 riots broke out when plans were made to build a traffic artery over a Muslim graveyard. The French squelched the unrest and occupied the city. The Europeanization of Casablanca began in earnest, but so did an economic boom. The harbour, which is the largest man-made port in North Africa, was built, phosphate deposits near the city were mined, colonial administrative buildings and French villas were erected. The wide boulevards and avenues that traverse the city to this day were also laid out at this time. Morocco gained its independence from France in 1956.

The mosque of Hassan II. In 1989, the ruler of Morocco, Hassan II, gave himself a truly royal gift for his sixtieth birthday: the Mosque of Hassan II. The second largest mosque in the Islamic world – only the Great Mosque at Mecca is larger – was built on a peninsula extending into the Atlantic, beginning in 1980. It currently boasts the highest minaret in the world, stretching 210 metres into the air. The area of the mosque is so vast that it can contain 100,000 worshippers at once, with 25,000 people in the main prayer hall alone. One of its main attractions is its retractable roof, which can be opened and closed to cool the interior depending on the time of day or season. From its roof, a projected laser beam that is visible for miles points towards Mecca.

FACTS

* **Name in the national language (Arabic):** Dar el-Beida ("White House")
* **Population of Casablanca:** *circa* 2.93 million
* **Population of the metropolitan area:** *circa* 3.63 million
* **Places of interest:** Sacre Coeur Cathedral, Sidi el Kairouani Cemetery (Koubba), Mahkama, Royal Palace, Anfa District, Habous District, Mosque of Hassan II, New Medina, Central Market

FAMOUS CITIZENS

* **Jean Reno** (b. 1948), actor
* **Guy Forget** (b. 1965), tennis player
* **Richard Virenque** (b. 1969), racing cyclist

EGYPT

Alexandria

WHEN ALEXANDER THE GREAT LAID THE CORNERSTONE FOR ALEXANDRIA IN 331 BCE, HE PLANNED FOR IT TO BE THE CENTRE OF HIS EMPIRE. HE COULD NEVER HAVE ANTICIPATED THE ALEXANDRIA OF TODAY, A CITY SEEMINGLY ALWAYS UNDER CONSTRUCTION.

Eight years later, Alexander's dead body was returned to Alexandria for burial; his grave has yet to be found. Today, Alexandria is the second largest city in Egypt and the third largest in North Africa. It is one of the major Mediterranean harbour metropolises, with three-quarters of all Egyptian exports passing through its gates.

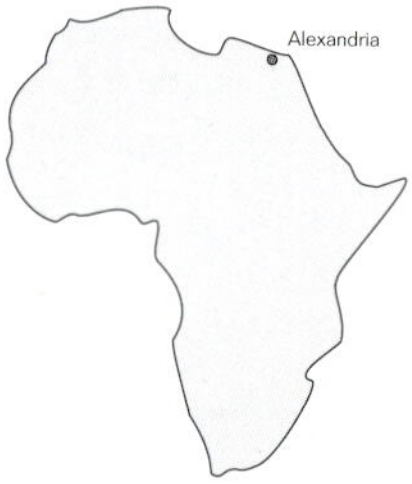

Alexandria is a big city that combines modernity with hints of the glamour of days gone by. Everything that one expects from a Mediterranean metropolis can be found here: extensive beaches, luxury hotels and nightclubs coexist with traditional coffee houses and markets, and of course all the commercial activity of a harbour city. The early Islamic caliphs also left an architectural legacy in Alexandria. The Abu al-Abbas al-Mursi Mosque is one of the city's most important religious buildings, incorporating both local styles and the love of detail that is more typical of the caliph's Islamic kingdoms in Spain. The later Tirbana Mosque, Ottoman in style and purely functional, could hardly be more different.

A wonder of the world. A good starting point for a tour of Alexandria is Midan Saad Saghlul, a square that opens onto the East Harbour. Hotels and several venerable coffee houses dating from the turn of the

The imposing Abu al-Abbas al-Mursi Mosque is the most important religious building in Alexandria.

FACTS

✱ **Name in the national language (Arabic):** Al-Iskandariyah

✱ **Population of Alexandria:** *circa* 3.8 million

✱ **Places of interest:** Tombs of al-Anfushi, Library of Alexandria, el-Shatbi Cemetery, Graeco-Roman Museum, Kom el-Shoqafa, Abu al-Abbas al-Mursi Mosque, Pompejus Column, Qa'it Bay Fortress

FAMOUS CITIZENS

✱ **Omar Sharif** (b.1934), Egyptian actor

✱ **Georges Moustaki** 934) and ✱ **Demis Roussos** (b.1946), singers

✱ **Haim Saban** (b.1944), international media entrepreneur

✱ **Dodi Al-Fayed** (1955–1997), heir and financier

nineteenth to the twentieth century can be found here. From the Boulevard 26th of July, called the Corniche, you can walk all the way out to the former Isle of Pharos, once the site of a lighthouse that was one of the Seven Ancient Wonders of the World. Over the centuries, the silting of the harbour has transformed the islet into a peninsula. Ptolemy II, an ancestor of Cleopatra, commissioned the lighthouse around 299 BCE.

The Pharos Lighthouse ends up as building material. The coinage of that era does not give us any clues as to what the lighthouse looked like. It was said to be 100 metres tall, with a beacon of fire blazing to help guide ships safely into the harbour. Along with the Great Pyramid of Cheops, the Pharos Lighthouse is one of only two of the Seven Ancient Wonders to have survived into the second millennium, when it was badly damaged by a series of catastrophic earthquakes. Arab travellers in the late twelfth century still reported that it was intact, and it was probably present as a ruin until the late fifteenth century, when a fort was built on the site. Blocks salvaged from the lighthouse and used to build the fort can be identified in its walls.

Cleopatra, the last pharaoh of Egypt, was born in Alexandria, and she took her own life here in 30 BCE. Today she is widely known for her stormy romances with Julius Caesar and Mark Anthony, whose bitter power struggles over Roman rule along the Nile can surely be traced in large part to her intrigues. In Egypt, however, Cleopatra was known as the first of the Ptolemaic Dynasty of rulers, the successors of Alexander the Great, who spoke Egyptian, instead of Macedonian Greek. She also adopted Egyptian customs and worshipped Egyptian gods, to whom she built elaborate temples.

Ancient wisdom. The most famous library of antiquity was in Alexandria, but no trace of it remains today. Full of flammable manuscripts, it was repeatedly destroyed by fire. The library was commissioned by Alexander the Great to serve as the repository of all the world's wisdom. It was Ptolemy II who made it not only the greatest library the world had ever seen, but also its first university. The famous mathematicians and scientists Euclid and Archimedes taught there, and Eratosthenes was its librarian. In 2002, the new library of Alexandria was built near the site of the original in collaboration with UNESCO.

Centre: The new Library of Alexandria.

Bottom: The Qa'it Bay fortress was built from the remains of the Pharos Lighthouse.

EGYPT

Cairo

WHILE IT IS CERTAIN THAT CAIRO IS THE MOST POPULOUS CITY ON THE AFRICAN CONTINENT TODAY, NO ONE, NOT EVEN THE EGYPTIAN GOVERNMENT, KNOWS JUST HOW MANY PEOPLE LIVE IN AND AROUND THIS TEEMING CITY.

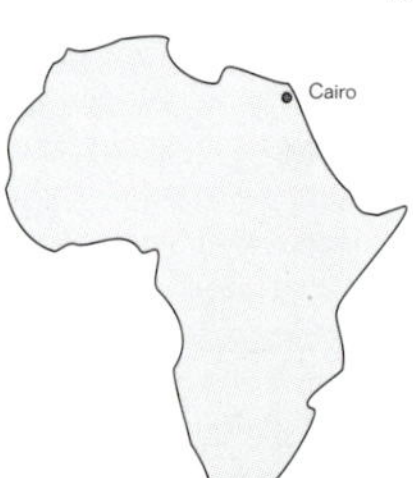

Cairo is the cultural capital of Africa. Three worlds meet here, or, better said, the cultures of three continents. Africa, Asia and Europe are all part of the city's architectural legacy. Antiquity, tradition and modernism are all present here as in no other city in the world. The ancient pyramids of Giza lie on the outskirts of Cairo; Arab bazaars, mosques and Koran schools dominate its Old City; and Western glamour distinguishes the centre of town.

From Cheri aha to Cairo. In the time of the pharaohs, what is today the centre of Cairo was known as Cheri aha, the place where the gods Horus and Seth fought their ultimate battle. Probably just a small settlement on the Nile, it did not achieve any lasting significance. This would change during the period of Roman rule, when an important fortress was built here around 100 CE to oversee important trade routes. Little of Roman Cairo survived the Arab sack of the city in 641. The city was given the name we know it by today by the Fatimid commander, Jafar, who conquered Egypt in 969 CE. He named the city El Qahira, "The Victorious One", and made it his dynastic residence.

The metropolis on the Nile. Africa's largest city is presently overwhelmed with dust, dirt, noise and smog. Traffic noise, car horns, the screeching of tyres

FACTS

*** Name in the national language (Arabic):** El-Qahira

*** Population of Cairo:** *circa* 7.7 million

*** Population of the metropolitan area:** *circa* 15.5 million

*** Places of interest:** Egyptian Museum, Al-Arayes Puppet Theatre, Mosque of Al-Hakim, Television Tower, Gabalaya Park, Gomhouriya Theatre, Great Sphinx at Giza, Ibn Tulun Mosque, Mahmoud Khalil Museum, Mohammed Ali Mosque, Oman Makran Mosque, Opera House, Pyramids of Giza, Citadel

FAMOUS CITIZENS

*** Naguib Mahfouz** (1911–2006), author (Nobel Prize 1988)

*** Boutros Boutros-Ghali** (b. 1922), former Secretary-General of the United Nations

*** Yassir Arafat** (1929–2004), Palestinian leader

*** Mohamed ElBaradei** (b. 1942), International Atomic Energy Agency

The Sphinx stands guard in front of the famous Chephren's Pyramid.

and the clash of fenders are many a visitor's first impressions of Cairo. Few would deny, however, that Cairo nevertheless remains one of the most beautiful cities in the world. Its museums, nearby archaeological sites, universities and important works of Islamic architecture rightly attract tourists from all over the world.

Bargaining as a way of life. Once acclimatized, visitors should begin their journey in the old part of town. Old Cairo, which was added to the UNESCO list of World Heritage Sites in 1979, is the heartbeat of the city. All the traditional bazaars are in the Old City. While Cairo has no shortage of modern shopping centres, wandering through an Egyptian bazaar is an experience not to be missed. The Tentmakers' Bazaar, Cairo's only remaining covered bazaar, and the thirteenth-century Khan el-Khalili Bazaar are especially worth seeing. The latter is famous for its spices, whose aromas waft tantalizingly though the air. Traditional music can be heard everywhere. Visitors are advised to keep in mind that bargaining is a way of life in Cairo, and absolutely required in its Old City bazaars.

A lion with a human face. No stay in Cairo would be complete without a trip to Giza. The Great Pyramid, belonging to the pharaoh Cheops, is the last of the Seven Ancient Wonders of the World standing. Next to it are the pyramids of Mycerinos and Chephren. The Sphinx, with its human head and lion's body, guards the middle pyramid, the one built for Chephren during the Fourth Dynasty (2550–2500 BCE). Modern researchers are still not sure of its purpose. Presumably, the head is an idealized portrait of Pharaoh Chephren. Whether his nose was removed for political reasons, fell off during an earthquake or was shot off by Napoleon's soldiers is one of the Sphinx's many unsolved mysteries.

Above: The City of the Dead, Imam al-Shafei, is a large cemetery and the oldest in Cairo.

Left: The Sultan Hassan Mosque in Old Cairo.

KENYA

Nairobi

NAIROBI, WHOSE NAME MEANS "COOL RIVER", IS THE LARGEST AND FASTEST-GROWING CITY IN EAST AFRICA. FOUNDED AS A RAILWAY WORKERS ENCAMPMENT, THE CITY IS NOW HOME TO OVER 3 MILLION PEOPLE.

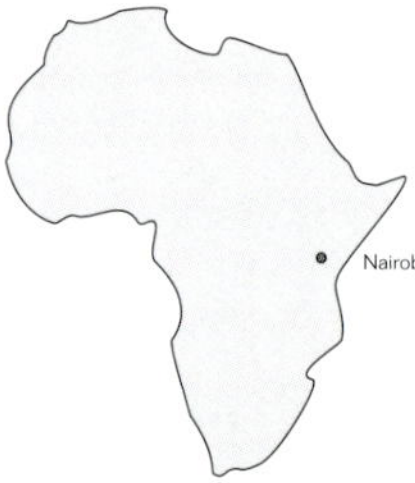

This city of millions has an impressive skyline incorporating several important buildings, including the striking Kenyatta Conference Centre. From the observation deck on its 28th floor, visitors look out on a marvellous panorama of city and countryside. Nairobi is the cultural, economic and communications centre of Kenya. The country's most important institutions of higher learning are found here, and its tourist industry continues to grow.

The role of the railway. Kenya's history is closely connected to Britain's colonial railway projects in Africa. The site for the railway encampment that became Nairobi was carefully chosen. Nairobi lies at an altitude of 1,700 metres. This elevation keeps Nairobi's average temperature too low for malarial mosquitoes to survive. When workers were hired for the Uganda Railway project to connect Lake Victoria with the coastal port of Mombasa, they were housed in Nairobi, which grew in importance after the railway was completed in 1900. It is no surprise that there is a Railway Museum in Nairobi today. It includes a diverse collection of objects from the history of the railway, including wonderful old photographs.

An international city. The modern city of Nairobi is the economic linchpin of East Africa. International

Right: The Jamia Mosque is one of the most impressive structures in Nairobi.

Below: Uhuru Park is in the central business district.

businesses and organizations base their operations here, among them UNO (United Nations Environment Program, UNEP) and UN HABITAT (United Nations Human Settlements Program). With so many international residents, it's little wonder that the restaurants in Nairobi rival those in major European and American cities.

Rich and poor. There are few places in the world where the contact and contrast between extreme wealth and extreme poverty is as glaring as in the Kenyan capital, though the severity of the situation is rivalled in South Africa's Johannesburg. Cynical commentators call the city "Nairobbery" because of its high crime rate. Accordingly, tourists are well advised only to leave central Nairobi, where it is relatively safe to walk around, if they are going on an official safari tour or driving back to the airport.

The best of Nairobi. The majority of tourists who visit Kenya see very little of Nairobi. They usually go straight from the airport to the countryside to set off on safari. In addition to stopping by the popular Railway Museum, those who are interested in getting acquainted with the city should definitely visit the National Museum. Everything worth knowing about Kenya is on display, from its abundant flora and fauna to the lifestyles and cultures of its native peoples, in particular, the Massai. The museum also houses a delightful exhibit of works by the artist Joy Adamson (1910–80). Adamson is best known for her book *Born Free* about her rescue of the lioness Elsa. Her deep love for Africa is vividly expressed in the exhibit.

Green Nairobi. Moi Avenue begins not far from the Railway Museum and leads directly into the centre of Nairobi. The central business district is punctuated by two large green spaces–Uhuru Park and Central Park. Both invite people to rest and relax under their shady trees, sit on a bench or stroll along a gravel path. Uhuru Park even has a small artificial lake. Environmentalist and 2004 Nobel Peace Prize winner Wangari Maathai saved Uhuru Park from development by organizing a series of locally and internationally supported protests in 1989.

At safari's end. Anyone who returns to the Kenyan capital after a week or two of the hard life on safari will appreciate the amenities of Nairobi's full service, Western-style hotels. Nairobi is ideally suited as a starting point for day trips and tours to the country's spectacular national parks. Nairobi National Park, the nation's first, is located only 8 km from Nairobi. Founded in 1946, it has an area of approximately 120 km^2.

FACTS

* **Name in the Massai language:** Engar Nyarobie ("Cool River")
* **Population of Nairobi:** *circa* 2.75 million
* **Places of interest:** Central Park, Kenyatta Conference Centre, Nairobi National Park, National Museum, Railway Museum, Uhuru Park

FAMOUS CITIZENS

* **Roger Whittaker** (b. 1936), singer and songwriter
* **Wangari Maathai** (b. 1940), activist and Nobel Peace Prize winner
* **Richard Dawkins** (b. 1941), biologist
* **Richard Leakey** (b. 1944), anthropologist
* **Jimmy Ogonga** (b. 1977), artist

SOUTH AFRICA

Johannesburg

GOLD RUSH TOWNS ARE OFTEN NOT AROUND TERRIBLY LONG – AS SOON AS THE GOLD IS GONE, MOST ARE ABANDONED. THE HISTORY OF JOHANNESBURG, HOWEVER, SITUATED ON THE EASTERN WITWATERSRAND OF SOUTH AFRICA, IS ANOTHER STORY ENTIRELY.

The area around Johannesburg has yielded a wealth of fossilized hominid remains, but the first settlement of any size began as a gold-rush town, one of many throughout South Africa in the late nineteenth century. When gold was first discovered in 1886, miners had no idea they had stumbled on the largest deposit of gold-bearing ore in the world. Thousands of workers and fortune seekers flocked to the region known as the High Veld, an upland plateau at an altitude of 1,750 metres. In just ten years, the number of people living there increased from a few hundred to 100,000.

It is not the capital. Johannesburg is still the economic and financial centre of today's South Africa and an influential banking city. It is not, however, the capital of the country. The capital, Praetoria, lies 50 km further north; Johannesburg was not beautiful enough to be chosen as capital. The southern border of the city is disfigured by old slag heaps, while the city centre is a concrete and glass jungle with streets like canyons. Nevertheless, the city still has charm, as well as outstanding hotels and restaurants, shopping districts, galleries, museums and theatres. Its society and zest for commerce are reflected in its residents' palpable lust for life. The real beauty of the region lies just outside of the

Right: The Nelson Mandela Bridge was opened in July 2003.

Below: The Township of Alexandra in the southern part of the city.

Johannesburg city limits, its "free hunting grounds". A unique landscape can be found there, the real African Bush.

The modern centre of South Africa. The heart of Johannesburg is a microcosm of the country, a cultural kaleidoscope of past and future. Modern towers, multi-storey buildings and skyscrapers – especially in the Joubert Park quarter, Berea and Hillbrow – stand in strong contrast to the older buildings built during the gold-rush era. Newer African stores and street peddlers scramble for business in the districts where established Portuguese, Indian and Chinese retailers have long owned shops, factories and markets. The symbol of the city is the Hillbrow Tower, located in the district of the same name. Due to the constant clash between the wealthy residents of the city and poor inhabitants of the surrounding slums, Johannesburg unfortunately has a very high crime rate. The crime problem has proved difficult to bring under control, with the city left in an unenviable position as a result.

Nobel quarter and townships. Over the course of the last twenty years, many companies have chosen to move to the suburb of Nobel. The Sandton district is currently the city's most important business centre, as well as the financial centre of the country. Since the end of the 1990s, the South African stock market, known as the Johannesburg Stock Exchange, or JSE, has been based here. Once again, the contrasts could not be more glaring. The very poorest township in the country, Alexandra, is right next door to Sandton. During the apartheid era in South Africa, townships were the slum areas designated for blacks, coloureds and Indian people. Only a narrow strip of highway, the M1 freeway, separates Alexandra from Sandton, but the real differences between the two are vast.

Sights and attractions. Johannesburg has a multiplicity of sights worth seeing. The most impressive is certainly Africa's tallest reinforced concrete building, the Carlton Centre Office Tower. It is approximately 223 metres high and has 50 floors. There is an observation deck at the top, which provides the best view of Johannesburg. A completely different sort of attraction lies about 25 km outside the city of the north-west: the Cradle of Humankind. The name alone is an attention-getter. A UNESCO World Cultural Heritage Site since 1999, it marks the location of the Sterkfontein Caves, where archaeologists and palaeoanthropologists have uncovered more early hominid skeletons than at any other site on Earth.

FACTS

* **Name in the Zulu language:** iGoli; **in Tswana:** Gauteng; **in slang:** Joburg
* **Population of Johannesburg:** *circa* 3.2 million
* **Population of the metropolitan area:** *circa* 8 million
* **Places of interest:** Art Gallery, Botanical Gardens/The Wilds, Carlton Centre, Cradle of Humankind, Gold Reef City, Lion Park, Market Theatre, Museum Africa, The Fort, Transvaal Snake Park

FAMOUS CITIZENS

* **Nadine Gordimer** (b. 1923), author, 1991 Nobel Prize winner
* **Gary Player** (b. 1935), professional golfer and course architect
* **Manfred Mann** (b. 1940), rock musician
* **Basil Rathbone** (1892–1967), actor

SOUTH AFRICA

Cape Town

CAPE TOWN WAS FOUNDED ON 6 APRIL 1652 AS THE FIRST DUTCH CITY IN WHAT IS NOW SOUTH AFRICA. ITS LANDMARKS – TABLE MOUNTAIN, SIGNAL HILL, LION'S HEAD AND DEVIL'S PEAK – ARE ALL FEATURES OF CAPE TOWN'S DRAMATIC NATURAL TOPOGRAPHY.

Cape Town is happy to be known as South Africa's "Mother City", and its location at the southern end of the African continent has earned it the sobriquet, "Most Beautiful End of the Earth". Its exciting mixture of cultures and styles, as well as its superb flora and fauna, exotic even by African standards, make Cape Town a unique destination. While the popular slogan, "washed by two oceans", is not literally true, as only the Atlantic meets its shores, Cape Town's dramatic setting and cosmopolitan urban life can make it seem as if anything is possible here.

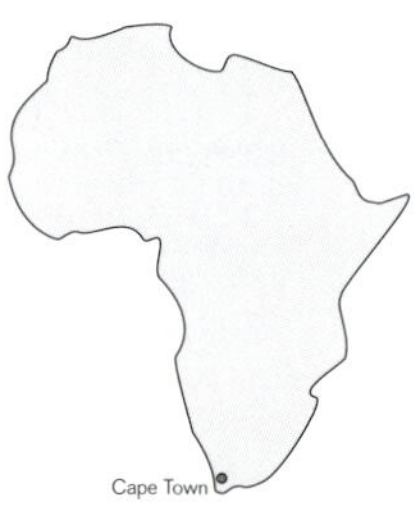

City on the Cape of Good Hope. Between October and March each year, the city is packed with tourists enjoying the warm sun of the southern hemisphere summer. In addition to the obligatory cable-car trip up the 1,087-metre-high Table Mountain, an excursion to Cape Town's Victoria and Albert Waterfront is highly recommended. The shipyard and harbour districts near the two historic docks on Table Bay have been thoroughly restored, and the nearby streets are full of souvenir shops, museums, hotels and restaurants. Also nearby are an exclusive yacht harbour, the Two Oceans Aquarium and a small outdoor theatre.

The centre of Cape Town is also alluring with its many historic structures and museums, including

The old City Hall with palm trees growing in front of it and a rugged, mountainous backdrop.

FACTS

* **Population of Cape Town:** *circa* 854,600
* **Population of the metropolitan area:** *circa* 3 million
* **Places of interest:** Kirstenbosch Botanical Garden, Castle of Good Hope, City Hall, Grande Parade, Houses of Parliament, Old Town House, Robben Island, Cathedral of St. George, Table Mountain, Two Oceans Aquarium

FAMOUS CITIZENS

* **Richard Rive** (1931–89), writer
* **John M. Coetzee** (b. 1940), writer
* **Sir Antony Sher** (b. 1949), actor, writer and artist
* **Sarah Poewe** (b. 1983), world champion swimmer

the oldest surviving building in South Africa, the Castle of Good Hope, dating back to 1666. Other places worth seeing include City Hall, the magnificent Cathedral of St. George, the National Gallery and the National Museum. The entertainment district of Cape Town is also close by. On Long Street, a wide range of restaurants, nightclubs, cafés and concert venues are on offer.

Wine and flowers. Tourism is not Cape Town's only source of revenue. The capital of Westkap Province is a power in the world of modern information technology, as well as a leader in textile production. Agricultural products from this region are exported worldwide, including wine from Constantia, a wine-producing district south-west of Table Mountain. Kirstenbosch, with its famous botanical gardens, is not far from Constantia. Flowers are another of Cape Town's most profitable exports.

Apartheid and its aftermath. Cape Town has another side, as can be said of all South African cities. The consequences of the racial separation policies of apartheid, which were officially abolished in 1994, are still highly visible today. While the predominantly white, affluent society lives in central Cape Town, most of the black majority still live in distant suburbs and townships. One of these is Nyanga, which visitors may notice because it is located just to the south of the airport. It is sadly obvious in Cape Town, as elsewhere in South Africa, that too little has changed.

Twenty-six years in the penitentiary. The prison on Robben Island is one relic of the apartheid era, and is currently one of Cape Town's top tourist attractions. The prison island, located in the middle of Table Bay about 12 km from the coast, was declared a national monument in the mid-1990s. The walls of what was once a penal colony now house a museum. The most famous inmate at Robben Island was Nelson Mandela, the African National Congress leader who began serving a life sentence there in 1964. Mandela was released on President Frederik de Klerk's orders in 1990, having been imprisoned for a total of twenty-seven years. Mandela was elected president of the country in the first post-apartheid elections in South Africa, held in 1994, and remained in office until 1999. Robben Island was declared a UNESCO World Heritage Site in 1999.

Centre: View of Cape Town Harbour.

Bottom: The prison facility on Robben Island where Nelson Mandela was long imprisoned.

Asia is a continent replete with contrasts – it changes with every mile travelled from east to west and back again. Western Asia's sun-drenched Mediterranean atmosphere gives way to the dusty mystery of the realm of 1001 Nights, and the crowds and chaos of South-East Asian cities lead one further into the serene, even austere, cities of the Far East.

ASIA

TURKEY

Istanbul

ISTANBUL STRADDLES BOTH SIDES OF THE BOSPORUS, AND IS THE ONLY CITY ON TWO CONTINENTS. EUROPE AND ASIA LITERALLY MEET HERE, AND ON THE CITY'S STREETS. THE FIRST SETTLEMENT IN ANCIENT TIMES WAS PROBABLY EUROPEAN IN ORIGIN.

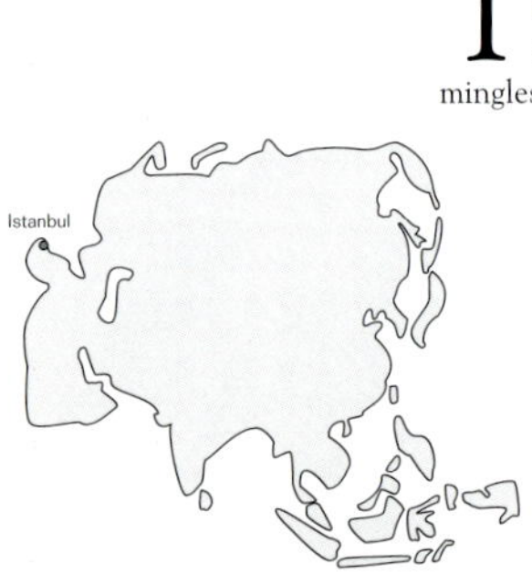

The first Greeks to settle on the inlet of the Bosporus, known as the Golden Horn, arrived sometime around 658 BCE. Turkish culture mingles with classical and pre-Ottoman architecture in contemporary Istanbul, and sites sacred to many different religions stand side by side. Greek Orthodox, Armenian Christian and Jewish minorities still live among Istanbul's Muslim majority.

Sacred structures and museums. In Istanbul, it is not unusual to find a Christian church or Jewish synagogue right next to a mosque, but sacred structures are not the only interesting sites that Istanbul has to offer. There is certainly no shortage of fascinating museums in the great city on the Bosporus. Hagia Sophia, or the Church of the Holy Wisdom, was once the most important church in Christian Byzantium. Today it houses the Ayasofya Museum, which, along with the even more renowned Topkapı Museum, is famous the world over. Some people may recall Jules Dassin's classic film *Topkapı*, in which Sir Peter Ustinov and Maximilian Schell conspire to steal a jewelled dagger from the former Ottoman palace.

Old Constantinople. To list everything worth seeing in Istanbul would fill an entire book. The architecture dating from after 200 CE deserves

Right: View of the entrance to Topkapı Palace.

Below: Hagia Sophia – at one time a cathedral, then a mosque, today a museum.

mention, despite the fact that most of it is in ruins. The Roman era Valens Aqueduct (*Bozdogan Kemeri* in Turkish) stands where it always has, now spanning a busy Istanbul street. It was begun during the reign of Emperor Valens, a successor of Constantine the Great. Of the original antique water conduit, parts of which were 26.5 metres high, just 800 metres remain standing, about half of its original length. Another Roman relic is the Theodosian Wall, completed in 424, which once encircled the entire city. Its 96 towers kept invaders at bay for centuries. Large stretches of it are preserved along the northern and southern borders of the city.

Ottoman architecture in Byzantium. The church of St. Saviour in Chora, located in the Edirnekapi district of Istanbul, it an outstanding example of Late Byzantine architecture. The church was later transformed into a mosque and is now known as the Kariye Camii. It has been home to one of Istanbul's many museums since 1948. Its glittering mosaics and monumental paintings are among the best-preserved examples of Byzantine art in the world. The Ottoman rulers set about placing their stamp on the city as soon as they conquered it in 1453. Particularly in the sixteenth century, countless buildings designed by the prodigious architect Sinan (or Mimar Sinan) went up all over the Ottoman Empire. Born Christian, he converted to Islam. In Istanbul, Sinan built the Sehzade Mosque in 1548 and the Suleyman Mosque in 1557. These are only two of the 136 sacred buildings he bequeathed to the Muslim world.

The bazaar – a city within a city. As in most Eastern cities, Istanbul's covered bazaar – the Kapalı Carsı – is more than just a collection of shops. It is an arched and domed city within the city, complete with streets, columned squares, eighteen "city gates", five mosques and six fountains. Covering an area of 200,000 square metres, it is one of the most expansive covered markets in the world.

Football fanatics. Istanbul would not be Istanbul without football. No fewer than four World Club championship teams are based here: Galatasaray, Besiktas, Fenebahce and Istanbulspor; and between them they have won nearly fifty championships. Galatasaray was the UEFA (European Cup Football) champion in 2000. A number of famous international players have come from the ranks of the Istanbul teams, including Fatih Akyel. Istanbul's many professional basketball teams also attract international attention. Currently, three Turkish players from Istanbul's powerhouse Efes Pilsen team play in America's NBA (National Basketball Association).

FACTS

* **Population of Istanbul:** *circa* 9.8 million
* **Population of the metropolitan area:** *circa* 12 million
* **Places of interest:** Blue Mosque, St. Saviour of Chora Church, Galata Bridge, Galata Tower, Great Bazaar, Hagia Sophia, Kapali Carsi, Mahmut Pascha Mosque, Nuru Osmaniye Mosque, Sehzade Mosque, Topkapı Museum, Valens Aqueduct

FAMOUS CITIZENS

* **Sinan** (1489–1588), architect
* **Osman Hamdi Bey** (1842–1910), artist and archaeologist
* **Bülent Ecevit** (b. 1925), writer and politician
* **Orhan Pamuk** (b. 1952), journalist and writer (Nobel prize 2006)

CHINA

Beijing

BEIJING GREETS ITS VISITORS WITH A FRIENDLY *NI HAO* AND A CHARACTERISTIC CHINESE SMILE. WHILE SHANGHAI SERVES AS CHINA'S ECONOMIC CENTRE, BEIJING IS ITS CULTURAL AND POLITICAL CAPITAL.

Nevertheless, Beijing finds itself in the throes of modernization and the changes that go along with it. The appearance of entire precincts can change within a short period of time, and this process has intensified since Beijing was awarded the 2008 Summer Olympics. It is fascinating to experience dynamic growth and three millenia of history coexisting and interacting with each other so closely. Beijing is home to a number of places and buildings that UNESCO has identified as being of particular cultural and historical significance in their World Heritage List.

The City of Khan. The trading town of Ji was founded in the northern part of what is now Beijing around 1121 BCE. It commanded a strategic location near the border between Manchuria and Mongolia. Over the centuries, many conquerors came and went. The city continued to change hands until 1215, when the Mongols, under the command of Genghis Khan, finally conquered it decisively. Once they entered the city they had besieged for so long, they razed it to the ground and built a new "City of the Khans" in its place.

Definitely the capital. The city was not given its present name until the reign of Emperor Yongle (r.1402–24), who was also the first to declare it an

The only man-made structure that can be seen from outer space, the Great Wall of China, passes 100 km north of Beijing.

FACTS

* Name in the national language (Chinese): Beijing
* Population of Beijing: *circa* 7.5 million
* Population of the metropolitan area: *circa* 14.9 million
* Places of interest: Old Summer Palace, Great Wall, Courtyard Gallery, Temple of Heaven, Lama Temple, Ming Tombs, Summer Palace, Beihai (North Lake) Park, Palace Museum, Tiananmen Square, Forbidden City

FAMOUS CITIZENS

* Lao She (1899–1966), writer
* Pu Yi (1906–67), last emperor of China
* Jet Li (b. 1963), martial artist and actor
* Michael Shapiro († 1986 in Beijing), English translator of Mao Zedong's writings

imperial residence and capital of China. Yong Le was the ruler who laid the cornerstones for the Forbidden City and the Temple of Heaven, which is why historians refer to him as the true architect of modern Beijing. Beijing has borne witness to it all, from corruption scandals to the Boxer Rebellion, the revolt of the warlords and invasion by the Japanese during World War II and the civil war between the nationalists and communists. Each of these events shook and influenced the city in a lasting way. Only when the Peoples Republic was proclaimed in October of 1949 did peace return to the city built around the Tiananmen (Heavenly Peace) Square.

The Forbidden City. Mao's mausoleum borders Tiananmen Square on the south. The Gate of Heavenly Peace stands at the north end, and functions as the south gate of the Imperial Palace in what is known as the Forbidden City. The palace has been on the list of UNESCO World Heritage Sites since 1987. From 1406 onwards, the rulers of the Ming and Qing dynasties governed all of China from the Imperial Palace. The procurement of building materials to build the Forbidden City took over ten years, since wood had to be imported from southern China and slowly floated northwards along canals that were dug especially for that purpose. The firing of hundreds of thousands of roof tiles in what is now Liulichang was child's play by comparison. The Imperial Palace has been converted into a museum that exhibits the imperial and palace treasures.

World Heritage Site of a great nation. There are countless places of interest in Beijing and the surrounding area, three of which are on the UNESCO World Heritage List. The first is the Summer Palace of the Jin emperors (1115–1234) on the outskirts of Beijing. A large lake, covered walkways, historical structures, pavilions and ornate gardens offer respite to tired tourists. Also on the list are the Ming Tombs in Shisanling, about 70 km north of the city. Another 30 km further north, the Great Wall (Chinese: *Chang Chen*) winds its way through the hills of northern China. The origins of this immense symbol of Chinese power go back more than two thousand years.

Centre: Panorama of the Forbidden City in the heart of Beijing.

Bottom: The Summer Palace of the Jin emperors above Kunming Lake on the outskirts of the city.

SOUTH KOREA

Seoul

OVER 20 MILLION KOREANS LIVE IN AND AROUND SEOUL, YET IT IS ONE OF FEW ASIAN CITIES THAT HAS SUCCESSFULLY PRESERVED ITS BUILDINGS FROM THE PAST AND INTEGRATED THEM INTO THE SKYLINE OF A GROWING GLOBAL CITY.

Seoul is loud and bustling, as befits one of the most densely populated metropolises on Earth. Lines of cars and throngs of people press their way through the cavernous streets. Oversized illuminated advertising marks the way, selling products in a foreign script. The underground system is Seoul's new and perfectly organized underworld. In the midst of all this chaos, visitors may suddenly come upon an oasis of stillness in one of the city's numerous temples, parks and pavilions.

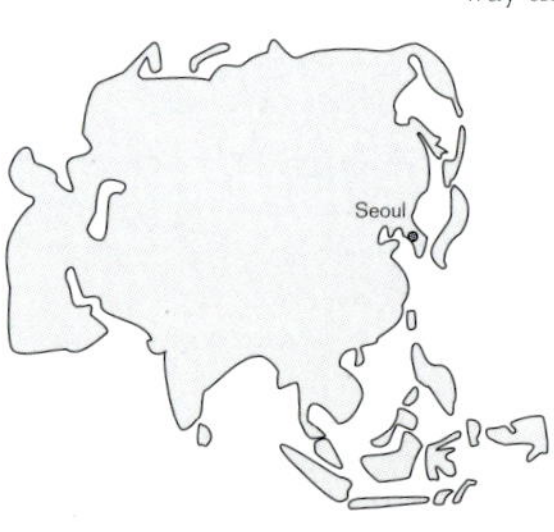

City on the river. Seoul was founded in 1394, following the demise of the Koryo Kingdom 1392). Its progress was long associated with the rise and success of the Choson Dynasty (1392–1910). After searching for a suitable location for his city, King Taejo, better known as Yi Seong-gye, decided on the north bank of the Han River. A small village named Hanyang was the only settlement in the area at that time. The name of the renowned Hanyang University, one of over 300 institutions of higher learning in Seoul, recalls that small village.

A modern sports city. Contemporary Seoul came into existence during the first half of the twentieth century, and largely through the influence of the Japanese. The old city wall gave way to modern

FACTS

* **Name in English:** "Capital City"

* **Population of Seoul:** *circa* 10.3 million

* **Population of the metropolitan area:** *circa* 21.7 million

* **Places of interest:** Namhansanseong (Mountain Fortress), Bongeunsa Temple, Bukhansanseong Fortress, Changdeokgung, Deoksugung, Gwangneung Sepulchre, Gyeongbokgung, Jogyesa Temple, National Folk Museum, National Theatre, Seoul Tower, Sejong Cultural Centre, Seonyudo Park, Seoul Historical Museum, Seoul Metropolitan Museum of Art, War Memorial Museum

FAMOUS CITIZENS

* **Yun Seondo** (1587–1671), poet and artist

* **Lee Byung-chul** (1910–87), businessman (Samsung)

* **Nam June Paik** (1932–2006), artist, video-art pioneer

The Secret Garden of Biwon in Chandeokgung Palace.

buildings, with only the ancient city gates preserved. After the catastrophic Korean War (1950–53), nearly all of Seoul had to be rebuilt. From that point onwards, Seoul grew at a very rapid pace. The city underwent massive changes, at times with little planning and consideration of their long-term impact. Trams ran until 1968, only to disappear almost overnight. They were quickly replaced by an underground system. The economic upswing of 1988 that followed in the wake of the Seoul Summer Olympic Games was a boon to the cultural, financial and sporting life of the city, and the sports world again turned its eyes to Seoul in 2002, when the FIFA World Cup football championship was held here.

Kings' palaces with curious names. But Seoul is much more than a showcase for sporting events: it is the cultural heart of South Korea, where universities, theatres, museums and more abound. When Seoul was founded in 1394, the Gyeongbokgung (Palace of Shining Happiness) was the first royal residence built. Happiness did not, unfortunately, shine on the palace and its inhabitants forever. Serfs burned the palace to the ground in 1592, and the death of Queen Min in 1895 led to the relocation of the royal family to Deoksugung (Palace of Virtuous Longevity). In 1997, the Changdeokgung (Palace of Prospering Virtue) was added to the UNESCO World Heritage List. It was built as an addition to Gyeongbokgung, and was the only structure destroyed in the 1592 uprising that was immediately rebuilt. Until 1872 and again from 1907 to 1910, it served as the seat of government of the Korean kings. The Secret Garden of Biwon is also especially worth seeing. The impressive burial cairns of King Sejo and his wife Yun Chon-hi are located there, just 30 km north of the city.

Above: The Namdaemun (Great South Gate) is a testament to Seoul's great past.

Left: The royal family moved to Deoksugung (the Palace of Virtuous Longevity) in 1895.

JAPAN

Tokyo

TOKYO IS NOT A CITY FOR THE HURRIED TOURIST MAKING A QUICK STOPOVER EN ROUTE TO OTHER DESTINATIONS IN JAPAN. TOKYO COMES AS A REAL SURPRISE TO MOST TRAVELLERS. MUCH MORE THAN A CITY, IT IS A COMPLETELY DIFFERENT WORLD.

When visitors to Japan first arrive at Narita International Airport, they often experience immediate culture shock. Signs point the way in Kanji (Japanese characters), but most tourists can't read them. Without a few helpful signs in English, it would be easy to get quite lost. At first sight, Tokyo itself is crowded, loud and not especially beautiful. The air quality is not particularly good. Men wearing white gloves shove people inside the regional transit cars in order to fit more people inside, and most Japanese respond with a blank stare when spoken to in English. Tokyo can be hard to negotiate, and travel around town can be stressful – but it is also a unique and exhilarating experience.

Kagemusha, the Shadow Warrior. Prior to (1456–57), there is very little salient knowledge available about the city of Edo, Tokyo's predecessor. With the building of the Edo Fortress during these years in the mid-fifteenth century, the city on Hibiya Bay gained in importance. The greatest advance, however, came in 1653, when the shogun Tokugawa Ieyasu established his centre of government here. Director Akira Kurosawa staged the life and work of this prominent, powerful shogun in his 1980 film *Kagemusha – The Shadow Warrior*. George Lucas did

Right: Shinjuku is pure contrast, with a peaceful park in the foreground and the prominent skyline behind it.

Below: The Ginza area is a hive of activity.

not shoot the backdrop of the film, but he spun the threads, so to speak. In his novel Shogun, writer James Clavell also painted a portrait of the most imposing figure in Japanese history. Ieyasu is considered the founder of modern Tokyo, even though the city did not take its official name or become the "Capital of the East" until the emperor moved there in 1868.

Beginnings of Western influence. The population of the city is said to have already exceeded a million by the beginning of the eighteenth century. Edo was not only the capital city under the Tokugawa shogunate, it was also the economic centre of Japan. The end in the shogunate is closely connected to the history of Edo and, by association, Tokyo. The balance of power changed under the Meiji emperors. Shogun Yoshinobu Tokugawa, who was rather weak with regard to the West, especially the United States, abdicated in 1867 and left Edo to the emperor. But

the actual goal of sealing Japan off from the West was never implemented by the shogun's adversaries, headed by the emperor. In fact, just the opposite occurred: a very active period of modernization based on the Western model began.

Destruction and rebuilding. In Tokyo, European-style houses were built right in between traditional wooden houses. Some of the most famous examples are the houses on Ginza Street, which were built from red brick in order to create more European surroundings for foreign residents in the capital. In spite of everything, such changes were mainly superficial. The city plan and homes of the native Japanese remained closely tied to the Edo tradition of the Shogun Era. But that changed in 1923, the year of the Great Earthquake, measuring more than 8.0 on the Richter scale. The earthquake itself and the fires that resulted from the it reduced nearly all of Tokyo to ruins. However, destruction has always represented an opportunity for change in Japan. Tragically, the World War II came quite soon after the earthquake, signalling yet another period of devastating destruction.

The new development of Tokyo began after the end of the World War II, and literally began on top of debris and ashes. On the basis of new technologies, a modern Tokyo cityscape consisting of skyscrapers, steel and concrete emerged. Special construction methods had to be used, because Tokyo lies in one of the most active earthquake zones in the world. Earthquakes are nothing out of the ordinary here, and smaller tremors can be felt in the city almost daily.

FACTS

*** Name in the national language (Japanese):** Tokyo

*** Population of Tokyo:** *circa* 8.3 million

*** Population of greater Tokyo:** *circa* 12 million

*** Population of the entire metropolitan area:** *circa* 36.5 million

*** Places of interest:** Yebisu Beer Museum, Edo-Tokyo Museum, Electric City, Money Museum, Hama Rikyu Garden, Imperial Palace, Meiji Shrine, National Museum, Omiya Bonsai Village, Opera House, Rainbow Bridge, Senso-ji, Shiba Park, Shinjuku Gyoen, Tamagawa Josui Hamura (Canal and Herb Gardens), Tama Zoo, Tokyo Disney Resort, Tokyo Metropolitan Museum of Art, Tokyo Sea Life Park, Tokyo Tocho (City Hall), Tokyo Tower, Ueno Park

Tokyo's oldest temple, Senso-ji, is in Asakusa and was built in 645.

By the time of the Olympic Summer Games in 1964, the war damage was no longer visible. The train and underground systems that were built for the Tokyo Olympics are still in use today and remain exemplary. In the 1970s and 1980s, more and more skyscrapers sprang up, but the following decade saw the stagnation of Tokyo's economy, and many companies and banks had to struggle just to survive. In fact, in Japan the 1990s are often referred to as the "lost decade".

Many cities are closely associated with greater Tokyo, making it a megalopolis. Only a few of the places of interest that the "Eastern Capital" has to offer are known outside of Japan; the main attraction is the opportunity to experience a metropolis that seems so similar to a Western city at first glance, but is fundamentally different at its core. It has no central square, no prominent symbol and no special landmark for tourists. Tokyo is a collection of various districts, an agglomeration of cities, some of which have seven-digit numbers of inhabitants themselves.

Ginza: quarter of the rich and famous. Chuo-ku, the central district of Tokyo, stands on deeply historic ground. Unfortunately, almost none of the historical sites remain. The heart of the district is the exclusive shopping area of Ginza, with its elegant boulevards, boutiques, department stores and the large crowds that go with them. Ginza, or "Silver Site", was the location of the mint during the Edo Period and of great importance for the city of the shoguns. The central district has remained the financial centre of the country, and the Shoken Torihikisho (Stock Exchange) is located here. There are rumours that plans to turn Ginza into a pedestrian zone are being considered, but it doesn't seem to have happened so far.

Centre City is similar in many respects to other districts, such as Shinjuku. This is probably the best place to experience the younger aspect of Tokyo. During the day Shinjuku swarms with workers, but it is tranformed into a neon-lit social strip after dark. In Shibuya and Harajuku there is a seemingly infinite selection of places to eat and drink, everything from gigantic beer halls to tiny, intimate theme bars, as well as modern shops, sports facilities and beautiful parks. Shinjuku Gyoen Park is one of the largest in Tokyo (58 hectares), and is both a playground and a peaceful oasis. There is an entrance fee, but it is

Right: The Rainbow Bridge across Tokyo Harbour, 570 metres long, was completed in 1993.

Below: The Imperial Palace.

worth investing the small sum of money to experience an oasis away from the hectic pace of the train-station district. The park was already laid out as early as 1906, but was reserved for use by the royal family in those days, and was only opened to the public after 1945.

Old Edo. In the shadow of soaring skyscrapers – Tokyo Tower, Tocho (city hall) and all of the other giants – the historical structures of Tokyo almost entirely disappear from view. Most of them are in Ueno and Asakusa, to the north of the erstwhile Edo Castle, in the lower part of Shitamachi. Senso-ji in Asakusa is a temple dedicated to the Kannon Buddha (Buddha of Mercy), built in the midst of a very crowded area, and next to it are many rows of shops in traditional architectural style.

The Old Edo Castle was replaced by the Imperial Palace under the Meiji emperors. Today there are only a few gates, towers and imposing graves and ramparts that remain to be seen. Of special interest in the Shibuya District are the Meiji Shrine and the lush, extensive park areas surrounding it. A shrine (Japanese: *jingu*) is to Shintoists what a church is to Christians, which is why this shrine is visited often, particularly by locals.

Theatres everywhere. The Japanese have a strong tradition of theatre, and there are numerous theatres in the capital. Traditional forms of theatre remain the favourite of many, and the most beloved is Noh drama, a legacy of the old samurai era in which only men perform. The works are mainly derived from Japanese and Chinese mythology; only very few Noh dramas deal with modern themes. Kabuki theatre is somewhat less traditional and includes lots of song, pantomime and dance.

No geisha romance. The faces of Tokyo are many and disparate: unrestrained consumerism and peaceful oases, overstimulation of the senses and gentle, unobtrusive beauty. Tokyo is an incredibly progressive city, which is nevertheless haunted by the past. Most of all, it is a fascinating city. Tourists who arrive laden with prejudices expecting to encounter the traditional Japan of samurai swords and geisha romance are sure to be disappointed. But those who are willing to experience the new may never want to leave Tokyo again, because there is always something unsual and unique to experience here.

FAMOUS CITIZENS

* **Saburo Moroi** (1903–77), composer
* **Olivia de Havilland** (b.1916), American actress
* **Mishima Yukio** (1925–1970), writer and politician
* **Yoko Ono** (b.1933), Japanese American artist and singer
* **Liv Ullmann** (b.1938), Norwegian actress
* **Takuma Sato** (b.1977), Formula 1 racing-car driver

IRAN

Tehran

TEHRAN IS CURRENTLY AMONG THE MOST DENSELY POPULATED CITIES ON EARTH, YET FOR MANY CENTURIES TEHRAN WAS NOTHING MORE THAN A SMALL, INSIGNIFICANT CITY ON THE STAGE OF WORLD HISTORY.

Aga Muhammad Khan, founder of the Qajar dynasty, chose Tehran as the capital of the Persian Empire in 1795, largely because of its location on the cool Elbur hillsides. And so it has remained to this very day. Only after a terrible earthquake in May 2004 was there heated discussion of moving the seat of government from Tehran to a less earthquake-prone region of the country.

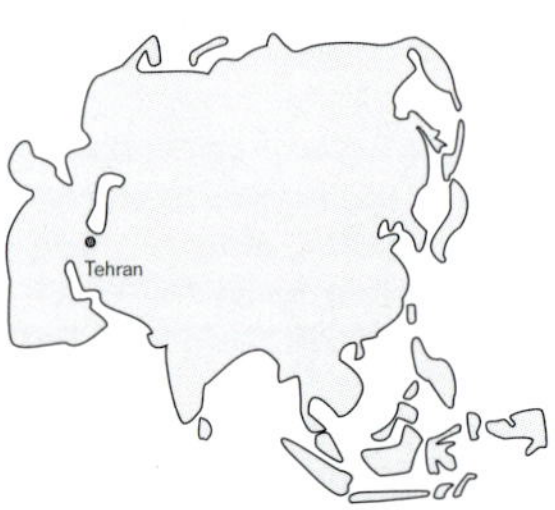

Palaces and museums. The bulk of Tehran's older buildings date back to the period of Qajar rule in the nineteenth century. Foremost among these structures is the Golestan, or Rose Garden Palace, the old seat of the shahs until 1979. Today it serves as a museum, and its most famous exhibit is the stunning Peacock Throne. Exactly 26,733 precious stones decorate this sumptuous throne of the former Persian rulers. While there are always crowds in the museum, the palace garden is a peaceful and beautiful oasis in the heart of Tehran. The Iranian capital has a large number of museums worth seeing in addition to the Golestan Palace, including the Archaeological Museum and the National Museum. Many other cultural sites are inviting and worthy of a sojourn.

Tehran's bazaar is legendary and one of the biggest in the world. The traditional Zurkhaneh (House of

FACTS

* **Name in the national language (Persian):** Tehran
* **Population of Tehran:** *circa* 7 million
* **Places of interest:** Archaeological Museum, Ayatollah Khomeini Mausoleum, bazaar, Behest-e Zahra (burial grounds), Freedom Tower, Golestan Palace, Green Palace, Crown Jewel Museum, Peacock Throne, Shah Mosque, Carpet Museum, White Palace

FAMOUS CITIZENS

* **Mohammad Mossadegh** (1882–1967), politician
* **Mohammad Reza Pahlevi** (1919–1980), the last shah of Iran
* **Jasmin Tabatabai** (b. 1967), actress
* **Vahid Hashemian** (b. 1976), football player

The bazaar in Tehran is a bustle of activity.

Strength) in the middle of the bazaar is a special kind of sports venue: up to 25 athletes at a time emulate their forebears, swinging maces and rings to the accompaniment of drums and ritual songs. This distinct form of athleticism, called *bastani* in Persian, originated under the yoke of the Mongols, who forbade the locals to engage in any kind of physical training. The Persians trained in secret in order to be ready for the day when they would free themselves from Mongolian rule.

Modern Tehran. Impressive testaments to Persian rule in this city include not only historical monuments and the traditional souk, but also numerous modern structures. The symbol of modern Iran is a more recent building, the Shahyad (Freedom) Tower on Azadi Square, built in 1971 during the reign of the last shah. From the observation deck one has a fantastic view of the entire city, and can see all the way to the distant, snow-capped Elbur Mountains. Another important symbol of the Islamic Republic of Iran, the Ayatollah Khomeini Mausoleum, is located in the southern part of the city. Four narrow minarets, each 90 metres high, surround its shining gold cupola.

Those who would prefer to flee the noise of the city leave Tehran travelling north, towards Darband and Darrake at the foot of Tochal Mountain in the Elbur Range. While en route through the northern neighbourhoods of Tehran, a visit to the Saadabad Palace, the summer residence of the last shah, is definitely worth making. Once you reach your final destination, there is a chance to enjoy the clear mountain air and to sojourn at one of many traditional cafés and restaurants. For a taste of adventure, you can also take the longest cable car ride in the world up Mt Tochal, and come down via one of in five ski slopes.

Above: The Fire Temple, a gathering place and cult site for followers of Zoroastrianism, stands not far from the city.

Left: View of the magnificent Golestan Palace.

LEBANON

Beirut

THE WESTERN WORLD MAINLY KNOWS BEIRUT FROM TELEVISION NEWS IN WHICH, SINCE THE 1970S, IT HAS BEEN THE ARCHETYPAL WAR-RAVAGED CITY. FEW WESTERNERS ARE AWARE THAT BEIRUT WAS ONCE ONE OF THE MOST BEAUTIFUL, SOPHISTICATED METROPOLISES IN THE EASTERN MEDITERRANEAN.

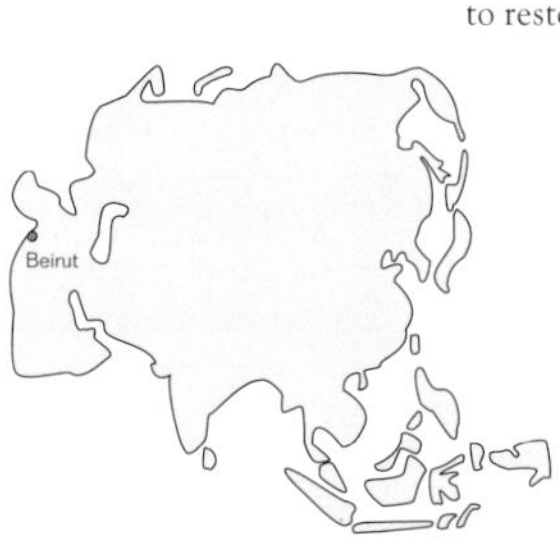

Once acclaimed as the "Paris of the Near East", Beirut may yet recover its former splendour. Efforts have long been under way to restore the damaged parts of the city and restore its broad boulevards to life. The spirit of modernism pervading the Levant, however, means that the ancient lanes and covered bazaars of the Old City will not be reconstructed. Beirut has always been notably unsentimental and less interested in reminiscing than in moving forwards.

A city under reconstruction. A quick trip through Beirut's city centre makes clear just how much has been destroyed by the years of civil war. Shelling and aerial bombardment have damaged nearly every building in the heart of the city past the point where simple restoration is possible. The Lebanese want their capital to return to the golden years of the 1960s, when it was a flourishing commercial city, a financial metropolis and a gateway between European and Arab culture. Razing of the rubble and rebuilding of Beirut's heavily damaged infrastructure was well under way when fighting broke out anew in July 2006. Once again, the citizens of Beirut were forced to confront the reality of life in a war zone.

Archaeological opportunity. The Place des Martyrs (Martyrs' Square), once the heart of Beirut's

Beirut's famous 'Pigeons' Rock is a favourite meeting spot for lovers.

FACTS

* **Arabic:** Bayrut
* **Population of Beirut:** *circa* 1.7 million
* **Places of interest:** Aanjar, Al-Amin Mosque, Beirut City Centre, Cathedral of St George, Corniche, Commodore Hotel, National Museum, Pigeon's Rock

FAMOUS CITIZENS

* **Nicolas Hayek** (b. 1928), entrepreneur (Swatch)
* **Bachir Gemayel** (1947–82), politician
* **Suleman Taufiq** (b. 1953), Syrian writer

financial district and thus of international finance for the entire Middle East, was left a heap of tangled rubble by the civil war. Prior to rebuilding on the site, archaeologists brought in to investigate uncovered the remains of the city's glorious and eventful history amid the destruction. Phoenician burial chambers, Persian and Roman temples, Byzantine mosaics and the foundations of Crusader fortresses were unearthed. In 1993, archaeologists, government officials and developers agreed to cooperate in further investigation of the remains of Ancient Beirut. More extensive excavations followed and development plans were altered to integrate the newly uncovered finds into the rebuilt modern city.

Historically, Beirut served as a bridge between the Middle East and Europe. Prior to the recent re-emergence of violence, Beirut had made great strides towards regaining its position of influence. International conferences and events were held here, emphasizing the cosmopolitan outlook of the city and its inhabitants. The AFC Asian Cup football championships held in Beirut in 2000 were a major success, even though the home team was eliminated early on.

Beirut has always been a city of contrasts. This was never more evident than in 2002, when Beirut was chosen as the site for the 2002 Arab League Summit. While it was under way, security precautions (including nearly 15,000 police and soldiers on high alert) turned Beirut into a hermetically sealed fortress. In the same year, the Miss Europe pageant took place in Beirut. The contrast between a serious political conference attended by stern politicians and a light-hearted contest with Europe's most beautiful young women could not have been greater. That both events could take place in the same city was emblematic of Beirut's commitment to regaining its reputation as the place where East meets West in an atmosphere of peace and prosperity.

Beirut's unique flair has always blended Western influences and its Middle Eastern location. Along the legendary Corniche, Beirut's seaside promenade, the *joie de vivre* of the city and country were apparent at every turn. Nearby is Pigeons' Rock, an arching limestone cliff rising from the surf. A symbol of Beirut, Pigeons' Rock is a favourite meeting spot for young and old. Lovers are especially drawn to this romantic spot, where generations of bold young men have dived from Beirut's highest coastal cliffs into the sea.

Centre: Once the pulsating heart of the city, the Place des Martyrs was in ruins at war's end.

Below: The Corniche, Beirut's legendary beach promenade.

SYRIA

Damascus

DAMASCUS LOOKS BACK ON 10,000 YEARS OF HISTORY, MAKING IT THE OLDEST CITY IN THE WORLD. DURING ITS GOLDEN AGE, BUBBLING FOUNTAINS, LUSH GARDENS AND MAGNIFICENT ARCHITECTURE WOULD GREET CARAVANS ARRIVING AT ITS GATES.

Damascus: the name alone conjures up a fairy-tale city of the Orient. In spite of more recent European influences, the Syrian capital has kept its Eastern outlook. The streets and bazaars of Damascus still preserve an ancient charm. Despite centuries of government by foreign powers as diverse as Ottoman Turkey and colonial France, Damascus remains an Arab city, the mother of all cities, the Pearl of the Middle East.

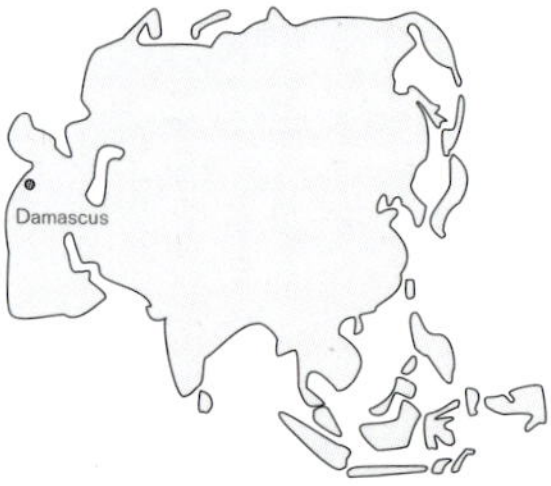

The souk and Turkish baths. Damascus stands in the shadow of the Jebel Qasiyn Mountains near the Oasis of Ghuata, one of the largest and most fertile in the Near East. The region has been settled for millenia and it has long been an important link between the Persian East and Mediterranean West. The past is palpable in the narrow lanes winding through the Old City, a UNESCO World Heritage Site since 1979. Visitors will pass at least one caravanserai, a kind of travellers' hotel catering to merchants from all over the world. Koran schools, palaces and gardens hidden in court-yards behind ornate walls can still be found through-out the city. Damascus' ancient souk is a vast, arcaded expanse devoted to trade. With its merchants, crafts-men and winding lanes, the souk is truly the heart of the city. Damascus' many *hamams*, or Turkish baths, are another popular destination for dusty travellers.

FACTS

✻ Name in the national language (Arabic): Dimashq

✻ Population of Damascus: *circa* 2.8 million

✻ Places of interest: Old City, Chapel of St Ananias, Al-Azim Palace, Bab Touma, Khan Asad Pasha Caravanserai, Umayyad Great Mosque, Chapel of St. Paul, National Museum, Saladin's Mausoleum, Sayyidah Zeinab Shrine

FAMOUS CITIZENS

✻ Abd ar-Rahman (731–788), first Umayyad emir of Cordoba in Andalusia

✻ Rafik Shami (b. 1946), writer

The magnificent prayer hall of the Umayyad Great Mosque.

The Umayyad Great Mosque. Damascus enjoyed its golden age in the eighth century when it was the capital city of the Umayyad caliphs. Many of the city's most magnificent buildings date from that period. The most important is the Umayyad Great Mosque, built by Caliph al-Walid in 705–715 on the foundations of a Christian church formerly shared by Christians and Moslems. The Great Mosque in Damascus is one of the oldest monumental religious buildings in the Islamic world. Three minarets in different architectural styles frame an arcaded inner courtyard and spacious prayer hall. The interior walls of the courtyard and arches of the arcades are adorned with glittering mosaics depicting the landscape of paradise and the golden canopy of heaven.

A great hero. Saladin (1137–93), an Abbasid general, sultan of Egypt and ruler of Damascus, was one of the Middle East's greatest heroes. Born to a Kurdish family in Iraq, his political skill and bravery gained him the respect even of Europeans he met in battle during the Crusades. After his death in 1193, Saladin was laid to rest in a simple wooden coffin below a red cupola in the courtyard of the Umayyad Great Mosque.

From Saul to Paul. The old Christian quarter of Bab Touma (St. Thomas's Gate) also lies in the Old City, including the ancient Chapel of St. Ananias, said to be the house cellar of the disciple who restored Paul's sight after he was blinded on the road to Damascus. Lying 6 metres underground, Ananias' house is one of Christendom's oldest sacred structures

Mohammed's granddaughter. One of the most exquisite monuments in Syria, the Sayyidah Zeinab mausoleum, is just 10 km south of Damascus in Rawia. Zeinab bint Ali, granddaughter of the Prophet Mohammed and sister of the Shi'a martyr Hussein, was laid to rest here. Her shrine with its golden cupola is one of Shi'a Islam's most important pilgrimage sites.

Above: The Sayyidah Zeinab Shrine in Rawia near Damascus.

Left: The Umayyad Great Mosque is at the heart of the Old City in Damascus.

IRAQ

Baghdad

THE TIGRIS RIVER SET THE STAGE FOR THE FOUNDING OF ONE OF THE WORLD'S MOST SPLENDID CITIES IN 762 CE. BAGHDAD, "GIFT OF GOD" IN PERSIAN, WAS BUILT BY ABBASID CALIPH AL-MANSUR AS HIS CAPITAL AND AS THE CENTRE OF THE MOSLEM WORLD.

In just four years' time, the palace of the Abbasid caliphs and its mosque rose along the west bank of the Tigris River. An important Middle Eastern capital, until recently Baghdad was the second largest city in the region after Tehran. Today, however, Baghdad is in turmoil. Large parts of the city have been destroyed and depopulated as a result of the 1991 Gulf War and the recent Iraq conflict. This is not the first time Baghdad has come under attack. Once the centre of Abbasid culture and medieval Islamic intellectual life, its decline began centuries ago, when the most feared invaders came from the East.

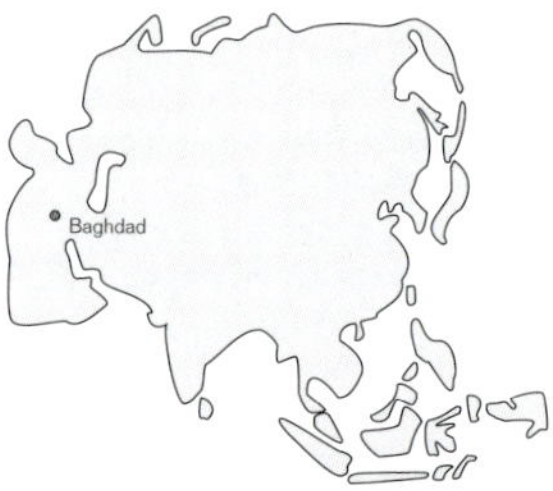

Decline and ruin. The decline of the city, and indeed the entire region, had already begun by the time of the Mongol invasion in the thirteenth century. The fighting between the invading hordes and Baghdad's defenders destroyed the regional irrigation essential to survival. Mesopotamia, which was aptly called the "fertile crescent" when irrigated, reverted to barren desert landscape almost overnight. Baghdad, one of the largest cities in the world at that time, sank quickly into oblivion.

Searching for Sheherezade. Baghdad's golden age had lasted for 500 years. Under its enlightened and educated Abbasid rulers, Baghdad thrived as a centre of science and the arts. It was the first of many

Opposite: A view of Baghdad in early 2003.

Right: The Gulf War monument.

Below: The Golden Mosque of Kadhimain.

medieval Arab cities to establish a *bayt al-hikmah*, or "house of wisdom", to house books and manuscripts collected from all over the known world. When it was burned to the ground by Mongol invaders, it is said that the Tigris River ran black with ink. The most famous Abbasid caliph is probably Harun al-Rashid (766–809), whose reputation as a wise, if brutal, ruler extended as far as Europe. Harun's court engaged in diplomatic relations with Charlemagne. Among the gifts Harun sent were a chess set, possibly the first ever seen in Europe, and an elephant. His reign and that of his son and successor Abdallah al-Ma'mun (813–833) are also the reason for Baghdad's reputation as a fairy-tale city. Both Harun and his son were inclined to extravagant expressions of their favour. As a result, this city of perhaps 65,000 people was richly endowed with bazaars, palaces and public baths. Many of the famous *Tales from 1001 Nights* told by Princess Sheherezade are set in Baghdad, including part of the story of Sinbad the Sailor. The events recounted in *Ali Baba and the Forty Thieves*, possibly part of a later, European addition to *1001 Nights*, take place in Baghdad as well.

Splendour of the caliphs. The oldest building in Baghdad is the Palace of the Abbasid Caliph. Both it and its mosque were continually enlarged over the course of many centuries. The parts of the palace preserved today were completed in the twelfth century. Mustansiriya University, now part of the University of Baghdad, was founded in 1227. Parts of it survive as the city's oldest remaining buildings. Several of its renowned professors were killed or forced to flee during recent sectarian violence. The Golden Mosque of Kadhimain, just north of the city centre, is a paragon of Islamic architecture. The third holiest site in Shi'a Islam, it was built in 1515 to house the graves of two important imams.

Modern Baghdad. Before the Iraq War in 2003, Baghdad was a busy, modern city with over 5 million residents. It also had some of the negative features of a large metropolis, such as heavy traffic on both banks of the Tigris River, smog and poorly designed high-rise buildings dominating the skyline. Karch, the city centre, was on the west bank of the river, joined with the historic centre of Rusafah on the opposite bank by eleven bridges. Most government ministries and the main railway station were located in Karch, which is today dominated by the "Green Zone", the heavily fortified military and government enclave where the present government of Iraq resides, near Saddam Hussein's former palace. The palace once extended more than 5 km along the banks of the Tigris.

FACTS

*** Name in the national language (Arabic):**
Baghdad

*** Population of Bagdad:**
circa 5.67 million

*** Places of interest:**
Mustansiriya University, Babylon, Imam Ali Mosque, Iraq Museum, Golden Mosque of Kadhimain, Abbasid Palace, Martyr's Monument, Presidential Palace

FAMOUS CITIZENS

*** Abd al-Karim Qasim**
(1914–1963), army general and first president

*** Bassim Salih Kubba**
(1944–2004), politician

*** Iyad Allawi**
(b. 1945), politician

*** Zaha Hadid**
(b. 1950), architect

CHINA

Shanghai

IN RECENT YEARS, CHINA'S LARGEST METROPOLIS HAS EXPERIENCED A TREMENDOUS BUILDING BOOM. SKYSCRAPERS HAVE SHOT UP FROM THE EARTH, GIVING WHAT WAS ONCE THE "PARIS OF THE FAR EAST" A BRAND NEW FACE.

Six thousand years ago, Shanghai's history began much more tranquilly. For many hundreds of years, the residents of the region lived by fishing in the East China Sea and the basin of the Yangtze River. An upswing began around the beginning of the second millennium BCE, when navigation up the Yangtze to the backcountry became increasingly important, and as a result Shanghai became the most important trade port on the route between inland China and Japan. This strategic location is also why Shanghai became an important piece of real estate for Europeans in the nineteenth century. As the city grew into its role as intermediary, it also acquired international flair.

Shanghai, city of adventure. The nineteenth century brought waves of Chinese emigration to Shanghai. Many people fled to the city during the upheaval of the furious Taiping Rebellion (1851–64), certainly among the worst in Chinese history. Others were attracted to the steadily growing city in the Yangtze delta in the hope of finding work or, even better, quick fame and fortune. And so it was that the population finally soared to above a million at the end of the nineteenth century. This caused a number of serious problems, including a steady increase in the unemployment rate and miserable living conditions

On the east bank of Huangpu River, the impressive towers and skyscrapers of Pudong rise up: Oriental Pearl Tower is one of the highest buildings in China.

FACTS

*** Name in English:** "City Leading to the Sea"

*** Name in the national language (Mandarin):** Dongfang Mingzhu (Pearl of the Orient)

*** Population of Shanghai:** *circa* 9.26 million

*** Population of the metropolitan area:** *circa* 18.25 million

*** Places of interest:** The Bund (Wai Tan), Chenghung Miao (Temple of the Town God), French Quarter, Huangpu Yuan, Yufo Si (Jade Buddha Temple), Lanxin Theatre, Longhua Ta (Pagoda), Shanghai Museum, Nanpu Bridge, Pearl of the Orient Tower, People's Square, Shanghai Centre, Shanghai Grand Theatre, Sun Yat-sen Residence, Yangpu Bridge, Yu Yuan Garden

for the great majority of people. Yet the influx of fortune seekers never wavered; regardless of the problems, Shanghai's economic significance continued to increase. After the abdication of the last emperor, Pu Yi, in 1911, Shanghai remained China's leading financial metropolis until well into the 1920s. Celebrated in early Hollywood films as the quintessential exotic Asian locale, it became synonymous with sin, adventurism and vast wealth.

Breeding ground for Communism. Frustration over the wide gap between the rich and the poor was expressed in ever-escalating conflicts, and it is no wonder that the richest of all China's cities should also be the breeding ground for the establishment of the Communist Party. The first Chinese Communists protested not so much against their own wealthy countrymen as against the "foreign imperialists" who lived a life of luxury in their segregated neighbourhoods. However, insurgencies that broke out in 1927 were put down with considerable bloodshed by the Chinese Nationalist Army.

Shanghai is bankrupt. In July 1937, the second Japanese-Chinese War broke out, and the Japanese marched into Shanghai in November of that same year. The Japanese did form a ring around the extraterritorial areas of the European Quarter, but even these did not get off scot-free. Beginning in 1943 – during World War II – the Japanese army rounded up foreign residents and put them into internment camps. At the end of the war, Shanghai was given back to the Chinese. The Communists gained control of Shanghai during the takeover in 1949, and this ushered in a new era for the European centres of commerce. Foreign capital was either heavily taxed or confiscated entirely. This is no surprise, because the Chinese Nationalists had plundered the gold reserves of the Bank of China in Shanghai during their flight from the Communists. The city was, in fact, bankrupt.

Decline and a new beginning. Shanghai was the centre of Mao's Great Cultural Revolution in 1966, as well as the scene of fierce battles between splinter groups of the Communist Party. Even following Mao's death in 1976, Shanghai remained the stronghold of the Maoists. The rulers in Beijing were opponents of the Maoists and, as a result, Shanghai was systematically suppressed by them until well into the 1980s. No progress was possible during that time.

Centre: The Bund in Shanghai with its colonial-era buildings.

Below: Yu Yuan Park is a place of rest and relaxation, as well as crowded walkways.

The Shanghai Museum, with its wealth of Chinese cultural exhibits, is a must-see for all visitors.

Only in the mid-1980s did things change for the better in Beijing. Shanghai was granted new privileges, and the city was again assigned a leading role in the modernization of China as a whole. Foreign companies were finally able to make the necessary investments, and Shanghai again boomed.

Two bridges unify the city. Today's Shanghai is an impressive blend of old and new. Skyscrapers, new construction, the harbour and the airport on the east side of the Huangpu River demarcate modern Shanghai. Puxi, or Old Shanghai, lies opposite it on the other bank, where lofty skyscrapers mount up again in the background. The two longest suspension bridges in the world connect these two districts, the old and the new: the Yangpu Bridge (7,658 metres long) and the Nanpu Bridge (8,346 metres). People can ride a lift up to the bridges and then walk across them – affording a wonderful view of Huangpu and the two riverbanks. You might even make faster progress on foot than driving if the cars are stuck in one of the frequent traffic jams.

Symbol of the city: the Bund. The Bund, or Waitan, a promenade along the Huangpu River, is the number one tourist attraction and symbol of Shanghai. This is the centre of what was once the "European Settlement" in Shanghai, but Chinese and foreigners alike enjoy promenading and wandering around the area nowadays. The old historical buildings in several architectural styles are found here, and the British Consulate at Number 29, built in 1873, is at the top of the list. A boat ride on the Huangpu River gives you an opportunity to view the historical buildings on one shore and the extensive new construction on the opposite bank from a number of angles.

Skylines everywhere. From the Bund, our eyes are naturally drawn to the opposite bank of the Huanpu River, where the modern buildings of Pudong are aligned. The view is truly amazing at night, when the skyscrapers are bathed in a colourful blaze of light. The television tower and the Jin Mao Tower (340 metres tall) are natural standouts. The latter reaches higher than any other building, and can be easily spotted from almost anywhere in the city. It is no coincidence that it has 88 floors, because eight is a lucky number in China.

At People's Square, which was a horse-racing track in colonial times, the city fathers approved the building of a beautiful opera house, the Shanghai

A familiar picture in Shanghai: in public places or parks, the entire personnel of a company gathers for Tai Chi during lunch breaks.

FAMOUS CITIZENS

* **Terence Young** (1915–94), movie director
* **George Atkinson** (1935–2005), founding father of video stores
* **Ingrid Noll** (b. 1935), German writer
* **Hu Jintao** (b. 1942), politician
* **Joan Chen** (b. 1961), actress

Grand Theatre, beginning in 1994. Standing some 40 metres tall, it is an impressive building. The dedication took place four years later in 1998. Western opera and chamber-music performances take place here, as well as Chinese operas and poetry readings. Typical Chinese acrobatic shows can be seen nightly at the Shanghai Centre on Nanjing Xi Lu.

Superlative public transport. But how does one get from point A to point B in this expansive metropolis? Numerous cars, taxis and buses are nearly always backed up on the streets. Shanghai is a car-lovers' city. All aspects of the car industry are concentrated in the Anjing District, including 180 domestic and foreign concerns thus far, with new ones still arriving. The Formula 1 racetrack is in this district, too. Since January 2003, residents and visitors are fortunate to have a new means of transportation at their disposal, the TransRapid or Maglev, which is definitely not standing in traffic. It connects Shanghai's underground network with the Pudong airport. With a current maximum speed of 430 km per hour, this high-speed train travels the 30-km stretch in just eight minutes. Although this top speed has only been sustained for about one minute, there is no doubt it moves people rapidly. Thus far, unfortunately, the TransRapid system does not travel into downtown Shanghai, but only to Pudong. From there, it is still almost thirty minutes by car to the city centre, and travellers must either transfer to the overcrowded underground or take a taxi.

Peace and health. Not only are the streets full of vehicles, the parks are full, too: full of people, especially on the weekends. Yu Yuan, the "Garden of Peace and Health", is no exception. Many local people come here to do Tai Chi or to practise some other Asian sport. The Yu Yuan Garden was constructed during the Ming Dynasty by Pan Yunduan (1559–77). Legend has it that he spent twenty years building the gardens to please his parents by giving them a place to rest during their old age. After Pan Yunduan's death, the garden fell into disrepair and suffered through extended periods of occupation by defending and invading troops. The city government decided to renovate the garden in 1956. Since 1961, the garden and all its amenities have been open to the public.Its pavilions, halls, stone buildings and ponds bear witness to the exceptional craftsmanship of the Ming and Qing dynasties in South China.

Centre: With more cars per capita than any other city in China, traffic jams are the order of the day in Shanghai.

Below: The ramps leading to the Nanpu Bridge resemble a maze.

ISRAEL

Jerusalem

JERUSALEM IS ONE OF THE OLDEST, CONTINUOUSLY INHABITED CITIES ON EARTH. THE CANAANITE PHOENICIAN "CITY OF PEACE" –URUSHALIM– BECAME JERUSALEM AFTER IT WAS CONQUERED BY KING DAVID AROUND THE YEAR 1000 BCE.

Living in Jerusalem has always been a bit of a gamble. The Ancient Babylonians, Egyptians and Persians all cast greedy eyes on Jerusalem's wealth. In the seventh century, Moslems conquered the "Holy Land" along with its city sacred to three faiths. During the Crusades, Jerusalem changed hands frequently. After the knights of the First Crusade succeeded in breaching Jerusalem's walls, they massacred nearly everyone within them, regardless of religion, killing as many as 40,000. Today, the Israeli and Palestinian states lay claim to parts of the city and Jerusalem's bloody, violent history continues.

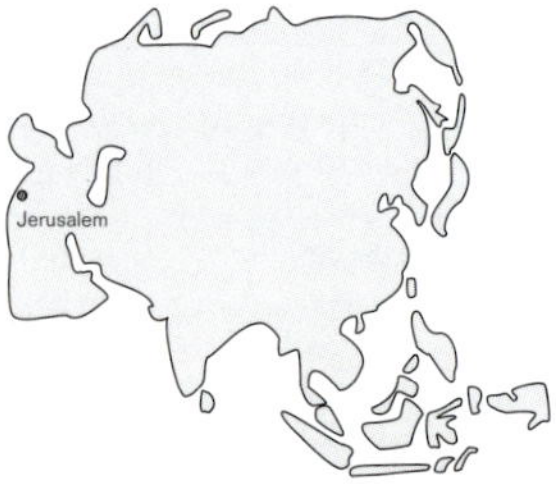

Since 1980, Jerusalem has been the seat of the Israeli government, although all foreign diplomatic missions are based in Tel Aviv in accordance with a UN resolution.

Three major religions coexist in Jerusalem, which naturally leads to a multiplicity of points of view. Each religious group is split and subdivided into factions and sects. There are as many as a dozen different Christian splinter groups, the largest of which is the Greek Orthodox community. This diversity of belief should contribute to Jerusalem's attraction, but, in reality, it too often leads to strife and violence.

The incredible concentration of sacred sites draw visitors, religious or not, from all over the world.

Right: The Mount of Olives with the Church of Mary Magdalene.

Below: The Wailing Wall with the Islamic Dome of the Rock in the background.

For Jews and Christians, Jerusalem is the Holy City and the centre of their faiths. For Moslems, Jerusalem is the third holiest city after Mecca and Medina. It was the destination of Mohammed's miraculous journey to and from Mecca in a single night. Its Temple Mount is the place from which Mohammed ascended to, and returned from, heaven.

Three architectural styles. The Old City of Jerusalem was declared a UNESCO World Heritage Site in 1981. It is divided into four districts. The Armenian Quarter occupies the south-west, the Christian Quarter, the north-west, the Jewish Quarter, the south-east and the Moslem Quarter, the north-east. The wall around the Old City was built on the order of the Ottoman sultan Suleyman the Magnificent in the sixteenth century.

Jerusalem's treasures are so many that only a few can be mentioned here. The most visited site is probably the Wailing Wall, a 400-metre-long section of the retaining wall of the terrace on top of the Temple Mount where Herod the Great built his great Jewish temple. This temple was destroyed by the Romans in the year 70 CE. Important pilgrimage sites for Christians include the Via Dolorosa, the name of the path Christ walked on his way to the crucifixion, and the fourth-century Church of the Holy Sepulchre. One of the most magnificent Islamic monuments is the Dome of the Rock. Erected on the Temple Mount over the place from which the Prophet Mohammed ascended to heaven, the Dome of the Rock is not a mosque. The remarkable Al-Aqsa Congregational Mosque, one of the largest and oldest in the world, is located nearby, also on top of the terrace of the destroyed Jewish temple.

More than a lookout point. The Mount of Olives (Hebrew: *Har Ha-Zetim*) is a famous hill on the eastern outskirts of Jerusalem. The ridge of hills is within sight of the Old City. The Temple Mount is actually higher than the Mount of Olives, which is just 809 metres above sea level. The Mount of Olives has great significance for all three major religions. According to the Jewish faith, the Messiah will cross the Mount of Olives to Jerusalem before the Last Judgement takes place in the Kidron Valley. Moslems also believe the Final Judgment will take place there. For Christians, the Mount of Olives is inextricably tied to the life and death of Jesus. Today it plays a more mundane role for many tourists, because its observation deck affords an incredible view of Old Jerusalem. Its olive trees and shaded slopes are a popular destination. Nearly all the best-known photos of the Temple Mount and Old City have been taken from the Mount of Olives.

FACTS

*** Name in the national language (Hebrew):** Yerushalayim

*** Population of Jerusalem:** *circa* 700,000

*** Places of interest:** Al-Aqsa Mosque, Old City, Bezalel Art Museum, Cardo Maximus (old road through the Jewish Quarter), Damascus Gate, Church of the Redeemer, Dome of the Rock, Golden Gate, Church of the Holy Sepulchre, Herod's Gate, Israel Museum, Western Wall, Mount of Olives, City Theatre, St. Stevens Gate, Via Dolorosa, Yad Vashem, Zion Gate

FAMOUS CITIZENS

*** William of Tyre** (1130–86), Archbishop of Tyre and historian

*** Abraham B. Jehoshua** (b. 1936), writer

*** Natalie Portman** (b. 1981), American actress

CHINA

Taipei

TAIPEI, THE CAPITAL OF TAIWAN, HAS UNDERGONE ENORMOUS CHANGE SINCE ITS FOUNDING IN THE EIGHTEENTH CENTURY. RICE FIELDS HAVE YIELDED TO SKYSCRAPERS, AND A MODERN, COMMERCIAL CITY OF MILLIONS HAS GROWN OUT OF ONCE QUIET SETTLEMENTS.

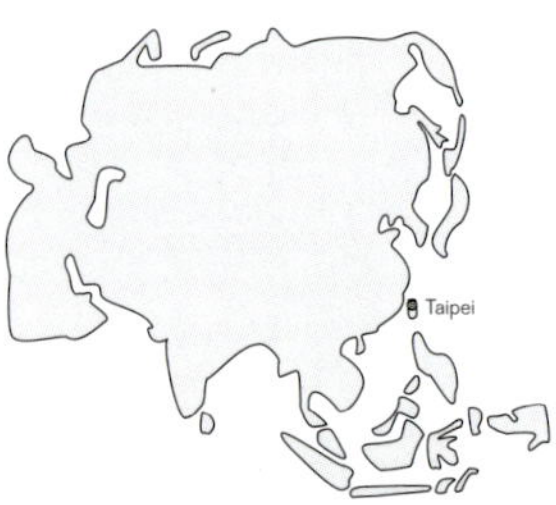

After climbing 508 metres up the Taipei 101 tower – the highest structure in the world, it can be seen easily from anywhere in the city – one can look down on the genuine Taipei amidst all the modern buildings: temples, markets, the National Palace Museum and, in between them, the many old streets and lanes where everyday life in Taipei actually unfolds.

First steps. There was a swamp here about 300 years ago, right where one of Asia's most modern cities now stands. Only the Pingpu – the original inhabitants of Formosa, who lived in the higher lying regions around the Taipei Basin – were able to reach this area by canoe. Han Chinese from the mainland came later to fish and trade, but they stayed on the banks of the Tamsui River and did not venture into the area of modern Taipei. In 1709, a Chinese farmer named Chen Lai-Chang from Chuanchou, laid the cornerstone of a farm in Takala, which is now central Taipei. From that point onwards, the number of settlers continually increased. The original settlement was known as Manka.

From Manka to Tataocheng. The administration of Manka and the surrounding region was mainly handled by emigrants from various parts of mainland China. Because of differing views regarding the future

FACTS

✱ Population of Taipei: *circa* 2.6 million

✱ Places of interest: Chiang Kai-shek Memorial Hall, Chi Nan Temple, Formosa Wonder World, Fort San Domingo, Peace Park, Jao Ho Street Night Market, Lungshan Temple, National Palace Museum, Seven Stars Mountain, Shilin Night Market, Shin Kong Observatory, Dr Yat-Sen Memorial Hall, Taipei 101, Taipei City Zoo, Taipei World Trade Centre, Taipei Financial Centre

FAMOUS CITIZENS

✱ Chieh Shih (b.1950), pianist and composer

✱ Jerry Yang (b.1968), one of the founders and board member of the Internet Service Provider, Yahoo!

At 508 metres, the Taipei 101 Tower is one of the highest structures in the world.

of the administrative structure, tensions between the residents soon escalated. The violent confrontations that resulted came to an end in 1823. One of the groups that was defeated fled from Manka, on the bank of the Tamsui River, to Tataocheng. There they began to make the land arable and laid the foundations for a flourishing community. Tataocheng surpassed Manka in the nineteenth century, and became the centre of the Taipei Prefecture in 1875.

Fast development. When the Japanese colonized Taipei in 1895, they built their main district in Taipei, and the city continued to develop steadily thereafter – even after the departure of the occupiers in 1945 and after the break with mainland China. Within a hundred years, the once rural district had developed into the administrative, economic and cultural centre of Taiwan. Manka, Tataocheng and Chengnei have all lost their original appearance, but a number of historically important sites have been preserved, including the Lin Family Villa and Garden, once the home of a very influential family in the nineteenth century, as well as the Peace Park and the 1919 Presidential Palace.

Modern city – old traditions. Today, all-glass office high-rises, luxury condominiums and modern shopping districts are situated along wide, tree-lined boulevards. Elegant restaurants, stylish nightclubs and appearances by international stars are all part of people's lives. Yet the traditional culture and way of life carries on below the contemporary surface. Everywhere you go, you stumble on timeless scenes: believers praying to their gods in ancient temples, long religious processions winding their way through the streets to the accompaniment of firecrackers, and little shops offering herbal medicines that have been relied upon for millennia. Clearly, this is one of the oldest cultures in the world.

Above: Two wheels are the best way to get around in Taipei.

Left: Traditional life mainly takes place in the temples, as seen here in the Lungshan Temple.

UNITED ARAB EMIRATES

Dubai

ACCORDING TO OFFICIAL FIGURES, 99 PER CENT OF THE RESIDENTS OF THE SMALL, ONCE INSULAR UNITED ARAB EMIRATES (UAE) RESIDE IN DUBAI CITY. THIS MAKES THE DISTINCTION BETWEEN CITY AND EMIRATE VERY SMALL INDEED.

Dubai is growing faster than any other city in the Persian Gulf region. New and luxurious hotel complexes, shopping centres and high-rise apartment buildings are being built daily. The face of this highly modern city with over a million inhabitants is constantly changing, yet always a bit eccentric. In addition to countless corporate headquarters, ultra-luxurious hotels and resorts and up-market shopping malls, Dubai is also home to the largest indoor snow park in the world, fittingly called Ski Dubai, itself located inside a gargantuan shopping mall. Opened in December 2005, the temperature inside the facility at the edge of the Arabian Desert is a constant –1°C, while the temperature outside soars to 40°C under the merciless desert sun. It would seem that in the city of Dubai, anything is possible.

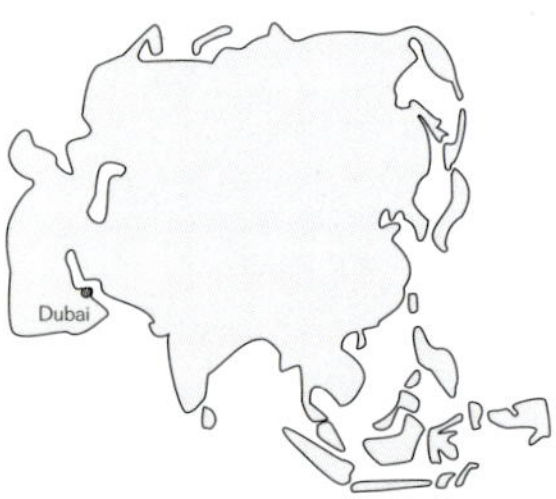

Oil – black gold of the emirs. Dubai has been governed for over 170 years by the Al-Maktoum clan. Under their leadership, and with substantial investment from Britain, the harbour of Dubai has become the most important commerical port in the Persian Gulf. The local inhabitants used to earn their living by diving for pearls. Their lifestyles changed drastically with the discovery of oil in 1966 and the economic boom that followed.

The Burj Al Arab Hotel, icon of Dubai.

FACTS

*** Population of Dubai:** *circa* 1.13 million

*** Population of the emirate:** *circa* 1.15 million

*** Places of interest:** Al Fahidi Fort, Bastakia Quarter, Burj Al Arab Hotel, Emirates Towers, Gold Souk, Great Mosque, Ibn Battua Shopping Mall, Madinat Jumeirah, Palm Islands, Sheikh Zayed Road, Ski Dubai Resort, Wild Wadi Water Park

FAMOUS CITIZENS

*** Maktoum bin Raschid Al Maktoum** (1943–2006), former emir of Dubai, succeeded by his brother in 2006

*** Mohamed bin Raschid Al Maktoum** (b. 1949), Emir of Dubai

Persian Gulf tourist destination. In addition to the oil industry, Dubai's economy relies on tourism, banking and trade. Great efforts have been made to promote Dubai as a tourist destination. The most exclusive residential quarter of the Emirate now boasts a number of world-class luxury hotels, including the famous Burj Al Arab, the "Arab Tower". Designed to resemble the sail of a traditional Persian Gulf ship, the 54-storey hotel is 321 metres tall. It is the tallest, most expensive and most luxurious hotel in the world. Visitors can play tennis at a dizzying height on top of the "helipad" overlooking the Arabian Gulf, 311 metres below. The Wild Wadi Water Park and Madinat Jumeirah shopping mall are located nearby in the suburb of Jumeirah. Then there are the Palm Islands, tear-shaped artificial landmasses built in the shallow gulf waters. They provide additional land for vacation homes, villas and hotels. Several nearby Gulf islands await similar development.

The river that is not a river. The wetlands known as Ras al-Khor divide Dubai into northern and southern sections. Ras al-Khor is not a river but a shallow inland bay. Small passenger ferries called *abras* carry people from one side to the other for a small fee, or traditional *lateen* sailing boats can be rented for a more extensive tour. A protected national wildlife area, the Ras al-Khor is home to over 100 species of birds, including a resident population of 500 greater flamingos.

Tourism promotes restoration. Most of the places of greatest interest to visitors in Dubai's Old City are found along the Ras al-Khor. Naturally, there are also many mosques in Islamic Dubai. The Great Mosque, built in 1998, is between the al-Fahidi Fort and Ras al-Khor. Al-Fahidi Fort was once the seat of the emirs of Dubai. Restored in 1970, it is now the National Museum. The Bastakia Quarter is one of the oldest parts of the city, making up the larger part of its historic centre. Having survived the twentieth-century building boom without sacrificing its ancient charm, the government now plans a complete restoration, including a museum, cultural centre, restaurants and art galleries. Houses in Bastakia are notable for their "wind towers", a traditional means of air conditioning. Cool air currents are pulled into the centre of the house through vents and windows. The system is so cleverly designed that even the smallest breeze circulates through the rooms below.

Centre: Boat trip across Ras al-Khor.

Bottom: The restful paradise of Madinat Jumeirah Beach Resort.

INDIA

Kolkata

KOLKATA, FORMERLY CALLED CALCUTTA, NEVER CEASES TO FASCINATE, DESPITE THE DIRT, STENCH AND CHAOS THAT MAY SHOCK WESTERN SENSIBILITIES. THE CULTURAL AND ARTISTIC CENTRE OF THE WEST BENGAL REGION IS STILL A HIGHLIGHT OF ANY TRIP TO INDIA.

Kolkata, capital of West Bengal, is still the centre of the high Indian arts and home to many of the nation's intellectuals. Serious and serene, Kolkata could hardly have less in common with the "Bollywood" atmosphere of Mumbai on the other side of the Indian subcontinent. Just how many people live in this famously overcrowded city? No one knows for certain. Most of the figures are based on conjecture rather than an accurate census. Nevertheless, according to the best recent estimates, Kolkata will soon be most populous city in India and, indeed, the largest city in the world, in part due to uncontrolled emigration from the surrounding regions.

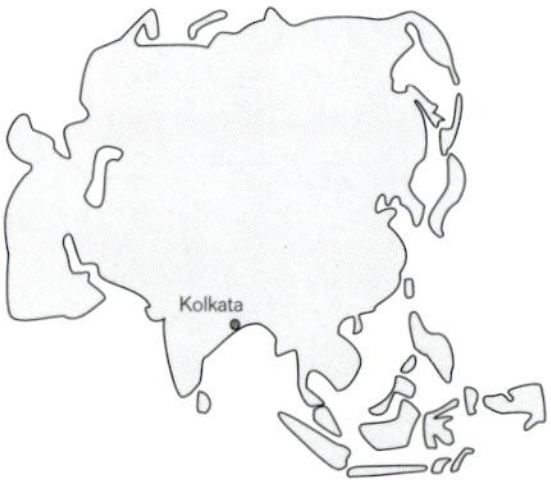

Kolkata in transformation. The British East India Company built its headquarters in the city they called Calcutta at the end of the seventeenth century. For more than a century the city was the seat of British colonial rule in India. Kolkata began to lose its leading role in 1911, when the capital was moved to the more centrally located city of New Delhi. Following the 1946 partition of the former British colonies into India and Pakistan, Kolkata found itself on the border with the Muslim nation of East Pakistan, today known as Bangladesh. Decades of civil strife within that country shut down the trade

Right: The Victoria Memorial, built in 1906 in honour of the empress of India.

Below: Belur Math is a church, mosque and temple all in one.

in jute, the raw material used in Kolkata's textile industry, which was by far the city's biggest employer. The result was unemployment and poverty for a large portion of the population. Overcrowding, which had been a problem since 1947, when Hindu refugees from Pakistan had poured into the city, became critical as unemployed mill workers from surrounding regions filled the streets. Almost overnight, the richest city in Asia became the poorest city in the world.

Proud and unyielding. The Bengali residents of Kolkata refuse to be brought to their knees by dirt, sickness and poverty. They are proud of their city, which they revere as a home to artists and saints. Two Nobel laureates are closely connected to this city on the Hooghly River. Poet Rabindranath Tagore (1861–1941), born in Kolkata, was in 1913 the first Asian recipient of the Nobel Prize for Literature. He was not only a writer, but also a painter, composer and musician. Nobel Peace Prize winner Agnes Gonxhe Bojaxhiu (1910–97), better known to the world as Mother Theresa, worked untiringly with the poorest of Kolkata's poor. Born in Macedonia, she died and was buried in Kolkata, which she made her home for nearly fifty years.

The temple complex of Belur Math. There is much more to this erstwhile British colonial capital than dirt and grime. Architectural marvels are everywhere. The Haora Bridge over the Hooghly River, for example, is the embodiment of the city's energy and strength. It has the heaviest traffic of any bridge in the world, used by over a million commuters per day, most of whom travel on foot or by pedicab. A "mere" 60,000 cars and buses cross it daily. One of the city's most important Hindu temple complexes is located in Belur Math, on the far side of the river. The renowned Hindu master Swami Vivekananda founded the Ramakrishna Mission here in 1897. Pilgrims journey here in large numbers to bathe ritually in the sacred waters of the Hooghly.

The Victoria Memorial. The colonial-era Maidan Park is still the heart of this city. Everyone gathers in the park, regardless of their social status, to play sport or just pass the time, and its gardens are some of the most extensive in the world. The architectural jewel of Kolkata is probably the Victoria Memorial, located at the park's south end. Constructed of the finest white marble, no photographs can do it justice. Not far from the memorial is the city's largest Christian church, St. Paul's Cathedral, built in 1847 with an iron and steel frame that was unique at the time. Despite its neo-Gothic design, in its day St. Paul's in Kolkata was considered a high-tech building.

FACTS

* **Official name since 2001:** Kolkata (Bengali: Kalkata)
* **Population of Kolkata:** *circa* 4.63 million
* **Population of the metropolitan area:** *circa* 14.45 million
* **Places of interest:** Academy of Fine Arts, Birla Planetarium, Dakshineswar Temple, Fort William, Haora Bridge, Indian Museum, Kali Temple, Maidan Park, Nakhoda Mosque, Pareshnath Jain Temple, Rabindra Sarobar Buddhist Temple, St. Paul's Cathedral, Victoria Memorial

FAMOUS CITIZENS

* **William Makepeace Thackeray** (1811–63), British writer
* **Rabindranath Tagore** (1861–1941), Bengali national poet (1913 Nobel Prize winner)
* **Swami Vivekananda** (1863–1902), philosopher

CHINA

Hong Kong

HONG KONG GREETS VISITORS FROM ALL OVER THE WORLD WITH A SMILE. THE URBAN EMBODIMENT OF THE BALANCING ACT BETWEEN CHINESE AND EUROPEAN CULTURES, HONG KONG HAS LONG BEEN ONE OF THE MOST EXCITING CITIES ON EARTH.

Few travel to Hong Kong for the sights; they come for business and excitement: Hong Kong is so lively it sizzles like the oil in the woks of its ubiquitous street vendors. Little has changed since the 1997 return of the British colony of Hong Kong to China. The city that flourished through cooperation between the Chinese and British societies is, if anything, more fascinating and colourful than ever before.

Opium highs and lows. In the early eighteenth century, the first British merchants to arrive at what would be Hong Kong found only a few fishing villages. The region had no importance at all within the Chinese Empire and had been ignored for centuries. The British built a trading port here in 1711, and it thrived during the early nineteenth century when goods from China were in vogue in Europe. As the fashion for things Chinese declined, the British began to deal in opium instead, growing it in India and importing it illegally into China, where the Qing Dynasty emperor had banned its sale. When the Chinese tried to halt the imports, the British responded with force. The resulting Opium Wars (1838–56) were disastrous for China. In 1842, the British took control of the city of Hong Kong and it became a British colony. An 1898 pact with China made Hong Kong and 234 nearby islands a British protectorate for 99 years.

FACTS

*** Name in the national language (Mandarin):** Xianggang

*** in Cantonese:** Heunggong

*** Population of Hong Kong:** *circa* 7 million

*** Places of interest:** Big Buddha, Flagstaff House, Heritage Museum, Hong Kong Cultural Centre, Hong Kong Disneyland, Hong Kong Museum of Art, Hong Kong Museum of History, Hong Kong Park, Lei Cheng Uk Branch Museum, Museum of Tea Ware, St. John's Cathedral, Statue Square, Supreme Court, Victoria Peak, Western Market, Wong Tai Sin Temple

FAMOUS CITIZENS

*** Amanda Lear** (b.1946), British-Asian singer, entertainer and dancer

*** Jackie Chan** (b.1954), actor

*** Chow Yun-Fat** (b.1955), actor

*** Leslie Cheung** (1956–2003), actor and pop star

The mighty bronze "Big Buddha" rises above Po Lin Monastery seated on a lotus throne.

The treaty expired in 1997. Negotiations took place in 1982 to modify the original agreement in order to protect Hong Kong's special status. China had originally demanded control not only of the so-called "New Territories" around the city, but also of Hong Kong itself. Through a series of agreements and concessions, Great Britain was able to prevent Hong Kong from being directly incorporated into mainland China. Instead, on 1 July 1997, Hong Kong was declared a Chinese Special Administrative Region.

Skyscrapers à la feng shui. Hong Kong's special status has allowed it to remain a modern economic metropolis. Despite its visible modernity, traditional ways of life are never far beneath the surface. The Ancient Chinese art of feng shui is still applied to new constructions, where measurements are configured according to lucky numbers and windows positioned so as to let prosperity in and bad luck out. Skyscrapers loom where splendid colonial buildings once stood, only a few of which have survived. In the central district, the Cathedral of St. John, the former French Residence and the Legislative Council Building are among the few pre-modern buildings that remain.

Omnipresent Buddha. Traditional life is a stronger presence in the New Territories than in the city itself. Superb temple complexes abound, built in traditional style in tranquil settings. 10,000 Buddhas Monastery is one of the most visited. This number represents "very many" or "countless" in Chinese, rather than a specific number of Buddhas. In fact, there are more, perhaps as many as 13,000. The enormous bronze Buddha towering above Po Lin Monastery on the island of Lantau is the largest Buddha in the world, at 26 metres tall. Visitors can climb a steep path of 260 steps to reach it. The panoramic view from the top definitely rewards the effort, as does the spiritual enlightenment achieved along the way.

Above: Many refugees came to Hong Kong by boat in the early 1980s, particularly from Vietnam.

Left: View of Victoria Harbour.

INDIA

Mumbai

MUMBAI, FORMERLY KNOWN AS BOMBAY, IS ONE OF THE MOST DENSELY POPULATED CITIES IN THE WORLD. IN 1533, WHEN THE PORTUGUESE FOUNDED BOM BAHIA, WHICH MEANS "GOOD BAY", NO ONE COULD HAVE IMAGINED A PLACE LIKE MUMBAI.

In India there is no official system in place to register individuals and addresses. This makes any estimate of the population of Mumbai a highly uncertain proposition. This sprawling city is modern India's centre for business and commerce, its financial capital and site of the the largest money market in the country. The Bombay Stock Exchange, founded in 1875 and based in Mumbai, is the oldest in Asia. Mumbai is also home to the largest film industry in the world – even Hollywood cannot match the sheer number of films that are produced in Bollywood.

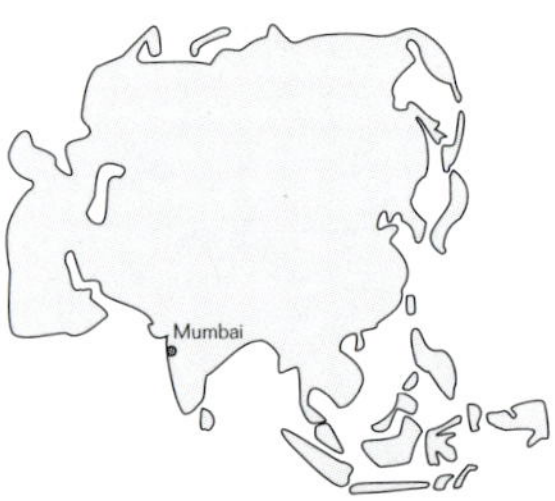

Mumbai is a city of contrasts where gleaming skyscrapers stand side by side with decrepit shacks, where air-conditioned tourist buses cruise along next to ox carts. Business goes on day and night. European-style shopping centres, recreation venues, bars, discos and pubs are everywhere. Whatever your taste, whatever you desire, you can probably find it in Mumbai. Multiplex cinemas are found on every street because Indians have a love affair with movies. As is the case with many large cities, Mumbai is also beset with a long list of social problems. At the top of the list is uncontrolled population growth. Land is scarce, and the cost of living is extremely high compared to the rest of the country. Approximately

The Gateway of India, symbol of Mumbai; to the left and behind it is the Taj Mahal Hotel.

FACTS

* **Official name since 1995:** Mumbai
* **Population of Mumbai:** *circa* 12.7 million
* **Population of the metropolitan area:** *circa* 19.5 million
* **Places of interest:** Babulnath Temple, Chhatrapati Shivaji Terminus, Crawford Market, Elephanta Caves, Fort Quarter, Gateway of India, Haji Ali Mosque, Hutatma Chowk, Malabar Hill, Jama Masjid Mosque, Mahatma Gandhi Museum, Mumba Devi

FAMOUS CITIZENS

* **Rudyard Kipling** (1865–1936), writer (1907 Nobel Prize)
* **Sir Nisargadatta Maharj** (1897–1981), religious teacher, guru
* **Rajiv Gandhi** (1944–91), politician
* **Salman Rushdie** (b.1947), writer

6 million people live in slums today, making up nearly half of the city's population. Many of the poor, unable to afford Mumbai's comparatively expensive housing costs, live far outside the city centre in impoverished commuter communities. Many spend several hours a day travelling to work via Mumbai's extensive rail and bus system.

A colonial metropolis. Mumbai is not an easy, relaxing city to visit and it is not exactly filled with typical tourist attractions. Nevertheless, if you are ready and willing to travel to every corner of the city, there are certainly some beautiful places to see. The home where Mahatma Gandhi lived from 1917 to 1934, for example, is open to the public. Known locally as Mani Bhavan, it includes a museum and research centre devoted to the life and work of its famous former occupant. The Gateway of India is also worth a visit. This monumental gateway directly on the harbour is a symbol of both Old Bombay and modern Mumbai. It was built in 1911 to welcome King George V and his queen, Maria von Teck on the occasion of their visit to the city. Boat tours of the harbour depart from this location, offering the best views of the Mumbai skyline, with the Gateway of India in the foreground and the Taj Mahal Hotel behind it. It is also possible to take a boat ride to Elephanta Island, where the Temple Cave of the Lord Shiva is found, one of the two UNESCO World Heritage Sites in the city.

The second UNESCO World Heritage Site in Mumbai is the Chhatrapati Shivaji Terminus, formerly known as Victoria Terminus. Dedicated in 1888, it has long been one of the largest and busiest railway stations on Earth. Its imposing scale was deliberately designed as an assertion of British claims to power and the right to rule. Architect Frederick Stevens designed a functional building that is nothing short of monumental, combining the neo-Gothic style of the early Victorian era with elements derived from traditional Indian architecture. Richly ornamented, with every detail precisely rendered, this magnificent behemoth is unfortunately under threat today from the damage done by smog and acid rain. From a purely practical point of view, the train station remains as important today as it once was to British colonial administrators. Over 1,000 trains pass through the station daily, carrying an average of 3 million passengers.

Centre: The Chhatrapati Shivaji Terminus (formerly the Victoria Terminus) is still a hub of activity.

Bottom: Stone sculpture of Trimurthi Sadasiva, a manifestation of Shiva, in the Elephanta Caves on an island near Mumbai.

THE PHILIPPINES

Manila

MANILA, CAPITAL OF THE PHILIPPINES, PRESENTS A CHALLENGE. BOTH BLESSED AND CURSED, SLUMS STAND ALONGSIDE VENERABLE CHURCHES AND SEVERAL UNIVERSITIES CONTRAST WITH THE MANY NIGHTCLUBS AND EXCITING, ROUND-THE-CLOCK STREET LIFE.

Manila is the political and economic nerve centre of the Philippines, and it serves as a magnet for people from all over the country. For most visitors from North America or Europe, this megacity does not seem to merit more than a few days' visit, after which the tranquillity of the provinces may seem all that much more attractive. Although a visit to Manila is taxing, it nevertheless gives the visitor important insights into the culture, history and current state of this island republic, insights that stem from its very wealth of contradictions.

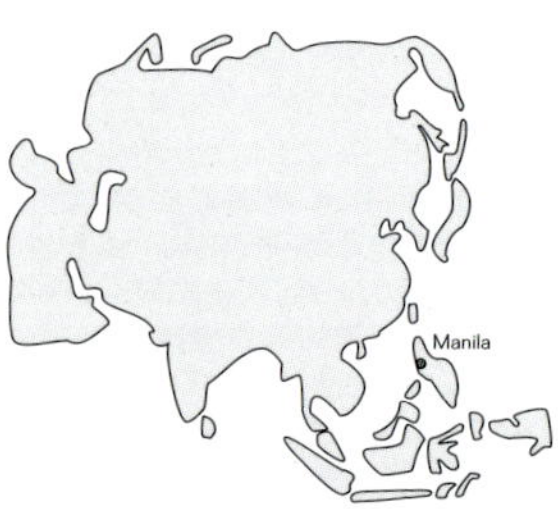

In the sights of foreign conquerors. Natives who settled at the mouth of the Pasig River in Manila have seen a great many rulers come and go. The first to come were the Malaysians, who arrived in the Philippines during the pre-Christian era. Hindu and Buddhist rulers from Indonesia followed. Islam reached Manila at the end of the fifteenth century. The Muslim sultanate established in the mid-sixteenth century had been in existence for barely a decade when Spanish Catholic seafarers appeared on the horizon.

Colonial Manila. Miguel de Legaspi conquered Manila in 1571, declaring it to be the capital of the Spanish colony of the Philippines. Despite the

Right: The impressive Romanesque architecture of Intramuros Cathedral.

Below: Jeepneys, mobile icons of Manila.

ravages of World War II, when Manila was heavily bombed, traces of the city's colonial past are still in evidence, particularly in the Intramuros district. The city centre, with its partially restored wall (*intramuros* = "inside the walls"), is the site of a number of sixteenth-century buildings, including Fort Santiago, Manila Cathedral and the church of San Augustin, the oldest in the city.

At the centre of power. The heart of Manila is now elsewhere, in Makati, the modern commercial and banking quarter. Elegant high rises, gorgeous residential estates, supermodern shopping centres and numerous international hotels can be found there. The modern development of this quarter began in the mid-twentieth century. Like much of the development in Manila, Makati is closely connected to the politically powerful Zobel de Ayala family. The family name is found throughout the city, on streets, buildings and public monuments.

They come here not only to pray. Pasay City is located in the south-west of Manila across the superhighway from up-market Makati. On Wednesdays, Pasay is overrun with people. In Baclaran, the faithful crowd into Redemption Church, where weekly services are held in honour of the Virgin Mary. But one suspects that even more Manilans make their way to Pasay in order to patronize the neighbourhood's famous *lechón* stands, known to be the best source of that quintessential Philippine specialty – roast suckling pig.

A bit of folk culture. Throughout Manila, a light rail station is never far away. If your stomach is complaining after a feast of suckling pig, a gentle ride on this elevated railway is highly recommended. The trip back to town can also be made by Jeepney, of course, though it will be slower and more crowded. Jeepneys were originally former US Army jeeps that had been converted into passenger vehicles with as many as fourteen canopied seats. These days, however, most Jeepneys come fresh from the factory. Skilful painting and ornamentation are a prerequisite for genuine Jeepney status. Most have religious motifs as their central theme, but they may include lighthearted comic-strip images. Many Jeepneys are so thoroughly covered in advertising that they resemble moving billboards, while others looks like temples on wheels. What's important for visitors to remember, however, is that Jeepneys follow specific routes, just like buses. It is always best to enquire about the route before getting on board.

FACTS

*** Population of the Manila metropolitan area:**
circa 15 million

*** Places of interest:**
Barrio San Luis, Binondo Church, Casa Manila, Chinatown, Coconut Palace, Corregidor Island, Fort Santiago, Intramuros, Malacanang Palace, Manila Cathedral, National Museum, Old Congress Building, Paco Park, Rizal Park (Luneta), Roxas Boulevard, San Augustin Church

FAMOUS CITIZENS

*** Carlos P. Rómulo**
(1899–1985), politician

*** Corazon Aquino**
(b. 1933), politician

*** Billy Crawford**
(b. 1982), entertainer

THAILAND

Bangkok

BANGKOK MAY BE THE MOST EXCITING METROPOLIS IN SOUTH-EAST ASIA. ITS CHARM IS ACCESSIBLE TO ANYONE WHO IS NOT PUT OFF BY ITS HECTIC ATMOSPHERE. BANGKOK DEMANDS THAT VISITORS DIVE IN AND ENJOY THE LIFESTYLE OF SOUTH-EAST ASIA.

Bangkok is a captivating, fascinating and dynamic city with countless places to see, terrific shopping opportunities, a diverse and exciting nightlife and thousands of restaurants. Since traffic is usually standing still, it is better to take the Skytrain and remain above street level. Even there, expect crowded platforms full of people shoving to board the cars.

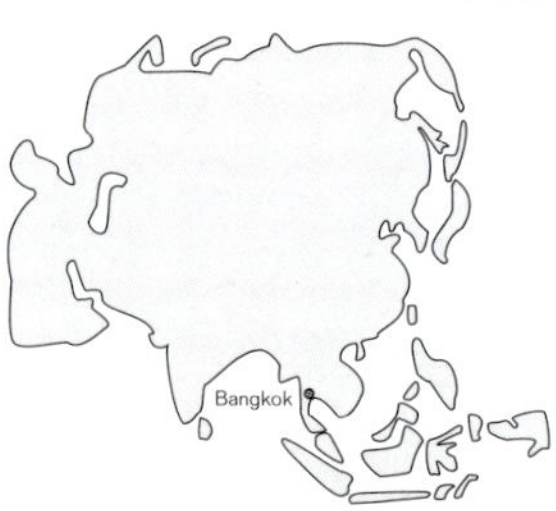

Siam's new beginning. Large parts of Thailand fell under Burmese rule during the eighteenth century. After the destruction of the former Thai capital, Ayutthaya, a handful of men under the leadership of General Taksin went in search of a new place to establish the government of the kingdom. In 1772, they settled on Thonburi, a small town on the west bank of the Chao Phraya River. The little town was built around an important temple. The site was well protected by the river and hastily erected land walls. Taksin expanded the temple complex into the royal temple of Wat Arun, in honour of the goddess Aruna. Wat Arun survives today as the landmark of Bangkok.

An inglorious end. Tak Sin ruled the Kingdom of Siam with an iron fist for ten years. Years of war transformed him into a merciless despot. He saw himself as Buddha's successor, and demanded to be

FACTS

* **Official name:** Krung Thep Mahanakhon
* **Name in the national language (Thai):** Krung Thep
* **Population of Bangkok:** *circa* 6.64 million
* **Population of the metropolitan area:** *circa* 10.78 million
* **Places of interest:** Ban Kamthieng, Chitralada Palace, Jim Thompson's traditional houses, Royal Palace, Lak Mueang Shrine, Lumpini Park, Memorial Bridge, National Museum, Puppet Museum, Queen's Gallery, Suan Pakkard Palace, Vimanmek Palace, Wat Arun, Wat Benchamabophit, Wat Pho, Wat Phra Kaeo, Wat Saket, Wat Trimit

FAMOUS CITIZENS

* **Seni Pramoj** (1905–97), politician
* **Tanin Kraivixien** (b.1927), politician
* **Sirikit** (b.1932), Queen of Thailand

The Royal Pantheon at Wat Phra Kaeo reflects the splendour of Old Siam.

worshipped as a god. This led to rebellion and to his execution on 6 April 1782. In accordance with time-honoured custom, he was placed in a sack and beaten to death, because royal blood could not be allowed to spill on the ground.

A city of temples. Following Tak Sin's death, Bangkok was founded anew as a different city on the opposite bank of the river. King Rama I used the old capital of Ayutthaya as a model for the construction of his new residence. There he built the Royal Palace and the Royal Temple of Wat Phra Kaeo, named after the statue of the Emerald Buddha, which Rama commanded be brought here from Wat Arun. Today, this is Thailand's most revered image of Buddha. The area around the Royal Palace is the historic centre of present-day Bangkok.

Canals, called 'khlongs', used to wind through and around the new capital, and much of the city's commerce took place directly on the water. Nearly all of the khlongs were filled in during the twentieth century to allow for the expansion of the city. All of Bangkok's busy streets and wide boulevards were originally canals. The first bridge over the Chao Phraya River, the Memorial Bridge, was dedicated in 1932, joining Thonburi with the constantly expanding city on the opposite bank. The last of the khlongs with their colourful floating markets can still be found in Thonburi. The face of the Bangkok metropolitan district, known as Krung Thep Mahanakhon in the Thai language, was mostly modernized in the 1980s, when an explosion of construction of high-rise buildings and skyscrapers forever altered the cityscape. The Skytrain now weaves its way through a concrete and steel jungle, with only the occasional glimpse of a golden stupa or ornately decorated palace to remind the visitor of Bangkok's glorious past.

Above: A merchant on one of the khlongs, or canals, that run through the city.

Left: The symbol of Bangkok, Wat Arun, illuminated by the setting sun on the north bank of the Chao Phraya.

CAMBODIA

Phnom Penh

PHNOM PENH WAS ONCE THE MOST BEAUTIFUL FRENCH COLONIAL CITY IN INDOCHINA. DESPITE DEVASTATION WROUGHT BY THE VIETNAM AND LATER CIVIL WAR, THIS MEKONG DELTA CITY ON THE TONLE SAP RIVER RETAINS MUCH OF ITS ORIGINAL CHARACTER.

Getting oriented in Phnom Penh is relatively simple. Most of the streets run perfectly parallel to each other, a legacy of the French colonial rulers who took what was a small, insignificant village and transformed it into a major Asian metropolis. In fact, the present-day Cambodian capital is bursting at the seams due to rural migration and unrestricted population growth.

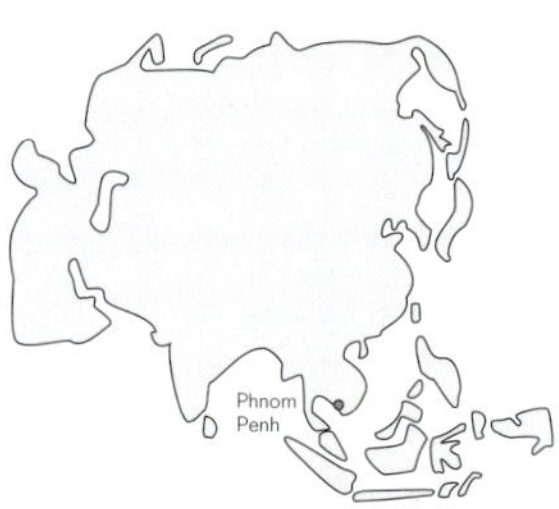

Myths and legends. Cambodian legends tell of a Widow Penh who lived by the river in the fourteenth century. In 1372, she saw a tree adrift on the Tonle Sap River. When, with the help of a friend, she finally managed to bring the tree onto the shore, she had been mistaken. What she had pulled from the current was not a tree, but four golden statues of the Buddha and a stone Buddha. The widow recognized the miracle as a sign, and in response she began to heap up a 'stupa' – a hill with a pagoda. The statues were placed in the pagoda of the temple complex known today as Wat Phnom Daun Penh (Hill of Old Penh). The town of Phnom Penh grew up around it. The legend does not explain just why the Widow Penh felt the need to rescue the "tree", rather than simply allowing it to drift further downstream. In Cambodia, it is enough to say that Phnom Penh exists thanks to Buddha.

The four legendary golden statues of the Buddha can still be seen in the temple of Wat Phnom.

FACTS

*** Population of Phnom Penh:** *circa* 1.5 million

*** Places of interest:** Foreign Correspondent's Club of Cambodia (FCCC), Choeng Ek Killing Field, Royal Palace, National Museum, Russian Market, Silver Pagoda, Tonle Sap River Promenade, Tuol Sleng Museum, Independence Monument, Wat Phnom

FAMOUS CITIZENS

*** Norodom Sihanouk** (b. 1922), king until 2004

*** Norodom Sihamoni** (b. 1953), king since 2004

Colonial Phnom Penh. The French established colonial rule in 1864, having been called in by the Cambodians to assist them in their fight against Siam (now Thailand) and Vietnam. In the process, and despite French military assistance, Cambodia lost about one-quarter of its territory. In 1884, Cambodia was declared part of the new French colonial territory of Indochina. Phnom Penh became the Cambodian capital in (1886–87). The small town grew into a city under French rule. Swamp areas in the surrounding region were drained, allowing Phnom Penh to expand and flourish. This all happened within a relatively short period, as French colonial influence lasted for just ninety years. The French planned and constructed the city according to their architectural tastes. With its wide boulevards and ornate façades, the city acquired something of a Mediterranean atmosphere in the process.

A royal gift. Many of Phnom Penh's colonial-period buildings are well worth seeing. First and foremost is the Royal Palace. Its throne room, constructed in 1917, is particularly magnificent. Not far from the throne room are the royal treasury and the villa of Napoleon III. The villa was built in 1866, but in faraway Egypt, rather than in Cambodia. It originally had served as lodging for the French empress Eugenia during the opening ceremonies for the Suez Canal. Napoleon III presented the building as a gift to the Cambodian king one year later, ordering that it be disassembled, transported to Phnom Penh by ship and then put back together again.

The wealth of the Cambodian kings. The Silver Pagoda is located in the northern part of the palace grounds. The pagoda, built for King Norodom in 1866, is mostly made of wood. King Sihanouk enlarged it in 1962. Its name is derived from the more than 5,000 silver tiles – weighing a total of more than six tons – that make up the floor of the pagoda. The most important image in the temple is the small, seventeenth-century Baccarat Crystal Buddha. Directly behind it stands a much larger statue of the Buddha, created in 1906 from 90 kg of gold and decorated with 9,584 diamonds. When visiting the Silver Pagoda, it is important to dress respectfully in the presence of so many holy images. Shorts and hats are strictly forbidden.

Centre: The throne room of the Royal Palace.

Bottom: The memorial at the Choeung Ek (the Killing Fields) reminds people of the horrors of the civil war (1975–79).

VIETNAM

Ho Chi Minh City

THE HEART AND SOUL OF VIETNAM IS NOT ITS CAPITAL, HANOI, IN THE FAR NORTH, BUT HO CHI MINH CITY. FORMERLY KNOWN AS SAIGON, THE CITY IN THE SOUTH WAS RENAMED TO HONOUR THE REVOLUTIONARY LEADER OF THE DEMOCRATIC REPUBLIC OF VIETNAM.

Ho Chi Minh City is an urban landscape full of life, a life that takes place mainly on the streets. Its clutter of shops, food stands, commercial vehicles and pavement vendors form the fascinating backdrop of Vietnam's most exciting city. Ho Chi Minh City, with an area of more than 2,000 km², is really more like a province, extending all the way from the South China Sea to the Cambodian border. To call it a mere "city" is almost a misnomer. To distinguish it from the larger associated area, the city's dense, urban centre is still officially known by its former name of Saigon.

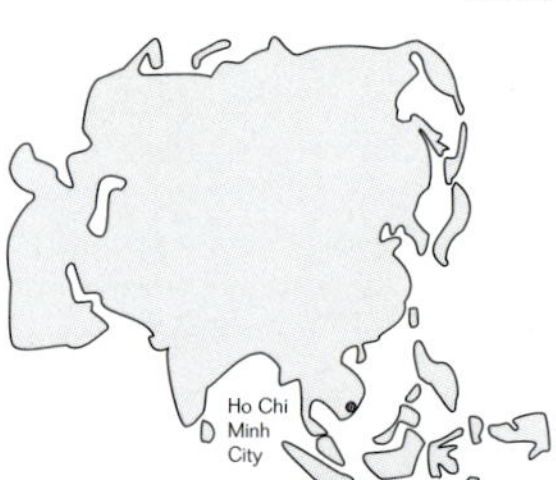

A village in the forest. The Vietnamese did not found Old Saigon; it developed from a village inhabited by Khmer fishermen sometime between the first and sixth centuries. They called their settlement Prei Nokor, which means "village in the forest". Prei Nokor grew during the period of the Khmer Empire, and by the seventeenth century it was already an important Mekong Delta trading centre. Even in those days, foreign merchants were drawn to the city, which soon had a resident population made up of Chinese, Malaysians and Indians. During this period, the Vietnamese Nguyen Dynasty began to expand southwards from its homeland in the north. The Vietnamese eventually conquered almost the entire

Right: Notre Dame Cathedral in Saigon.

Below: A flower market on Nguyen Hue during the Vietnamese New Year (Tet Festival).

southern region of present-day Vietnam, including, in 1698, the city of Prei Nokor, which they renamed Saigon.

The legacy of colonialism. In 1861, the city had new rulers following the French occupation. The French colonial administrators made Saigon the administrative seat of Cochin China, the one direct-rule colony within the larger Indochinese protectorate. The colony consisted of most of South Vietnam and eastern Cambodia. In the years that followed, the colonial rulers had the surrounding wetlands drained and set about creating a French-Mediterranean city in the middle of South-East Asia. The Cathedral of Notre Dame, built between 1877 and 1883, is one of the best examples of French colonial architecture in a city that is filled with impressive buildings. The old French Quarter of Ho Chi Minh City remains one of the principal tourist attractions to this day. Most of the sites can be admired along the famous, 1.6-km-long strip of Dong Khoi Street, where city hall, the cathedral, the City Theatre and the ornate main post-office are conveniently arrayed all in a row. The steel frame for the post-office building is the work of Gustave Eiffel, the engineer for a number of bridges and public buildings in French Indochina, as well as of the famous Eiffel Tower in Paris.

Living on in novels. There are three more buildings of note on Dong Khoi Street, all hotels that appeared in novels set in Vietnam. Two of them are connected to the famous British author Graham Greene. The Continental Hotel is the set for Greene's novel *The Quiet American*, later made into a 2002 film starring Michael Caine. Nearby is the Hotel Rex, where many journalists covering the Vietnam War lived. Graham Greene himself frequently stopped by for a drink in its famous rooftop bar. Further down the street is the Majestic Hotel, made famous by the French author Marguerite Duras in her novel *The Lover*.

The scent of Asia. Saigon's Chinese quarter, the Cholon, is entirely and genuinely Asian. *Cholon* means "large market", which is precisely what it is. Street barbers, ear cleaners, bird dealers and more ply their trade in its twisting, turning, narrow alleys and streets. Exotic aromas emanate from Chinese restaurants and apothecaries. Pungent incense drifts out into the street from the many Taoist temples along Nguyen Trai Street. Perhaps the most beautiful pagoda in Saigon is the Thien Hau Pagoda (Chua Ba), a masterpiece of southern Chinese temple architecture. The façade and roof are adorned with colourful, lifelike ceramic figures.

FACTS

* **Name in the national language (Vietnamese):** Thanh pho Ho Chi Minh
* **Name prior to the 1976 reunification:** Saigon
* **Population of Ho Chi Minh City:** *circa* 7.4 million
* **Places of interest:** Ben Thanh Market, Cholon, Dong Khoi Street, Main Post Office, Jade Pagoda, Le Duan Boulevard, Nguyen Hue Boulevard, Revolutionary Museum, Cathedral of Notre Dame, Quan Am Pagoda, Saigon Museum, Thien Hau Pagoda, Reunification Palace

FAMOUS CITIZENS

* **René Le Hénaff** (1902–2005), French movie director
* **Linh Dan Pham** (b. 1974), actress

MALAYSIA

Kuala Lumpur

KUALA LUMPUR IS INEXTRICABLY LINKED WITH THE PETRONAS TOWERS, THE LARGEST TWIN TOWERS IN THE WORLD, AND FORMULA ONE RACING FANS WILL KNOW THAT KUALA LUMPAR HAS HOSTED THE MALAYSIAN GRAND PRIX SINCE 1999.

There is much more to Kuala Lumpur than racetracks and skyscrapers. Because of its strategic location, Kuala Lumpur has been an important commercial and business centre for over a century. Tree-lined streets, parks and public flower gardens are brightly illuminated at dusk, transforming the city into a beautiful night-time wonderland. It is no wonder that Kuala Lumpur is called "Garden City of Lights".

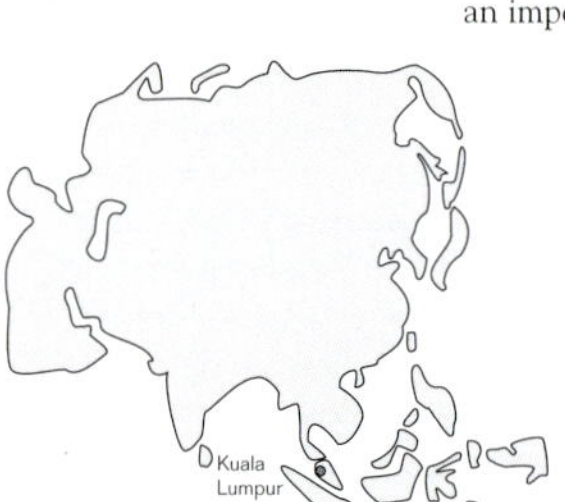

Riches based on tin. Kuala Lumpur, a name that can be translated as "muddy confluence", was founded in 1857 as a tin-prospecting camp under the protection of the Malay royal family. The discovery of tin brought prosperity and urban growth to the region. Everyone wanted a piece of the wealth, including the British. In 1895, Kuala Lumpar was made the capital of the British protectorate of the Malay Federated States. The British laid out Kuala Lumpar's streets, built markets and regulated the harbour traffic. The legacy of colonialism is still apparent everywhere one looks, and buildings from that period are among the city's top tourist attractions. Chief among these is the 1897 Sultan Abdul Samad Building, constructed in the Moorish architectural style complete with copper cupolas and a 130-metre-tall tower. Formerly the seat of the British protectorate administration,

FACTS

* **Population of Kuala Lumpur:** *circa* 1.45 million
* **Population of the metropolitan area:** *circa* 4.3 million
* **Places of interest:** Chinese Night Market, Istana Negara (official royal residence), Lake Gardens, Masjid Jamek Mosque, Masjid Negara Mosque, National Monument, Petronas Twin Towers, Independence Square, Sri Mahamariaman Temple, St. Mary's Cathedral, Sultan Abdul Samad Building, Suria KLCC (City Centre), Thean Hou Temple, The Golden Triangle

FAMOUS CITIZENS

* **Mei-Ling Ludi** (b. 1974), Miss Malaysia 2000
* **Alex Yoong** (b. 1976), motor sportsman

View of KLCC Park from the Skybridge that joins the Petronas Twin Towers.

it now houses the Malaysian Justice Ministry and a textile museum.

A city of towers. Visitors to Kuala Lumpur simply have to experience the Petronas Twin Towers and the Kuala Lumpur City Centre (KLCC). From 1998 until 2003, the 88-storey high twin towers were the tallest buildings in the world. Stretching 452 metres high towards the sky, incredibly, the two towers are joined between the 41st and 42nd floors by a 58-metre-long steel Skybridge. The upper storeys of the Petronas Towers, headquarters of Malaysia's national energy industry, are not generally open to the public, although a limited number of free tickets granting access to the Skybridge are given out every morning at 8:30 am. Anyone wanting to take advantage of this opportunity can expect long queues. The towers are more than just an architectural attraction for tourists, however. The lower floors and basement are occupied by bustling shopping centres, cinemas and restaurants. Anyone who would like to get a good view of the towers can walk over to the Menara KL Television Tower. This needle-like structure, reminiscent of a minaret, is located on top of a nearby hill. Because the television tower itself stands 421 metres tall, it offers a superb view of the Petronas "Twins".

A peaceful oasis. Kuala Lumpur has a tranquil heart. The Taman Tasik Perdana ("Lake Gardens") offer almost 100 hectares of green landscaping right in the middle of the city. The gardens are a popular destination for locals and visitors alike. Everyone in Kuala Lumpur needs a break from the stressful, hectic pace of daily life in the big city. Malaysia's National Monument is located in the centre of Taman Tasik Perdana. The largest freestanding bronze sculpture in the world, it depicts a heroic scene from World War II.

Above: The Suria Shopping Centre is in the lower levels of the Twin Towers.

Left: The Sultan Abdul Samad Building houses a textile museum.

SINGAPORE

Singapore

THE MERLION, THE HERALDIC ANIMAL OF SINGAPORE, SPOUTS A POWERFUL STREAM OF WATER INTO THE SINGAPORE RIVER. THIS MYTHICAL CREATURE HAS THE HEAD OF A LION AND THE BODY OF A FISH.

The Merlion's origins are a combination of the magical and mundane. Towards the end of the thirteenth century, a Buddhist prince from the Indonesian island of Sumatra founded the Kingdom of Temasek near what is today Singapore. One day, he arrived at a large island, where he saw a terrifying beast. He thought it was a lion, although no lions had ever been seen in the area, nor have they been sighted since. The city founded on the island was named Singha Pura ("Lion City") as a result. The Merlion's tail connects it to fishing, the traditional occupation of the local population.

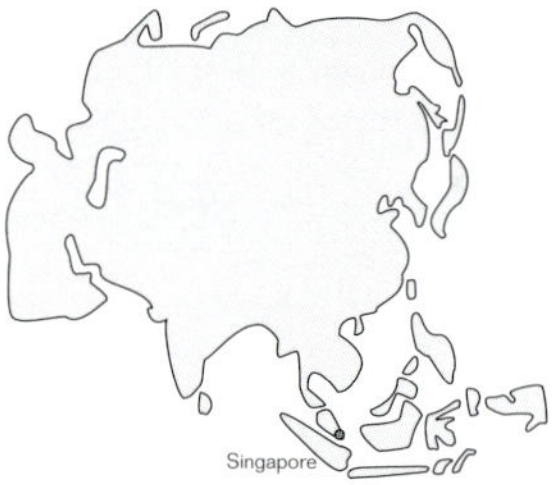

A British crown colony. In Singapore, drivers still follow the British practice of keeping to the left side of the road. British influence began in the early nineteenth century when Sir Thomas Stamford Raffles founded the first branch office of the British East India Company here in 1819. Raffles is a difficult man to forget in Singapore, where statues, streets and the Raffles Hotel all bear his name. Before Raffles arrived, the island had been a desolate place, occupied by only a few fishermen and the occasional Malaysian pirate. Singapore was a British crown colony as well as a commercial port belonging to the East India Company from 1867 to 1963. During those years, the city developed into one of largest commer-

The Merlion spouts a stream of water into the Singapore River against the background of the city's imposing skyline.

FACTS

✱ **Name in the national language (Malay):** Singapura

✱ **Population of Singapore:** *circa* 4.4 million

✱ **Places of interest:** Arab Street, Boat Quay, Botanical Gardens, Bukit Timah Nature Resort, Chinatown, East Coast Park, Esplanade Park, Financial District, Jurong Bird Park, Lau Pa Sat Festival Market, Little India, The Merlion, Orchard Road, Sentosa Island Resort, Sim Lim Square, Singapore Art Museum, Singapore Science Centre, Singapore Zoo, Suntec City, The Raffles Hotel

FAMOUS CITIZENS

✱ **Leslie Charteris** (1907–93), American author

✱ **Tony Anholt** (1941–2002), English actor

✱ **Vanessa Mae** (b. 1978), violinist

cial ports in South-East Asia. Since independence in 1964, Singapore has grown into a modern metropolis.

More than just business. Though Singapore enjoys a worldwide reputation as a hyper-successful economic powerhouse, "Lion City" is not usually listed among anyone's favourite tourist destinations. Many travellers only make a brief stop here en route to somewhere else. This is not really fair to Singapore, a city that has a great deal to offer. Its Chinatown Quarter, Arab Street and Little India have been tidied up and polished until they shine. Even the modern areas of the city centre have numerous places worth visiting. The cultural life of the city is diverse, and one runs into it at every turn. Singapore has never been more colourful or inviting.

Esplanade Park. A new cultural centre has sprung from the banks of the river delta in Singapore's Esplanade Park. Along with the Merlion, this facility is emblematic of Singapore, possibly in part because the complex is shaped like an enormous durian melon. This is a fruit with a famously awful smell, as many travellers to South-East Asia have learned from personal experience, but "stink fruit" is very popular with the locals.

Driving licence by auction. Owning a private car in Singapore is a rather costly proposition. Once all the expenses are tallied up, owning a car can cost more than twice as much in Singapore as it does in Europe. Among the additional costs is the purchase of a licence "at auction". This licence is valid for ten years, and is linked to the specific vehicle with which it is registered. If the owner purchases a new car, the whole process has to be started all over again. This method has so far proven very successful in keeping Singapore from being overrun with traffic jams and smog, the fate of so many other big cities.

A stroll through Singapore. Singapore has a rich array of historical buildings. A walk through Singapore should begin in the city centre with Chinatown. The colourfully decorated stores, restaurants and cafés invite a short stopover. Wandering to the other side of Cross Street brings one to the Lau Pa Sat Festival Market. A short detour to the river promenade, where the Merlion statue can be seen in action, is also recommended. Along the promenade, visitors can relax under an umbrella and get away from the bustle of the city. Later, the nightlife at nearby Boat Quay may prove more tempting.

Centre: A whirl of colourful activity on the streets of Chinatown.

Bottom: The concert hall in Esplanade Park, Singapore's cultural centre.

INDONESIA

Jakarta

THE INDONESIAN CAPITAL IS THE MELTING POT OF SOUTH-EAST ASIA. PEOPLE FROM ALL OVER THE REGION LIVE AND WORK IN JAKARTA: INDIANS, CHINESE, ARABS, AUSTRALIANS AND DESCENDENTS OF ERSTWHILE COLONIAL RULERS FROM THE NETHERLANDS.

Slowly but surely, Jakarta is becoming one of the most congested cities in the world. The steadily growing metropolis is located on the north-west Indonesian island of Java, the most densely populated island in the world. Jakarta, the great Islamic city, is a mixture of old and new, traditional and Western, wealthy and poor, modern and dilapidated. It continues to present a diverse and ever-changing countenance to the world.

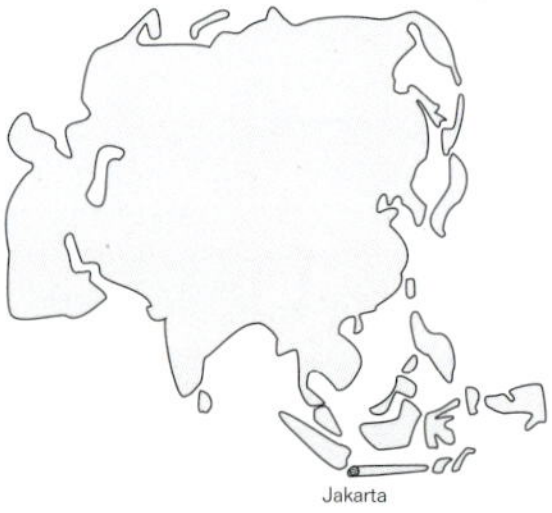

Foreign rulers. In the seventeenth century, the Dutch East India Company founded the commerical trading post of Fort Batavia on the site of what would one day be the megacity of Jakarta. The Dutch were not the first to recognize the strategic advantages of this place on the Ciliwung River, however. The river delta had already been settled for centuries by the time the Europeans arrived. Muslims had sacked the city of Sunda Kelapa in the spring of 1527, and founded the city of Jayakarta ("Great Victory") in its place a few months later. Soon after that, the Dutch arrived. They saw to it that the Dutch settlement at Fort Batavia was fully equipped with channels and canals, just like so many cities in their home country. Only a few years later, with the arrival of the first tsunami floodwaters, did the Dutch realize that the canals

Right: View of the city and the Istiqlal Mosque.

Below: Dutch architecture on Kali Besar, the Great Canal.

were perhaps not particularly well-suited to the location. Describing the aftermath of a tsunami, a travel companion of the British explorer James Cook wrote that, "When it [the floodwater] subsided, one found an unbelievable amount of mud and faeces in its place… Of one hundred Dutch soldiers who had come here from Europe, we were told that barely fifty had survived at the end of the first year… In all of Batavia, we did not see a single person who looked really flush and healthy."

Islamic modernity. The vast majority of Jakarta's residents are Muslim. The Istiqlal Mosque, Jakarta's largest, is both an impressive building in itself and the biggest mosque in South-East Asia. Nevertheless, there is little of the splendour of Arabian or Persian architecture in this modern structure. Like the mosque, the entire skyline of Jakarta is ultra-modern in design and supremely functional, if not especially beautiful. Skyscrapers and other new buildings line the streets of the busy harbour. The Jakarta Tower, scheduled to open its doors in 2009, is as yet unfinished. At 558 metres it will be the tallest, freestanding structure in the Southern Hemisphere.

The restored Dutch Quarter. Anyone who wants to experience the past must take a stroll through Jakarta's old Dutch Quarter. Working in cooperation with UNESCO, the city administration has restored many of the original colonial buildings. One of these is the Stadthuys, Batavia's city hall, which today houses a historical museum. Other museums of note in Jakarta include the Wayang Museum, which is dedicated to traditional Indonesian puppet theatre, the Balai Seni Rupa art museum and the Gedung Gajah (National Museum).

Merderka Square. Not far from the Old City is the Kali Besar, located directly on the Great Canal. Batavia's wealthy commercial offices were once located here, conveniently next door to storehouses that were filled with spices, tobacco and other exotic wares. In the nineteenth century, when rampant epidemics made the Old City uninhabitable, the Dutch relocated to the area they called Konings-plain, which has since been renamed Merdeka ("Independence") Square. Nearby, Indonesia's national monument, the Monas, a tower topped by a golden flame, stretches 132 metres into the air. The presidential palace and a number of government ministries are also in the area, making Merdeka Square the political and administrative centre for all of Indonesia.

FACTS

* **Former name:** Batavia
* **Population of Jakarta:** *circa* 8.54 million
* **Population of the metropolitan area:** *circa* 17.6 million
* **Places of interest:** Chinatown, Gambir Station, Gedung Gajah (Elephant Building), Hoenderpasarbrug (Chicken Market Bridge), Istiqlal Mosque, Jakarta Museum, Jin De Yuan Temple, Kali Besar (Great Canal), Jakarta Cathedral, Merdeka Square, Museum of Art and Painting, Ceramic Museum, Pusat Museum, National Monument, Portuguese Church, Church of St. Emmanuel, Taman Impian Jaya Ancol, Wayang Museum, Willemskerk

FAMOUS CITIZENS

* **Eddy de Neve** (1885–1943), Dutch soccer player
* **Millane Fernandez** (b. 1986), pop singer

Europe's cities are as different from each other as their respective cultures. Most have developed into their present form over the course of centuries, or even millennia. Even the "younger" of the European cities are at least a thousand years old. European cities are usually defined by their shared Western outlook and Christian religion, as reflected in their abundance of sacred structures.

EUROPE

ICELAND

Reykjavik

REYKJAVIK IS ONE OF EUROPE'S "HOT" CITIES, THANKS TO ITS MUSIC SCENE AND FAMED NIGHTLIFE, WITH BUBBLING GEYSERS AND THERMAL SPRINGS NEARBY. REYKJAVIK'S SPECIAL ENERGY DRAWS ON ITS UNIQUE PHYSICAL AND CULTURAL LANDSCAPE.

The northernmost national capital on Earth is a city of breathtaking contrasts. Small wooden houses with corrugated-iron roofs stand alongside futuristic glass buildings. Sophisticated cultural centres are just minutes away from newly created lava fields. Reykjavik is also a city where international influences blend seamlessly with Icelandic traditions, creating a unique European culture with roots that are ancient, but an outlook that is supremely modern.

The founders. In 874, Ingólfur Arnason became the first settler to step onto Icelandic soil. He called the place where he settled "Smoky Bay" because ghostly vapours rose out of the earth near his home. Where they came from and why, no one knew. Over the next thousand years, very few people settled along the widely spaced inlets leading into Smoky Bay. Reykjavik would not prosper until well into the eighteenth century, when Governor Skúli Magnússon revitalized Iceland's economy by promoting wool manufacturing, fishing and shipbuilding. In 1749, he ordered that new harbours and shipyards be constructed on Smoky Bay, making Magnússon the city's founding father. Reykjavik received its city charter in 1786.

Independence. Once under way, Reykjavik thrived. Nevertheless, Iceland was still under Danish sover-

Austurvöllur is in the heart of the Old City. Sun worshippers and picnickers pass the time in front of the exclusive Borg Hotel.

FACTS

* **Name in English:** Smoky Bay
* **Population of Reykjavik:** *circa* 114,800
* **Population of the metropolitan area:** *circa* 185,000
* **Places of interest:** Ásmundarsafn Sculpture Centre, Domkirkja, Einar Jónsson Museum, Árbaejarsafn Open Air Museum, Hallgrímskirkja, Árni Magnússon Manuscript Collection, National Art Museum, National Museum, Perlan (The Pearl)

FAMOUS CITIZENS

* **Níels Finsen** (1860–1904), doctor (1903 Nobel Prize)
* **Halldór Laxness** (1902–98), writer (1955 Nobel Prize)
* **Magnús Magnússon** (1929–2007), TV presenter, journalist, writer
* **Arnaldur Indridason** (b. 1961), writer

eignty and subject to the ups and downs of political and economic decisions made in distant Scandinavia. Iceland danced to the tune of the Danes until 1944, when everything changed. British and American troops stationed in Reykjavik during World War II brought Iceland a level of prosperity it had never known, leaving Reykjavik poised to become an important commercial centre. On 17 June 1944, the city finally gained independence from Denmark. Since then, Reykjavik has continued to thrive, and there doesn't seem to be an end in sight.

Not just for the scenery. Many visitors to this far-flung island in the North Atlantic come for the amazing, unique scenery, but there are many sights to see in Reykjavik itself. The Old City, located on a small plot of land between Tjörnin Lake and the sea, has a number of eighteenth-century buildings, and Tjörnin Lake is a bird-watchers' paradise. The new city hall (1992) is located on its northern bank. The relief map of Iceland on display in its exhibition hall is a must-see. The Fógetinn (1751) is the oldest building in Reykjavik, and currently houses a restaurant serving traditional Icelandic food. Across the street is the newly restored monumental statue of Ingólfur Aranson, built in part with basalt columns said to be similar to those from his original homestead.

Hallgríms church. The modern Hallgrímskirkja is the symbol of Reykjavik, and a great place to begin a tour of the city. It was built on a hill between 1945 and 1986, and looks down over the entire city. Rising 73 metres, the church's central spire offers the best view of Reykjavik with the wide expanse of ocean in the background. A statue of Leif Ericson stands in front of the church's main portal. It was a gift from the United States in honour of the 1,000-year anniversary of the founding of Iceland's parliament, the Althing, the first democratic assembly in Europe.

Valley of the hot springs. The Laugardalur hot springs are just 3 km outside the city. Nearby are a huge camping site, a youth hostel, large open-air baths, a botanical garden, a zoo and a sculpture garden. Hot water is pumped from numerous holes drilled in the earth. The steaming water is then circulated to heat the turf of Reykjavik's football stadium, among other things. Geothermal heat is the basis of nearly every heating system in Iceland. For centuries, Reykjavik's residents have derived their hot water and winter heat from the Earth.

Centre: Tjörnin Lake.

Below: The Perlan Building's glass cupola straddles an enormous hot-water tank, part of the building's geothermal system.

NORWAY

Oslo

ONLY A QUARTER OF NORWAY'S CAPITAL CITY IS OCCUPIED BY ROADS AND BUILDINGS, INCLUDING MUSEUMS AND LIBRARIES DEVOTED TO HENRIK IBSEN AND EDVARD MUNCH. THE REST OF OSLO CONSISTS OF FORESTS, LAKES AND WORLD-FAMOUS SKI JUMPS.

The ski jumps on the mountain slopes of the Hausberg can be seen from just about everywhere in Oslo. From the Holmenkollen, another ski jump, visitors brave enough to climb to the top are rewarded with tremendous views of the entire Norwegian capital. In fact, one feels as though one could make a technically perfect jump from here and almost land in the centre of the city. Alas, the record jump by Sven Hannawald measures "just"132.5 metres, still far short of the centre of town.

Christiania. Although Oslo celebrated its thousand-year anniversary in 2000, today's city really came into being only after a devastating fire in 1624. Old Oslo, the residence of the Viking kings, was founded in approximately 1000 CE on the opposite bank of the Aker River. After the 1624 fire, King Christian IV, ruler of Denmark and Norway, had the city rebuilt across the river, where it now stands. He named it after himself, calling it Christiania. The new city grew quickly, thanks in part to a flourishing timber and shipping supply industry. Despite the fact that the king had issued an edict forbidding the use of any kind of wood as building material for the new city, Norway's most valuable – and combustible – natural commodity was an important part of its economy.

Right: The Norwegian Parliament meets in Stortinget.

Below: Ski jumps are the sport symbol of Oslo, and can be seen from everywhere in the city.

Capital of Norway. Denmark, allied with the French during the Napoleonic Wars, ceded Norway to the neighbouring country of Sweden after the British defeated them. Towards the end of the nineteenth century, Christiania became the centre of a Norwegian cultural renaissance. A wave of nationalism gripped the country when Norway gained its independence from Sweden in 1905. Prince Carl of Denmark became King Hakon VII of Norway, and Christiania was declared the capital of the new kingdom. The city reverted to its ancient original name of Oslo in 1925.

From city hall to the central railway station. The city hall with its two massive towers is a symbol of Oslo. It was built between 1931 and 1950 at Aker Brygge, an old shipyard in the harbour, and this is the building where the Nobel Prize ceremony takes place each year. Other places of interest nearby include the Royal Palace, National Theatre, the History Museum, the National Gallery, the University of Oslo and the central railway station.

Historical centre. Kvadraturen is the section of central Oslo located between the fourteenth-century Akershus Fortress, the cathedral (which dates from 1697), the Övre Vollgate and the Skippergata. Many beautifully preserved buildings from the seventeenth century can be admired in this area, and a great many historical and cultural institutions are located in the Kvadraturen, including the Theatre Museum, the Museum of Modern Art, the Stock Exchange, Café Engebret and Det Gamle Raadhus, a restaurant that is known for serving genuine Norwegian specialties.

The ubiquitous Edvard Munch. Edvard Munch is, without a doubt, Norway's most famous painter. While his work enchants many an art lover, others simply find his pictures exasperating. As polarized as opinions about his work may be, a visit to the Munch Museum is an absolute must for any visitor to Oslo, and not only to see his most famous painting, *The Scream*. There are numerous other Munch works there as well, including *Fear*, *Melancholy*, *Grief* and *Despairing Woman*. Munch also painted striking self-representations, such as *The Coffin is Carried Out*, *Self-Portrait with Wine Bottle* and the (rather inevitable) *Self-Portrait in Hell*. The museum's gift shop has recently started to offer for sale a take-home, inflatable balloon version of *The Scream* so that everyone, everywhere can be reminded that while modern life may not be a bowl of cherries, it is nonetheless best not to take it too seriously.

FACTS

* **Population of Oslo:** *circa* 550,000
* **Population of the metropolitan area:** *circa* 1 million
* **Places of interest:** Holmenkollen Ski Jump, Royal Palace, Kon Tiki Museum, Munch Museum, National Gallery, Oslo Bymuseum, Oslo City Hall, Akershus Fortress, Vigeland Sculpture Park

FAMOUS CITIZENS

* **Edvard Munch** (1863–1944), painter and graphic artist
* **Trygve Gulbranssen** (1894–1962), writer
* **Jostein Gaarder** (b. 1952), author
* **Kjetil André Aamodt** (b. 1971), Alpine ski racer, Olympic champion on numerous occasions
* **Bente Skari** (b. 1972), female cross-country skier

FINLAND

Helsinki

WHEN IT IS NOT BLANKETED IN WINTER WHITE, HELSINKI IS A GREEN CITY. LOCALS ENJOY LINNANMÄKI AMUSEMENT PARK AND OTHER ATTRACTIONS JUST OUTSIDE THE CITY, WHILE VISITORS MAY PREFER THE CHARM OF HELSINKI'S HARBOURS AND SHADED SQUARES.

Helsinki's museums offer art lovers a wealth of options. Its streets, especially in summer, are crowded with cafés and open-air galleries. With its many lovely parks, views of the water on every horizon and sea breezes, Helsinki is the unique European capital that feels like a small town. Its central square, the Kauppatori ("Market Square") is surrounded by quaint nineteenth-century buildings. There are no skyscrapers here. **In 1550, the city** that would be Helsinki was incorporated under the name of Helsingfors by decree of the Swedish king, Gustav I. The king founded the city to reinforce Swedish interests in the Baltic Sea region against the claims of the country's commercial competitors in the Hanseatic port city of Tallinn. Even today, much of Helsinki reflects its Swedish heritage, including a number of important buildings that survived the great fire of 1808 which destroyed most of the city. In 1809, following a disastrous war, Sweden was forced to cede most of Finland to Russia. It was under Russian sovereignty that Helsinki began to expand and prosper. Its proximity to St. Petersburg attracted important architects, who designed buildings that turned Helsinki into a neoclassical jewel on the Baltic. To this day, Swedish, Russian and Finnish cultural influences are visible in equal measure.

FACTS

* **Swedish:** Helsingfors
* **Population of Helsinki:** *circa* 559,300
* **Population of the metropolitan area:** *circa* 1.23 million
* **Places of interest:** Havis Amanda Fountain, Kaupungintalo (City Hall), Finlandia Concert Hall, Linnanmäki Amusement Park, Parliament, Seaworld Helsinki, Seurasaari Open Air Museum, Suomenlinna Fortress, Temppeliaukio Church, Uspenskij Cathedral

FAMOUS CITIZENS

* **Mika Waltari** (1908–79), writer
* **Mika Salo** (b. 1966), racing driver
* **Linus Torvalds** (b. 1969), founder of the Linux software project

Once thought scandalous, the nude mermaid by artist Ville Vallgren (1908) on the Kauppatori is now a symbol of Helsinki.

The mermaid on Market Square. Most places of interest in Helsinki can be found within the relatively small city centre located on the South Harbour. The Kauppatori is here, as is the city's symbol, sculptor Ville Vallgren's Havis Amanda Fountain, with its seductive mermaid. Her bare breasts were considered scandalous at her dedication in 1908. Just across from the fountain is the Kaupungintalo, the neoclassical city hall designed in 1833 by C. L. Engel. The dignified Presidential Palace sits two blocks further east, with a stoic guard stationed in front of it.

Orthodox and Lutheran. A canal connects the South and North Harbour districts. The Russian Orthodox Uspenski Cathedral, with its characteristic onion domes, stands on the bank of the South Harbour, stylistically somewhat out of sync with the buildings that surround it. The statue of Czar Alexander I on Senate Square, which portrays him like a prince out of a fairy tale, is the undisputed masterpiece of sculptor J. A. Ehrenström. Senate Square is one of most beautiful plazas in all of northern Europe. The former senate building, now the seat of the Finnish government, takes up the entire east side of the square, with the imposing neoclassical façade of Helsinki Lutheran Cathedral making up its western side.

Suomenlinna Fortress is next on the tour, built on six islands at the entrance to the harbour. A UNESCO World Heritage Site, it is one of the most popular destinations in Helsinki. The Swedes built the fortress in 1748 as protection against the ambitions of Peter the Great, who had recently established a strong Russian presence in the Baltic with the founding of St. Petersburg. Although the Russians never succeeding in capturing the almost impenetrable fortress, the Swedes were forced to hand it over to the Russians as part of the treaty of 1809.

Above: Never taken, Suomenlinna Fortress became a World Heritage Site in 1991.

Left: The Lutheran Cathedral and the Orthodox Uspenskij Cathedral stand harmoniously side-by-side.

RUSSIA

St. Petersburg

MAGNIFICENT PALACES, SUMPTUOUS, SHIMMERING FAÇADES AND GOLDEN CUPOLAS CHARACTERIZE THIS CHARMING CITY ON THE NEVA RIVER. PETER THE GREAT FOUNDED HIS CAPITAL WITH AN EYE TO EXPANDING RUSSIA'S INFLUENCE IN EUROPE.

St. Petersburg's city government, supported by a host of private investment, has worked hard to spruce up the city's main thoroughfare, the Nevski Prospekt. This famous boulevard enters the city via a series of bridges and canals. There are over 540 bridges in St. Petersburg, a planned city newly built in the seventeenth century across 44 islands at the mouth of the Neva River. This lyrical relationship between architecture and water makes St. Petersburg one of Russia's most stunning cities. The historical city centre was declared a UNESCO World Heritage Site in 1990.

Window to the West. Located on an important northern shipping route, St. Petersburg is by far the most European city in Russia. Founded by Tsar Peter the Great to serve as his "window to the West", its infrastructure and buildings were designed primarily by Western European architects. Throughout the eighteenth and nineteenth centuries, St. Petersburg's own particular style tempered the pomp of the baroque with a neoclassical sense of order. As a result, the city has aged well. It is still one of the most beautiful in Europe, although much of it is badly in need of repair and restoration: the work currently under way is at least eighty years overdue. Despite a history full of drama and considerable

Tsarina Elizabeth, daughter of Peter the Great, did not live to see the completion of the Winter Palace – which she had commissioned – in 1762.

FACTS

*** From 1924 until 1991:** Leningrad

*** Population of St. Petersburg:** *circa* 4.6 million

*** Places of interest:** Alexander Nevsky Cloister, Alexandrinsky Theatre, Resurrection Church, The Hermitage, Church of Our Saviour, St. Issac's Cathedral, Catherine Palace, Kunstkammer Museum, Mariansky Theatre, Menshikov Palace, Peterhof, Cathedral of Peter and Paul, St. Annen Church, Winter Palace, Woronzov Palace, Summer Palace

FAMOUS CITIZENS

*** Victor Hartmann** (1834–74), architect, sculptor and painter

*** Carl Peter Fabergé** (1846–1920), jeweller

*** Joseph Brodsky** (1940–96), author (1987 Nobel Prize)

*** Vladimir Putin** (b. 1952), politician

suffering, the residents of St. Petersburg remain powerfully attached to their city, which they affectionately call "Peter".

Built on mud. Peter the Great dreamed of making Russia a great naval power, but he needed a harbour on the Baltic Sea. With this plan in mind, he conquered the small Swedish fortress of Nienschanz in 1703. He built the first structure for his new city, the Peter and Paul Fortress, on nearby "Rabbit Island" in the Neva River. The cornerstone was laid on 16 May 1703, the official date for the founding of St. Petersburg. The city was named in honour of St. Peter, the czar's patron saint. Geological conditions presented a challenge to the city's expansion. The earth was so soft that tens of thousands of wooden stakes had to be driven into the ground to prevent buildings from sinking into the alluvial mud.

The Russian bear dances here. The days of Peter the Great are long gone. Tsars, revolutions, communism and Perestroika have all brought changes to the city. Once introspective and intellectual in atmosphere, St. Petersburg has today become a European tourist destination with a distinctive nightlife. London, Paris and Rome can hardly keep up with the pace of its street life on summer nights. The nightclubs are equally full during the winter months, when Russians and visitors alike head indoors to enjoy the fine entertainment on offer. St. Petersburg has something for every taste.

"White Nights". On the subject of the nightlife in St. Petersburg, the only city with over a million people located at near-arctic latitudes, the city's famous "White Nights" comes immediately to mind. Every summer, there is at least a month during which it never gets dark. A mystical, romantic atmosphere pervades the city during this time. The temperature is pleasant, and people wander through the city all night long, over its bridges and along its many canals. Because the city is situated in what are known as the high northern latitudes, the sun never really sets in the summertime. Twilight arrives shortly before midnight, and merges into the dawn. There is a silvery blue glow on the horizon, lending radiance to the city's busy streets. The Nevsky Prospekt is transformed into an open-air art gallery during the Festival of White Nights, held each year from the end of June through mid-July. Twenty-four-hour daylight can continue well into August.

Centre: Peterhof Palace.

Below: View of the former Russian capital from the Neva River with St Isaac's Cathedral in the foreground.

SWEDEN

Stockholm

STOCKHOLM IS BUILT ON WATER, INTEGRATING LAND AND SEA, PAST AND PRESENT, INTO A CITYSCAPE OF EXCEPTIONAL CHARM. THE SÖDERMALM HILLS OFFERING VISTAS OF THE CITY AND THE ANCIENT FORESTS OF DJURGARDEN ISLAND PROVIDE STRONG CONTRASTS.

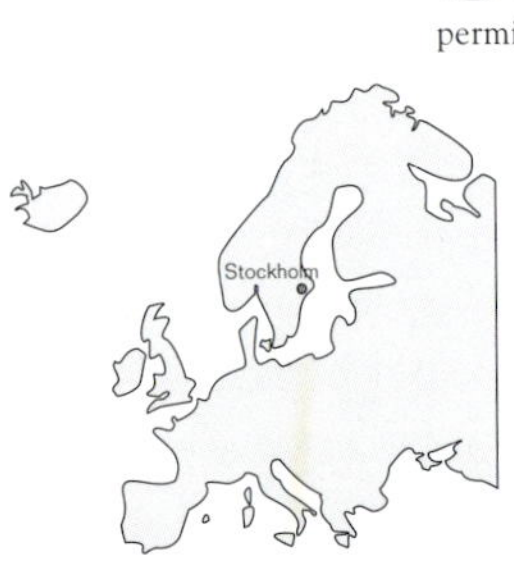

Stockholm's tall tower is called the Kaknästurm. The panoramic view from its 155-metre-tall observation deck is worth the trip. Weather permitting, it is possible to see as far as 60 km from the top, a view encompassing all of Stockholm, from city hall to the Globe Arena, past the skyscrapers to the Hay Market, over the city's many waterways all the way to the farthest reaches of the outer suburbs.

In the land of the Norsemen. Long before the city was founded, Vikings had settled in this place where the Baltic Sea and Lake Mälar meet. Viking culture expanded exponentially between 800 and 1050, and Lake Mälar became a busy trading port. One of the main trading posts, Björkö Island, was quite close to present-day Stockholm; it was declared a UNESCO World Heritage Site in 1993. The first written mention of Stockholm dates from the thirteenth century, and by 1270 it was already referred to as a city. Its strategic location made it one of the most important cities in Scandinavia well into the fifteenth century.

The Old City of Stockholm. Like Norway, the Danish crown ruled Sweden throughout the Middle Ages. Sweden became independent much sooner, however, and in 1523 Stockholm was the residence

Right: Drottningholm Palace, the Versailles of the north.

Below: The Centralbron over Lake Mälar is one of the most important bridges in Stockholm.

of its own royal court. By 1634, it was the national capital. Many of the great buildings and palaces in the Old City (Gamla Stan) of Stockholm were constructed during this period, including the Riddarhuset (House of the Nobility, 1641–74), the Oxenstierna Palace (1653–68) and the Tessin Palace (1692). Not far away are the old state bank and St. Gertrud's church, the latter the church of the German merchants along the trade thoroughfare of the Västerlanggatan. There are also much older structures in the Old City, such as the thirteenth-century St. Nikolai's Cathedral, which is the church where Swedish rulers are traditionally crowned. This is also where the current king, Carl Gustav XVI, married Queen Sylvia, his commoner bride, in 1976.

Kungliga Slottet, the royal palace. The changing of the Royal Guard is one of Stockholm's most popular attractions, but the royal palace has much more to offer. Its 608 rooms – three more than in Buckingham Palace – makes it the most extensive royal palace in the world. Designed and fashioned by some of Europe's best and most famous artists and artisans, its many beautiful chambers include the Hall of State, the palace chapel, the magnificent Bernadotte Apartment, the King Gustav III Antique Museum, the treasury and the Tre Kronor Museum. Today the royal family lives several km west of here at Drottningholm Palace, a baroque structure that became a UNESCO World Heritage Site in 1991.

Skansen, the world's oldest open-air museum. Young and old flock to Skansen, a favourite destination since it opened in 1891. It is one of the world's oldest living museums, a place where the past comes to life and people can have fun learning about Sweden's past. Visitors can stroll between beautiful old farmhouses, manor houses and workplaces showcasing crafts from all the provinces of Sweden. There is also a zoo on the grounds, with wolves, bears, wolverines, reindeer and elk, all housed in large outdoor enclosures.

A labyrinth of islands. Stockholm is above all a city of water, and would not be Stockholm without its fascinating conglomeration of 24,000 islands, islets and cliffs. Most boats to the islands take off from the docks of Strömkajen and Nybrokajen. A trip aboard one of the city's restored steamships is a special treat. The ride to the island town of Vaxholm takes about an hour, and the journey to Drottningholm Palace about fifty minutes. The latter should not be missed. Sandhamn and Utö, two rugged and heavily wooded islands, are popular destinations famous for their natural beauty.

FACTS

*** Population of Stockholm:** *circa* 766,700

*** Places of interest:** Bonde Palais, St. Katarina's Church, Royal Palace, Oxenstierna Palais, Palace of the Crown Princes, House of the Nobility, Skansen Museum, Stadsholmen Island, Stockholms Stadshus (City Hall), Storkyrkan (Cathedral), Tessin Palais, St. Gertrud's Church, Vasa Museum

FAMOUS CITIZENS

*** Alfred Nobel** (1833–96), inventor

*** Greta Garbo** (1905–90), actress

*** Ingrid Bergman** (1915–82), actress

*** Benny Andersson** (b. 1946), founding member of the pop group ABBA

ESTONIA

Tallinn

THE CAPITAL OF ESTONIA IS A MEDIEVAL JEWEL OF A CITY. CATHEDRAL HILL TOWERS OVER THE NARROW STREETS OF TALLINN'S OLD CITY. ACCORDING TO ESTONIAN LEGEND, THE HILL IS THE BURIAL MOUND OF THE HERO KALEVI.

What was formerly the German Hanseatic city of Reval is, in many travellers' opinion, the Baltic region's most beautiful city. It is one of the few anywhere in Europe with a well-preserved medieval city wall. Tallinn's pleasant atmosphere, aesthetic beauty and reputation for hospitality draw thousands of tourists each year.

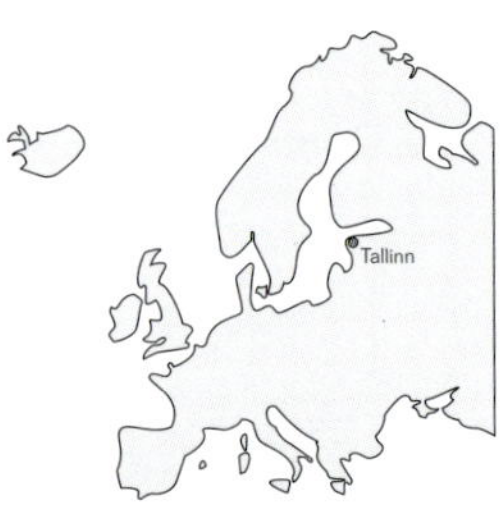

The Hanseatic city of Reval. The Arab geographer al-Idrisi already knew about the Estonian settlement of Reval, which he called Lindanise. It appears on maps as early as 1154. Located along the trade route between northern and eastern Europe, it quickly developed into a powerful trade city. Under the name of Reval, it became a member of the Hanseatic League in 1285. The city's wealth attracted conquerors as well as merchants. Danes, German knights, Swedes and Russians all invaded and occupied the city, some more than once. For most of the nineteenth century, Reval was politically part of Russia, but controlled locally by German land barons. Estonia's Independence Manifesto of 1918 temporarily freed the country from foreign control. At that time, the capital city of Reval was renamed Tallinn, one of its Ancient Estonian names.

Soviet Estonia. Tallinn did not remain free for long. Occupied by Germany from 1941 to 1944, Estonia

FACTS

✱ Population of Tallinn: *circa* 403,500

✱ Places of interest: Alexander Nevsky Cathedral, Church of the Holy Ghost, Naissaar Island, St. Nicholas's Church, City Hall, Katharinental Palace, St. Olai's Church, Teletorn Tower, Toompea (Cathedral Hill)

FAMOUS CITIZENS

✱ Fjodor Andresen (1806–80), Russian painter

✱ Robert Gernhardt (1937–2006), writer, painter, draughtsman, and cartoonist

✱ Neeme Järvi (b. 1937), conductor

St. Olai's church once boasted the highest tower in the world. It still towers above the medieval city walls and lower town.

became a member state of the Soviet Union after World War II, a status it retained until 1991. As was the case with the other Baltic states, Stalin at first subjected Estonians to strict "Russianization", although Estonian culture was never entirely suppressed. A UNESCO World Heritage Site since 1997, Tallinn has revived its traditions and renewed its relationship with the past. The legacy of the Hanseatic League is everywhere to be seen, particularly in the meticulously restored Old City. With a highly visible tower measuring 159 metres, St. Olai's church on the northern end of the Old City was once the tallest building in Europe. This was intentional: Tallinn's medieval merchants wanted to attract trade, and the soaring tower was designed with the goal of making the city famous. Over the centuries, the tower was badly damaged on many occasions. Today's version dates from 1830 and is just 123 metres tall.

Cathedral Hill. The 50-km ferry trip from Finland to Tallinn offers visitors one of the loveliest city panoramas on the Baltic Sea coast. Approaching the city, the massive, sharply sloping limestone block of Cathedral Hill (Toompea) with its onion-domed Alexander Nevsky Cathedral comes slowly into view. Closer to the harbour, Tallinn's massive lower city defensive towers and walls, Gothic spires and elegant baroque bell towers give an impression of strength and grace. For hundreds of years there was tension between the aristocrats who lived high on Cathedral Hill, and the merchant residents of the lower city. Both groups only grudgingly acknowledged each other on Sundays, from opposite sides of the church, through a haze of incense. Reval and Cathedral Hill were worlds apart, but there is no question as to who really ruled Tallinn. The clerics and nobles may have thought they were in control, but it was the merchants of the lower town who held the real power.

Above: Pikk Street is a popular tourist destination.

Left: Even Peter the Great left his imprint on the city. The Kadriorg Palace was built as his summer residence.

LATVIA

Riga

RIGA IS THE SECRET TREASURE OF THE BALTIC REGION. WHILE ITS MANY TOWERS MAY REMIND VISITORS OF LÜBECK, RIGA IS MORE CLOSELY ASSOCIATED WITH BREMEN, ALSO A HANSA CITY, WHENCE RIGA'S FOUNDERS ARE THOUGHT TO HAVE COME.

Despite any outward similarities to the German Hanseatic cities, Riga, the capital of Latvia, is a Russian city. Only one-third of the population is of Latvian descent, a legacy of the "Russianization" efforts of the Soviet Union under Stalin. For Riga, this involved the immigration of tens of thousands of ethnic Russians. Latvians are accustomed to being in the minority. During the medieval period, ethnic Germans made up the majority. Since the end of the Cold War, the resurgence of Latvian identity and cultural life, especially in Riga, has been especially pronounced.

Outside influence is not synonymous with cultural oppression here. Citizens maintain the Hanseatic cityscape despite the fact that it primarily represents a German heritage. Riga also treasures its unique Jugendstil buildings, most of which were designed by Latvian architects. Their work dominates the late nineteenth-century district known as the New City, where street after street of Jugendstil houses survive. The Hanseatic quarter of the Old City is less architecturally unified, largely due to damage it suffered during World War II; perhaps one-third of Riga's historical buildings were destroyed. Today, more than half of the most visited sights in Riga are located in the Old City, a World Heritage Site since 1997.

The Russian Orthodox Cathedral is located on Brivibas iela (Freedom Street).

FACTS

*** Population of Riga:** *circa* 731,700

*** Population of the metropolitan area:** *circa* 882,300

*** Places of interest:** Daugavgriva District, Vecriga, Freedom Monument, Large and Small Guild Houses, Museum of the Occupation of Latvia, Riga Palace, Hanseatic Schwarzhäupter House, St. Jacob's Church, St. Peter's Cathedral, Television Tower

FAMOUS CITIZENS

*** Sergey Eisenstein** (1898–1948), Soviet stage and film director

*** Heinz Erhardt** (1909–79), German comedian

*** Mariss Jansons** (b. 1943), conductor

*** Mikhail Baryshnikov** (b. 1948), ballet dancer, choreographer

Riga and the Hanseatic League. The first merchants came to the small settlement at the mouth of the Daugava River around 1158. The official founder of the city was Albert von Bekeshovede, a clergyman from the powerful Hanseatic city of Bremen who promoted Riga as the seat of the archbishopric of the Livonia Confederation. The city joined the Hanseatic League itself a hundred years later. Ships from all the Hanseatic cities, England and the Netherlands came to Riga, where they were loaded with raw materials from the East. Merchants built sturdy storehouses along the harbour to protect the treasures, which included furs, timber, honey and especially amber. Gazing up at Riga's brick church towers from the river, among them St. Peter's Cathedral, St. Jacob's church and St. Mary's Cathedral, it is not difficult to imagine oneself transported back to the city's golden age of wealth and prosperity.

Of all the magnificent buildings along the Daugava, Riga Palace is outstanding. The cornerstone for its massive walls was laid in 1330. Today it is the residence of the Latvian President, and home to three museums. The Anglican Church of the Holy Saviour, built alongside the palace in 1859, bears witness to the importance of trade with the British Empire. Buckets of earth were brought here from England so the church's foundations could rest on British soil.

Visible Soviet legacy. Riga came under Swedish authority during the seventeenth century. It was under Swedish rule that Riga grew into the largest city in the kingdom, with a larger population than Göteborg or Stockholm. Its prosperity attracted the Russian czars as well, especially after the Baltic port of St. Petersburg was founded in the eighteenth century. Annexed by Russia, Riga soon became the most important Russian military harbour on the Baltic Sea. It was the Soviet Russians who instituted the most enduring changes to the cityscape of the Latvian capital, and Riga's skyline is still dominated by Soviet hulks of buildings, most of which are charitably described as unimaginative buildings in poor repair. Among these is the crumbling complex known as "Stalin's Cake", which houses the Latvian Academy of Sciences. The Museum of the Occupation of Latvia is housed nearby, also in a former Soviet "block". Reflecting, perhaps, the still-majority Russian population of the city, it is by far the most frequently visited museum in the city.

Centre: The Hanseatic Schwarzhäupter House is a popular attraction.

Bottom: Middle-class homes in the Hanseatic quarter of the Old City.

RUSSIA

Moscow

MOSCOW IS A SHOWPLACE OF RUSSIAN CULTURE, REFLECTING EVERY TURN OF ITS COLOURFUL HISTORY. THE LONG TSARIST MONARCHY, COMMUNISM AND ECONOMIC REVIVAL HAVE ALL LEFT THEIR MARK ON THIS MOST RUSSIAN OF RUSSIAN CITIES.

Today's Moscow is a prosperous international city, but it is also one of blatant economic contrasts and deep social divisions. The cosmopolitan veneer laid over Moscow's ancient, impenetrable façade conceals an array of problems that have characterized Russian culture since the days of Ivan the Terrible. Nevertheless, the time-honoured, utterly unique charm of Moscow remains unchanged. Sacred structures, including a host of chapels, cloisters and cathedrals, have always played a prominent role in the city. Their presence lends this city on the Moskva River an atmosphere redolent of czarist romanticism and the splendour of the Eastern Orthodox Church.

Centre of the Russian Empire. Russia's capital celebrated its 850th anniversary in 1997 with great festivity. The jubilee had been calculated based on the first written reference to the city in a letter dated 1147. In it, the city's founder, Juri Dolgoruki – who was the Grand Duke of Kiev and sixth son of the powerful prince Vladimir Monomach – invites his ally, Sviatoslav Olegovitch, Prince of Novgorod-Severski, to "Come to me, brother, come to Moscow", promising to arrange a sumptuous feast in his honour. In the course of the following century, Moscow became an independent principality, and

Right: Many tsars are buried in the Cathedral of the Archangel.

Below: St. Basil's Cathedral towers over the south end of Red Square.

after another hundred years it became the centre around which the Grand Duchy of Moscow – and with it, all of Russia – coalesced. Moscow was declared a metropolitan residence of the Eastern Orthodox patriarchy and, in the second half of the fifteenth century, the capital of a united Russia.

The third Rome. The reigning prince at that time, Ivan III, called on Italian architects to beautify his new capital city. Uspensky Cathedral, the Cathedral of the Archangel and the Ivan the Great Clock Tower all originated during this period. These imposing edifices were designed to emphasize Moscow's new role as the most important city in Russia. Married to the daughter of the last Byzantine emperor, Ivan III saw himself as the successor to the Roman tradition. He took his role as emperor seriously, taking the title Tsar ("Caesar" in Russian) for the first time in 1478, after the defeat of Byzantium by the Ottoman Turks. Although Russian rulers were not officially crowned as tsars until 1547, the message he hoped to send was clear.

Prince Ivan IV was the first Russian ruler crowned as tsars. At his command, Moscow flourished. One of the most enigmatic czars of the Russian Empire, Ivan "the Terrible" had a famously violent temper that cost thousands of his subjects their lives. And although he initiated great projects and improved the city's economic foundation, he ultimately brought about its downfall by waging a costly war against Poland, Sweden and Lithuania as part of his desire for westward expansion. The Crimean Tartars used Ivan's preoccupation with the West as an excuse to attack Moscow in 1571, and as a result most of the city was burned to the ground.

Moscow vs. St. Petersburg. Reconstruction of the devastated city, including an expansion of the Kremlin, lasted through most of the final decades of the fifteenth century. Moscow quickly became as magnificent as it had been before the Tartar sack. To protect the city against similar assaults, an extensive system of defensive walls and moats was constructed around 1600. This level of security permitted seventeenth-century Moscow to experience an economic and cultural renaissance. After Peter the Great moved Russia's capital to St. Petersburg in 1712, Moscow retained its status as the country's most important historical and religious centre, with its political, economic and cultural life continuing very much as it had in the past.

Moscow continued to progress and expand, despite its loss of the royal residence to St. Petersburg. Many of the later tsars preferred Moscow to the

FACTS

*** Population of Moscow:**
circa 10.4 million

*** Population of the metropolitan region:**
circa 14.43 million

*** Places of interest:**
St. Basil's Cathedral, Bolshoi S, Borodino Panorama Museum, Federatsiya, Church of the Twelve Apostles, Kremlin/Red Square, Lenin Mausoleum, Lomonosov University, Assumption Cathedral (Uspensky Sobor), Palace of the Patriarchs, Pushkin Museum of Fine Arts, State History Museum, Tretyakov Gallery, Triumph Palace

Manezhnaya Square with the 1817 "Manège", an elite indoor riding school, is of the most exclusive addresses in Moscow.

damp, swampy environs of the new city on the Baltic Sea. Benefiting from unceasing royal patronage, Moscow became more beautiful with every passing year. In the late nineteenth century, it already boasted asphalt paved streets illuminated by electric lights. Moscow in no way lagged behind St. Petersburg, or for that matter, any other city in the world.

City of heroes. Invaders have always sought to control the beautiful city on the Moskva. In addition to the Mongols and Tartars, the French under Napoleon tried to take the city, as did Germany during World War II. Napoleon instigated Moscow's "Great Fire" of 1812, but Russia was ultimately victorious in this "Great Patriotic War" against the French, and Moscow was quickly rebuilt. Moscow was made the capital of the newly formed Soviet Union in 1918. Despite repeated attempts, invading German forces also failed to conquer Moscow. In 1941, Russian forces aided by the heroic efforts of its populace stopped the German army just outside the city. Throughout Russian history, Moscow has always been a city of heroes.

The heart of Russia. Moscow is currently Europe's biggest city, the political, commercial and cultural centre of Russia. It has universities, technical colleges, churches, theatres, museums, galleries and the 577-metre-tall Ostankino Television Tower. The Kremlin and Red Square were added to the UNESCO List of World Heritage Sites in 1990. Red Square is where every visit to Moscow should begin. The Kremlin, at the very heart of the city, has always played a central role in Russian history. Tsars and Soviet potentates alike have ruled over their enormous, intractable empire from within its walls.

A visit to the Kremlin. Uspensky Cathedral, dedicated to the Assumption of the Blessed Virgin Mary, where Orthodox patriarchs were buried and Russian tsars were crowned, is the largest of all the many sacred buildings inside the Kremlin. Its famous arched gables are its most distinctive feature. The lovely Church of the Annunciation, with its nine lustrous, gilded domes, was the private chapel of the tsars. Ivan the Terrible commissioned its famous Grosnensky Portal after he married for the fourth time, and the patriarchs forbade him entry through the front door. The Cathedral of the Archangel was built in 1505. It houses the mortal remains of the mighty princes and tsars who ruled from the Kremlin

Right: The new Tretyakov Gallery, directly on the Moskva River, houses the world's most important collection of Russian painting.

Below: The GUM shopping complex.

in the years before Peter the Great came to power. The State Armoury, which also houses the Diamond Fund, is where Russia's national treasures can be found. Items on display include a number of Fabergé eggs and the 180-carat Orlov diamond, a gift to Princess Sophie Frederick Augusta from her suitor, Count Grigory Orlov. Later, when the princess had become Empress Catherine the Great, she had the stone set in her royal sceptre. The tsar's cannon and bell are also found in the Kremlin. At 40 and 200 tons, respectively, they are the largest of their kind. They were cast purely for display: the cannon was never fired and the bell has never been struck. Modern structures are also present in the Kremlin. The congress hall, a business-like structure with a large hall capable of accommodating up to 6,000 people, was built in 1961. This is where public events and international conferences take place, as well as opera and ballet performances.

Red Square. The great May Day parades of the Soviet era all took place in Red Square, an enormous, rectangular-plan plaza. It was once Moscow's open-air market. Many people come here today to see the Lenin Mausoleum, a stepped pyramid housing the glass coffin enclosing the embalmed body of the deceased founder of the Soviet Union. The Kremlin's walls and towers form one long side of Red Square. The façade of the GUM shopping complex makes up its eastern side. St. Basil's Cathedral, the very emblem of Moscow, is located at its southern end. Each of St. Basil's towers is decorated with its own individual pattern, and their combined effect is truly remarkable. In the 1550s, Ivan the Terrible had St. Basil's built to memorialize his important victory over the Mongols at Kasan.

Nearly all of Moscow's most popular sites are located inside of Moscow's Garden Ring Road. The Moskva River flows within the ring, running alongside one wall of the Kremlin, and on through Gorky Park. Made famous by the novel and film of the same name, what is officially known as the Gorky Park for Culture and Recreation is the most popular of the roughly one hundred parks in Moscow. Among its numerous attractions are boat docks, restaurants, cafés, pubs and skating rinks. Artists perform on multiple open-air stages. Public entertainment is offered free of charge on weekends and holidays, accompanied by colourful fireworks displays. The original area of the park included the gardens of the old Golitsyn Hospital. Its picturesque hills, green groves and little bridges were once part of the country estates of Moscow's aristocracy.

FAMOUS CITIZENS

* **Alexander Pushkin** (1799–1837), poet
* **Fyodor M. Dostoyevsky** (1821–1881), writer
* **Vassily Kandinsky** (1866–1944), painter and graphic artist
* **Boris Pasternak** (1890–1960), writer (1958 Nobel Prize)
* **Boris Tchaikovski** (1925–1996), composer
* **Vladimir Ilyushin** (b. 1927), test pilot
* **Marat Safin** (b. 1980), tennis pro

DENMARK

Copenhagen

ALMOST EVERYONE WHO COMES TO COPENHAGEN VISITS THE LITTLE MERMAID IN THE HARBOUR. IN HANS CHRISTIAN ANDERSEN'S POPULAR FAIRY TALE, SHE GAVE UP HER VOICE TO EXCHANGE HER FISHTAIL FOR LEGS IN A VAIN ATTEMPT TO WIN A PRINCE'S LOVE.

Love is capricious. In the end, the unhappy mermaid looks on mutely as her beloved abandons her in favour of a princess. In Andersen's fairy tale, the little mermaid throws herself into the sea, dissolving in the foam. Today, the bronze mermaid sculpted by Eric Eriksen sits on a rock on the harbour at Langelinie Pier. Vandals have attacked the statue on several occasions, but luckily, city officials keep the original bronze moulds in a secure location. Identical replacement parts are always available.

From fishing village to capital city. When Denmark became a kingdom in the tenth century, what would later become the great city of Copenhagen was a small, insignificant fishing village named Havn. Located at the entrance to the Baltic Sea, its strategically advantageous location attracted the attention of the Danish crown. Havn was transformed virtually overnight into an important trading centre. The building of Slotsholm Fortress in 1167 is usually said to mark the city's founding. Three years later, Copenhagen was given its current name, which in Danish means "merchant's harbour". In 1443, the emergent city became the official capital of the Kalmar Union of Denmark, Norway and Sweden. When the union disbanded in 1523 it became capital of the Kingdom of Denmark.

A visit to the Little Mermaid is an absolute must in Copenhagen.

FACTS

* **Name in the national language (Danish):** København
* **Population of Copenhagen:** *circa* 501,200
* **Places of interest:** Trinity Church, Frederiks Church, Tivoli Gardens Amusement Park, Holmens Church, Statens Museum of Art, Little Mermaid statue, Ny Carlsberg Sculpture Gallery, Round Tower, St. Petri's Church, Amalienborg Palace, Christiansborg Palace, Rosenborg Palace

FAMOUS CITIZENS

* **Sören Kierkegaard** (1813–1855), philosopher and theologian
* **Martin Andersen Nexö** (1869–1954), writer
* **Niels Bohr** (1885–1962), physicist (1922 Nobel Prize)

The Octagon. Amalienborg, the famous winter palace of the Danish royal family, stands on a broad, paved, octagonal plaza. Four nearly identical palaces were built along the four diagonal sides of the octagon. At the centre of this beautiful rococo complex, one of the loveliest in Europe, is an equestrian monument honouring King Frederik V. A changing of the guard takes place outside the palaces each noon.
The Round Tower. The best view of the Old City of Copenhagen may be from the wide platform on top of the Round Tower. Although the tower is only 36 metres high, the spiral staircase to the top winds around 209 metres. It was once possible to ride to the top on horseback, as Peter the Great did when he visited. Unfortunately, horses are now banned from the tower. Trinity Church is adjacent to the tower, with the shopping districts of Strøget and Straedet nearby. Most of the Old City is off limits to vehicles, making it one of Europe's biggest pedestrian zones.
Christiansborg Palace is on the small island of Slotsholm, the site of the original fortress, which is today joined to the rest of the city by several bridges. The palace was once home to the Danish royal family, and is now the seat of the Danish government and its parliament, the Folketing. This is the sixth building to stand here since the 1167 founding of the city. Invading armies, fires and modernization have all taken their toll. While the first castle on the site stood from 1417 into the late eighteenth century, rebuilding and renovation has been fast and furious ever since. The present Christiansborg was built in the early twentieth century.
Accessible from every quarter of the city, Tivoli Gardens amusement park first opened on 15 August 1843. Visitors can take a trip in a small boat on the moats once used for Copenhagen's defence or take a pleasant ride on the big wheel looking down at the city from on high. It has a new, zero-G roller coaster ("the Demon") and twenty-five other rides, as well as many restaurants and concert venues. The mime presentations in the Pantomime S are extremely popular. After 150 years of continuous operation, neon signs are still banned in Tivoli. Instead, more than 110,000 incandescent lanterns brilliantly illuminate one of Europe's oldest surviving pleasure gardens. The white bulbs hung from trees contribute to Tivoli's uniquely old-fashioned atmosphere, even as the Demon screams by.

Centre: Amalienborg Palace.

Bottom: The colourful promenade at Nyhavn.

SCOTLAND

Edinburgh

NOWHERE IS SCOTTISH IDENTITY AS HIGHLY CULTIVATED AS IN EDINBURGH, THE CAPITAL CITY ON THE FIRTH OF FORTH. THE NARROW HOUSES OF THE OLD TOWN RUN UP THE HILL TO CASTLE ROCK LIKE A STRING OF PEARLS.

Edinburgh Castle, perched on Castle Rock's highest point, protects a blood-soaked piece of land, the site of countless battles between Scotland and England. Great King Street, the Royal Mile, leads from the castle down to Holyrood House, residence of Scotland's royalty. State carriages once rode this street alongside the hangman's carts bringing prisoners to and from the castle. In the summer, Edinburgh hosts renowned arts festivals that transform Great King Street into a single enormous stage.

Castle Rock is the basalt "plug" of a volcano that became extinct over 340 million years ago. Three of the mountain's sides are nearly vertical, making the site a natural choice for a well-defended settlement. The earliest dates to the ninth century BCE, and Roman-influenced settlement dates from the first and second centuries. The first fortress was built on the site in the seventh century by Celts. This fortress was in turn besieged and taken, not by Scots or Picts, but by Angles, an immigrant group from the south. Clearly, this fortress on the border between "civilized" Britain and "wild" Scotland has always led a precarious existence.

Edinburgh became Scotland's capital in the mid-fifteenth century. At that time, its Old Town already occupied its present area, with its buildings densely

FACTS

✻ Name in the national language (Scottish Gaelic):
Dùn Eideann

✻ Population of Edinburgh:
circa 435,800

✻ Places of interest:
Arthur's Seat, Bellevue Chapel, Edinburgh Castle, Grass Market, Greyfriars' Churchyard and Tolbooth and Highland Kirk, Holyrood House Palace, Princes Street Gardens, Royal Botanic Garden, Royal Mile, Royal Museum of Scotland, Scotch Whisky Heritage Centre, St. Giles' Cathedral, University of Edinburgh

FAMOUS CITIZENS

✻ Sir Walter Scott
(1771–1832), writer

✻ Alexander Graham Bell
(1847–1922), inventor of the telephone

✻ Sir Arthur Conan Doyle
(1859–1930), writer and doctor

✻ Sean Connery
(b. 1930), actor

✻ Tony Blair
(b. 1953), British politician

Whisky and music are a firm part of life in Edinburgh. Lovers of traditional music meet in the many pubs, such as Sandy Bell's on Forrest Road.

crowded together. Land for the city's growth has always been in short supply, but everything else was abundant in Edinburgh; its moneyed aristocrats, merchants and industrious workers prospered. Immigrants had been welcomed since the High Middle Ages, giving this geographically isolated northern city a cosmopolitan air. Living space was so scarce that they began to build blocks of rental units as high as twelve storeys, likely the first high-rise buildings in Europe.

Great King Street is a fine place to stroll from Castle Hill to Holyrood Palace, a stretch known as the Royal Mile. St. Giles' Cathedral is here, where Protestant reformer John Knox gave fiery sermons. Mary Queen of Scots, his greatest adversary, was the object of his frequent and unbridled fury. The vivacious queen, raised in the French court, was always something of a stranger in her own realm. She spent most of her years in Edinburgh in Holyrood Palace.

James Craig's New Town. By the eighteenth century, Edinburgh was bursting at the seams. The Royal Mile was entirely lined by tightly staggered rows of towering tenements, half of them on the verge of collapse. Mayor George Drummond was the first to try to find a solution. In 1767, he called for an architectural competition for an expansion of the city. The surprise winner was the twenty-two-year-old architect James Craig. His plan for what would become Edinburgh New Town was amazingly simple. Instead of the rambling streets and alleys of the Old Town, he proposed a linear street plan based on the principles of neoclassical design. His New Town is now the centre of modern Edinburgh. In 1772, North Bridge was built to cross the old loch separating Edinburgh's old and new districts. Once the heavily polluted loch was drained in the early nineteenth century, Craig's plan was complete. Both the Old and New Towns were declared UNESCO World Heritage Sites in 1995.

Above: Many festivals take place in Edinburgh Castle, including the Edinburgh Military Tattoo, with performances by military bands from all over the world.

Left: View of St. Giles' tower from the East Princes Street Gardens.

LITHUANIA

Vilnius

THE LITHUANIAN CITY OF VILNIUS RADIATES SOUTHERN CHARM UNDER THE NORTHERN SUN. NESTLED IN THE NATURAL AMPHITHEATRE OF THE SURROUNDING HILLS, VILNIUS HAS MUCH TO OFFER VISITORS INTERESTED IN HISTORICAL ARCHITECTURE.

Vilnius, which can look back on a thousand years of Lithuanian history, boasts one of the largest historical town centres in Eastern Europe. Among its almost 1,500 buildings are representatives of nearly every European architectural style and historical period. Vilnius has wonderful examples of architecture from the Gothic, Renaissance, baroque, neoclassical and Jugendstil periods, all of which are located within easy walking distance of the city centre. The uniqueness of the Old City of Vilnius led to its inclusion on the UNESCO World Heritage List in 1994.

Heathens and Christians. After most of Europe had adopted Christianity and prayed to a single God, the people of Vilnius continued to pay homage to their pantheon of heathen deities. For centuries, it mattered little. Founded in the eleventh century as a walled fortress at the convergence of the Vilnia and Neris rivers, the city has always been well protected from invaders. Nevertheless, it wasn't until Vilnius became the capital of the Grand Duchy of Lithuania under Prince Gediminas in 1323 that other nations took an interest in its economic potential. The German confederation, Poland and the Russian tsar all cast their greedy eyes on Vilnius, each wanting a portion of its wealth and prosperity. Merchants,

Right: A modern office and business quarter is developing on the north bank of the Neris.

Below: The statue of Prince Gediminas keeps watch to the south of the Neris.

businessmen and priests arrived in droves, and with them came Christian missionaries. Soon afterwards, most Lithuanians finally became Christian.

The Jesuits in Vilnius. As a result, unlike many of the other cities in the Baltic region, Vilnius became an eastern outpost of the Roman Catholic Church, and a multitude of glorious baroque churches and buildings greets visitors today. In the wake of the Reformation, a period of intensive building activity was begun under the patronage of the Jesuit order. Jesuit activities were also at the heart of Vilnius' intellectual revival, as the first Jesuit University was founded in 1579. Today, the University Quarter is recognized as a one-of-a-kind architectural ensemble. Its buildings were inspired primarily by the styles of the early Italian baroque. Its courtyards, the church of St. John the Baptist, the clock tower, the observatory and the library are unparalleled anywhere else in the Baltic region.

City of churches. Vilnius lost its political significance following the union of Lithuania with Poland in 1569. From this point onwards, rulers and occupying façades came and went. The city suffered greatly, again and again bowing to the will of more powerful nations. The construction of churches, however, continued unabated and Vilnius became known as "the Rome of the East", a city noted for its abundance of churches and cloisters. Rapid growth continued to attract craftsmen, artists and labourers to the city, and by the beginning of the nineteenth century, Vilnius was the third most populous city in eastern Europe: only Moscow and St. Petersburg were larger.

Vilnius today. After fifty years of occupation by the Soviet Union, Lithuania obtained its independence in 1990, and Vilnius was declared the capital of the modern, democratic state. Lithuanians are busy restoring their city today, in full awareness of the weight of history. More than buildings need to be restored; the very identity of Vilnius needs to be revived as well. As the Lithuanian government proudly proclaims: 'Here we are not only repairing the façades, but also the foundations'. The president of Lithuania resides in a palace near the towers of the university, in the midst of the lively Old City. An office and business quarter has recently been established nearby, on the opposite bank of the Neris River. Vilnius, already a growing tourist destination, has set its sights on once again becoming the economic centre of the Baltic.

FACTS

*** Name in the national language (Lithuanian):**
Vilnius

*** Population of Vilnius:**
circa 542,300

*** Places of interest:**
Old City Hall, Gediminas Fortress, European Park, Cathedral of St. Stanislaw, Church of St. John the Baptist, St. Kazimir's Church, Church of Sts. Peter and Paul, University, Trakai Castle

FAMOUS CITIZENS

*** Eduard Flegel**
(1855–86),
African wayfarer

*** Maximilian Steinberg**
(1883–1946),
Russian composer

*** Jascha Heifetz**
(1901–87), violinist

ENGLAND

Manchester

THE DAYS WHEN MANCHESTER WAS DEFINED BY ITS WORKING-CLASS NEIGHBOURHOODS AND FOOTBALL TEAMS ARE LONG GONE. NOWADAYS, MANCHESTER IS ONE OF BRITAIN'S MOST MODERN CITIES, BUT ONE THAT IS ALSO PROUD OF ITS ROOTS.

The long shadow of London makes it difficult for other British cities to get the attention they deserve. Manchester, for example, has a great deal to offer – a lively arts scene, historically noteworthy buildings, miles of shopping districts and ultra-hip nightlife – yet the attractions of this city in north-western England are still among Europe's best-kept secrets. Potential visitors just don't know what they're missing.

Founded by Brigands. Not "brigands" as in outlaws, but a group of Celtric tribes by that name settled here long before 79 CE, when Roman general Gnaeus Julius Agricola built Mamucium at the confluence of the Irwell and Medlock rivers. One wonders if Agricola had a sense of humour, because "Mamucium" means "breast-shaped hill". Remains of the Roman fortress were visible until the eighteenth century, but railway construction has since destroyed every trace. A reproduction of the Roman castle has been recreated in Manchester's Castlefield district.

Wool and linen. After the Romans left Britain in 407, the hill fortress of Mamucium was deserted until the Anglo-Saxons arrived in the seventh century. They named the village they founded near the old fortress Mameceaster, later spelled Manchester. The town continued to grow into an important city. Wool manufacturing and linen production were the basis of

The Lowry Centre on Salford Quays with its striking pedestrian bridge over the Irwell has become the symbol of Manchester.

FACTS

*** Population of Manchester:** *circa* 422,300

*** Population of the metropolitan region:** *circa* 2.5 million

*** Places of interest:** B of the Bang (England's tallest sculpture), Bridgewater Hall, Chinatown, Chorlton Park, Cornerhouse Gallery, Free Trade Hall, Imperial War Museum North, Manchester Art Gallery, Manchester Cathedral, Museum of Science and Industry, Old Trafford Stadium, People's History Museum

FAMOUS CITIZENS

*** David Lloyd George** (1863–1945), politician, prime minister

*** Norman Foster** (b. 1935), architect and designer

*** Steven Patrick Morrissey** (b. 1959), pop singer ("The Smiths")

*** Noel Gallagher** (b. 1967), rock musician ("Oasis")

the economy, supported by skilled tradesmen and labourers. The city boomed in the late eighteenth and early nineteenth centuries. The Industrial Revolution and, in particular, the invention of the steam engine improved the efficiency of the factories and transportation of goods. Manchester would remain England's number one textile city until World War II.

Peaceful coexistence. Then as now, Manchester has been a place where people worked and lived together in peace and harmony. The glass skyscrapers of Manchester's new Millennium Quarter are not far from the historical Old Town, most of which dates to the Victorian era. Anyone wishing to explore the compact city centre need not walk the entire way. There are no London taxis here, but there are metro shuttle buses and a modern light rail network called the Metrolink.

Parts of the city resemble large shopping malls. Stylish boutiques and charming cafés are concentrated in particular near Exchange Square. For the more fashionable, the North Quarter at the other end of the city offers designer clothing at discount prices. Manchester's many small designer stores are on a par with those of London. Excursions to the legendary Old Trafford Stadium of Manchester United, the Velodrome or the Country Cricket Club may be of interest to sports fans. The souvenir shops, which do a rousing business in team jerseys and autographed equipment, are alone worth the visit.

The ultra-modern Millennium Quarter is full of new steel, concrete and glass structures that are well ahead of their time. Crossing the new Trinity Footbridge over the Irwell River to the renovated Salford Quays is an experience in itself. Designed by Spanish architect Santiago Calatrava, it curves and bends across the narrow waterway, offering a new perspective with every step. New office buildings house seemingly endless companies, businesses and museums. The Urbis Cultural Centre is located in one of them. Its glass elevator rises at a disorienting 45-degree angle from the ground to just below the roof. The city's arts and cultural scene ranks high on the list of Manchester's priorities for municipal development. Already, over fifty galleries and museums are open to visitors free of charge. Of special interest are the Manchester Art Gallery, specializing in twentieth-century works, and the Old Library, which has been in continuous use since the fifteenth century.

Centre: The glass walls of the Urbis Cultural Centre.

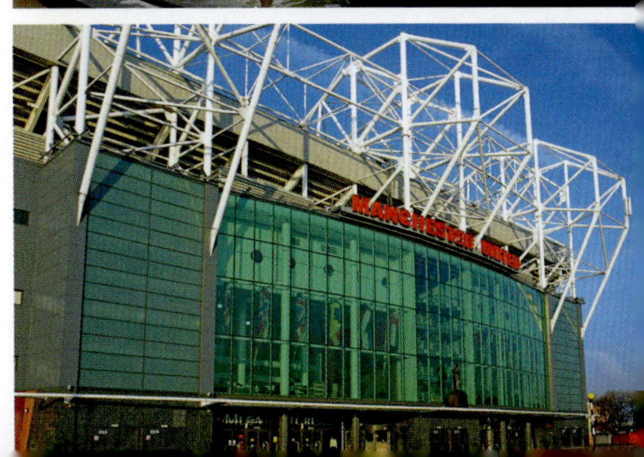

Bottom: Manchester United plays in time-honoured Old Trafford Stadium.

IRELAND

Dublin

THE CAPITAL OF IRELAND IS ONE OF EUROPE'S LIVELIEST CITIES AND WAS AT THE FOREFRONT OF IRELAND'S RAPID ECONOMIC EXPANSIONS. THIS LED TO THE REVIVAL OF DUBLIN - ITS CAPITAL AND BIGGEST CITY.

While Dublin may not be Europe's biggest city, it does have delightful charm and boasts many important historical attractions. The most interesting places to visit are south of the River Liffey in the vicinity of elegant St. Stephen's Green and Grafton Street, where stately Georgian villas line wide, green boulevards.

Heritage of conquerors. Ireland possesses a rich, multi-layered heritage and a large number of unique historical sites. Among these are the megalithic tombs of Ireland's earliest inhabitants, dating to *circa*. 3000 BCE. The many Gaelic "ring forts" date from the Bronze and Iron Ages. The Vikings also left traces here: it was they who founded the city of Dublin in 832, enclosing the new settlement inside a massive fortification wall. The Norman conquerors rebuilt the city's fortifications when they enlarged the area of the city in 1169. Christianity in Ireland is responsible for its many monastic retreats and cloisters, as ubiquitous in the Dublin area as the famous Celtic crosses.

The Book of Kells. The pagan Celtic period in Ireland ended with Christianization in the fifth century, and was followed by a flowering of what is called the Celtic Church in early Christian Ireland. The Celtic Church only fully merged with the Roman Catholic

FACTS

✻ **Name in the national language (modern Irish):** Baile Átha Cliaths

✻ **Population of Dublin:** *circa* 495,800

✻ **Population of the metropolitan region:** *circa* 1.6 million

✻ **Places of interest:** Abbey Theatre, Christ Church Cathedral, Dublin Castle, Four Courts, Grafton Street, Guinness Brewery, Half Penny Bridge, Irish Museum of Modern Art, James Joyce Museum, Malahide Castle, Merrion Square, National Gallery, National Museum, St. Patrick's Cathedral, St. Stephen's Green

FAMOUS CITIZENS

✻ **Oscar Wilde** (1854–1900), writer

✻ **George Bernard Shaw** (1856–1950), writer

✻ **James Joyce** (1882–1941), writer

✻ **Samuel Beckett** (1906–89), writer (Nobel Prize 1969)

✻ **Brendan Behan** (1912–64), writer, journalist and IRA activist

Trinity College is located on the south side of the Liffey River.

Church in the twelfth century. One of the most important manuscripts of the Middle Ages, the Book of Kells, dates to this Christian Celtic period. The Book of Kells, completed around the year 800, is a spectacularly illuminated copy of the four Gospels. According to legend, its original bindings were of solid gold. The Book of Kells is now on display in Dublin's Trinity College.

Trinity College, the most prestigious of Ireland's universities, looks back on a remarkable past. Queen Elizabeth I founded it in 1592 to keep students from going to continental Europe for their studies, where it was feared young minds would be influenced by revolutionary and Roman Catholic ideas. For centuries, Trinity College was a centre of Protestantism, but today, three-quarters of its students are Catholic. Many famous Irish writers studied here, including Samuel Beckett, Oliver Goldsmith, Bram Stoker, Jonathan Swift and Oscar Wilde.

Christ Church Cathedral now stands on the spot where the Vikings laid the first stones of Dublin's fortification wall. The first cathedral was built in 1050 and was made of wood. The stone structure we see today was finished around 1240 by the Normans, and has been the seat of Dublin's archbishops ever since. The city's second cathedral and primary Protestant church is St. Patrick's, located in the city centre. It was built between 1191 and 1270.

A view from the bottom of a glass. Anyone who comes to Dublin should not miss a visit to the Guinness Brewery. Built in 1876 in the heart of the Old City, it was soon the largest brewery in the world. An exhibition and cultural centre has been located on the site since 1957. Needless to say, visitors can always "get to the bottom" of Guinness's secret methods by draining a glass of stout in the pleasant atmosphere of the Gravity Bar.

Above: A busy street in front of a Dublin pub.

Left: St. Patrick's Cathedral stands on the spot where St. Patrick is said to have baptized the first Irishmen.

THE NETHERLANDS

Amsterdam

THE AMSTERDAM MELTING POT HAS BEEN ATTRACTING IMMIGRANTS FOR CENTURIES: VISITORS MAY FIND THEMSELVES NOT WANTING TO LEAVE. BE WARNED: ONCE YOU'VE SEEN AMSTERDAM, OTHER CITIES MAY SEEM DULL AND LIFELESS IN COMPARISON!

Amsterdam unites so many threads: historic and long-established, typically Dutch and yet multicultural, calm and yet dynamic, this "Venice of the North" with its narrow canal homes, patrician villas, imposing brick facades and steel-and-glass skyscrapers is like no other city in Europe. Its rise to prominence began in the seventeenth century, when its merchants and sailors had the world at their command.

Built upon pilings. Amsterdam began as a town on the banks of the Ij Bay at the mouth of the Amstel River. The city has always had a special relationship with the sea, and much of the city's land lies below sea level. Special measures were needed to make this strategic and commercially advantageous location inhabitable. Amsterdam rests on millions of pilings made of fir trunks sunk deep into the mud. The very first dam, the one on the "Amstel" (or "Amster") that gave the city its name, still exists today. Paved over, it is now a popular town square. Myriad canals run through the city, fronted by red-brown brick homes that are often barely wider than their bright red front doors. As is true throughout Holland, living and dining rooms seldom have curtains or draperies. No one minds being seen inside their four walls, sitting at the table, reading a newspaper or slurping a bowl of soup.

Right: Narrow canal houses in the harbour.

Below: The Rijksmuseum is the gateway to Amsterdam's museum district.

Wealth built on beer. The earliest inhabitants of Amsterdam were farmers and fishermen who tamed the Amstel River with canals, dams and dykes. The city grew rapidly after 1300, when commerce between the North Sea, Baltic Sea and southern Europe flourished. Count Floris IV of Holland first permitted the import of beer in 1323, leading to increased contacts with the cities of the Hanseatic League and boosting Amsterdam's ascent as a trading centre.

Rulers of the seven seas. The golden age of Amsterdam (1580–1740) began when the Spanish occupied Amsterdam's trading rival, Antwerp, decreasing that city's access to the sea. Ships from Amsterdam quickly moved in to take over the sea trade and fishing. With the establishment of its overseas colonies in the seventeenth century, Holland expanded its horizons in every sense of the word. The Dutch East India Company, one of the largest, most profitable trading corporations the world has ever seen, was founded in 1602. Amsterdam merchants provided 50 per cent of its initial financing, and its continued success made the city one of the wealthiest in the world.

World creditors. Banking and finance became more important in the eighteenth century. Amsterdam's dominance in trade and fishing came to an abrupt end in the early nineteenth century when, during the Napoleonic Wars, the French occupied the city, leading to a British blockade of the harbour. By the time the French departed in 1814, Amsterdam had been reduced to a local market city, and British merchants, who had taken advantage of Amsterdam's absence, ruled the waves. Amsterdam quickly rebounded by becoming an important financial centre. Any European prince needing money for a war went to Amsterdam bankers to borrow it.

1928 Olympics. In the late nineteenth and early twentieth centuries, Amsterdam increasingly turned its back on the sea, reinventing itself as an industrial and manufacturing centre. Railway connections encouraged steel production, and the population grew. The diamond industry also contributed to a booming economy in the early twentieth century, as did Dutch neutrality during World War I, which kept it relatively free of debt. Indeed, much of the war debt burdening other European nations was owed to Amsterdam banks. Amsterdam's glorious golden age, one of many it has enjoyed in the course of its history, was crowned in 1928 when it hosted the Summer Olympic Games. The years of World War II were devastating, but as before, Amsterdam recovered again, regaining its place as one of Europe's most important cities.

FACTS

*** Population of Amsterdam:** *circa* 742,000

*** Population of the metropolitan region:** *circa* 1.2 million

*** Places of interest:** Amstelkerk, Amsterdam Zoo, Anne Frank House, Begijnhof, Beurs van Berlage Café, Central Station, Concertgebouw, De Duif, Old Weighing House, Botanical Garden, Amstelkring Museum, Rembrandt House, Rijksmuseum, Scheepvaart Museum, Stadtschouwburg, St. Nikolaaskerk, Van Gogh Museum

FAMOUS CITIZENS

*** Alfred Heineken** (1923–2002), brewer

*** Rinus Michels** (1928–2005), football coach

*** Paul Verhoeven** (b. 1938), movie director

*** Ruud Gullit** (b. 1962), football player and coach

THE NETHERLANDS

Rotterdam

UNTIL 2004, ROTTERDAM HAD THE BUSIEST HARBOUR IN THE WORLD, THE DRIVING FORCE BEHIND THE CITY'S GROWTH AND PROSPERITY. THE HARBOUR EXTENDS 40 KM FROM THE CITY LIMITS TO THE MOUTH OF THE MAAS RIVER ON THE NORTH SEA.

Rotterdam's immense harbour and striking modern architecture are among its most impressive features. A walk through Rotterdam offers a glimpse into the future of city planning. Graceful, modern buildings make up the entire city centre and cutting-edge, modular housing contrasts with the historic buildings of the old harbour area. Among Rotterdam's most interesting architectural sights are Piet Blom's *kubuswonigen* ("cube houses"). The architect turned giant steel, glass and concrete cubes on their corners, and set them on pedestals creating what he called "a forest of houses" along Rotterdam's Overblaak Street.

A young city by European standards. The oldest settlement in the Rotterdam area dates back to the early eleventh century, with no permanent settlement established for another 200 years. Dykes were built to prevent damage from the frequent floods that had kept the region uninhabitable. The 1230 construction of the dykes on the Rotte River is considered the founding date of the city, which received its official charter on 7 June 1340. From that point on, its advantageous geographical location enabled Rotterdam to rapidly develop from a fishing village into a wealthy commercial port city.

Manhattan on the Maas. The city centre and harbour area were completely destroyed during World

A genuine historic lighthouse still stands alongside the modern structure that houses the Rotterdam Maritime Museum.

FACTS

*** Population of Rotterdam:** *circa* 589,200

*** Places of interest:** Delfshaven, Diergaarde Blijdorp (Rotterdam Zoo), Erasmus Bridge, Euromast Television Tower, Laurenkerk, Kop van Zuid District, Cube Houses, Rotterdam Art Gallery, Boijmans van Beuningen Museum, Netherlands National Building, Netherlands Institute of Architecture, Old Gothic Church, Provenierswijk (pre-WW II Old City), Schiedamsedijk, City Hall, Willems Bridge

FAMOUS CITIZENS

*** Erasmus of Rotterdam** (1469–1536), philosopher

*** Willem de Kooning** (b. 1904–97), artist

*** Ruud Lubbers** (b. 1939), politician

*** Rem Koolhaas** (b. 1944), architect

War II. Reconstruction in the post-war decades produced an impressive modern metropolis with eclectic architecture. From the ruins of the war, an entirely new city came into being, one that bears scant reference to the nineteenth-century city that stood there before. With its expansion inventively and creatively managed by master architects and city planners, the city continues to grow. Once-abandoned harbour areas were transformed into commercial and residential districts. These new parts of the city were connected to the old city centre by a magnificent new bridge, named the Erasmus Bridge, after the city's greatest son, philosopher Erasmus of Rotterdam.

Rotterdam harbour. Although Shanghai has now become the number one harbour in the world in terms of freight turnover, Rotterdam still has the largest harbour area in the world: an amazing 11 km^2, including the adjacent industrial zone. A number of smaller towns are located along the harbour, including Schiedam, Vlaardingen and the well-known passenger-ferry port Hoek van Holland (The Hook of Holland). Hundreds of millions of tons of cargo from approximately 30,000 container ships pass through Rotterdam Harbour annually. New on the scene is the high-tech Europoort, designed to facilitate oil tankers and refineries. It lies well away from the mouth of the Maas, across the harbour from the Hook.

Netherland's tallest building. The observation deck at the top of the 185-metre Euromast Television Tower in the Parkhaven district provides a beautiful view of Rotterdam's harbour. The Euromast also has a panoramic restaurant, The Flying Bridge, decorated with nautical instruments. The tower is the highest structure in the Netherlands. It was built in 1960 on the occasion of an international horticultural exhibition (The Floriade), and was at first a mere 104 metres tall. As taller buildings shot up around it, the Space Tower was added to extend it to its present height.

A green city. Parks are evenly distributed throughout Rotterdam, inviting people to stroll. Many of the city's green spaces have a particular theme, such as Museum Park. What they have in common is their tranquillity, except during festival time. Rotterdam's summer festivals turn many of its parks into stages for singing, dancing or poetry reading. Kralingse Bos, the largest park, has a lake where one can rent boats and sail along with a magnificent view of Rotterdam's modern skyline towering over the surrounding trees.

Centre: Rotterdam's cubic houses are wonderfully unique.

Bottom: The old Voorhaven area, no longer as busy as it used to be, is almost peaceful today.

GERMANY

Berlin

IN BERLIN, HISTORY IS PROUDLY ON DISPLAY AS IN FEW OTHER CITIES IN THE WORLD. THE WALL IS GONE, TO BE SURE, AND A UNITED BERLIN IS ONCE AGAIN THE CAPITAL OF GERMANY, BUT THE CITY REMAINS DIVIDED AT HEART.

The physical transition between East and West Berlin is much easier to navigate today than it was during the years of the Cold War. Today, glamorous and glitzy downtown West Berlin connects directly to the centre of the former East Berlin with its opera houses and museums. Before the Berlin Wall came down, the city's barbed wire, checkpoints and heavily patrolled no man's land served as a potent reminder of the alienation of an entire country. Today, few physical reminders of those years survive. Berlin has always been open to change. From the chaos of the Thirty Years' War to the bombing and firestorms of World War II, the city has often found itself either under siege, completely destroyed or in a phase of rebuilding.

Berlin-Cölln. The first written record of a settlement in the location of modern Berlin dates back to 1237. It mentions a village called Cölln on the banks of the Spree to the south of what is now known as Museum Island. Spandau (1197) and Köpenick (1209), two less central districts of the city today, are actually a bit older. The name Berlin is not mentioned until 1244, when it refers to a town along the Spree near the church of St. Nicholas, extending as far as Alexanderplatz. Berlin and Cölln were joined in 1307. The city name was often

Right: A modern sculpture in front of the Europa Centre.

Below: The Berlin Reichstag (parliament building).

hyphenated, with Berlin soon becoming the more popular designation.

The residence of the House of Hohenzollern. In 1415, the House of Hohenzollern took control of the government of the Duchy of Brandenburg. It would remain the power base in Berlin and Potsdam for over 500 years, first as electors of Brandenburg, later as kings of Prussia and, finally, as the kaisers (emperors) of Germany. When Berlin became the Hohenzollerns' official city of residence, it was obliged to give up its status as a member of the Hanseatic League. Instead of an economy devoted to import, export and trade, business in Berlin began to focus on the production of luxury goods catering to the tastes of the court aristocracy.

The Club War. Following the Protestant Reformation, property formerly held by the Roman Catholic Church was seized for sale and redevelopment. Joachim II, Elector of Brandenburg, instigated a number of ambitious building projects. It was he who laid out the earliest version of the Kurfürstendamm, for example, and he also commissioned the Grunewald Hunting Lodge and Berlin City Palace. A rather strange episode took place during Joachim's reign. To bolster city pride, the elector set up a series of war games as part of a competition between Berlin and neighbouring Spandau. The games had been rigged so that Berlin would win, or at least that was the plan. Both sides were allowed only short clubs as arms, which is why the events have been called the "Knüppelkrieg" ("club war"). What had been planned as a civic entertainment became three days of slaughter when it became clear that the Spandauers did not agree with the planned outcome. Increasingly violent fighting raged in the Havel River and continued on land. The "war" ended when the Spandauers drew the Berliners into an ambush and beat them with their clubs to the point of surrender. Joachim II was so furious that he had Spandau's mayor thrown into jail for several months.

City and capital. Berlin suffered greatly during the Thirty Years' War, when its population declined precipitously. Not until the time of "Great Elector" Friedrich Wilhelm did Berlin begin to grow once again. The founding of the Kingdom of Prussia in 1701 set off a building boom. Charlottenburg Palace is just one of many important buildings in Berlin that date to this period. On 1 January 1710, Berlin and its semi-autonomous districts of Cölln, Friedrichswerder, Dorotheenstadt and Friedrichstadt were proclaimed the capital of the Kingdom of Prussia by royal decree.

FACTS

*** Population of Berlin:** *circa* 3.4 million

*** Places of interest:** Berlin Cathedral, Berlin City Palace, Brandenburg Gate, Checkpoint Charlie, Holocaust Memorial to European Jews, German Opera, Friedrichstadt Palace, Gendarm Market, Gropius City, Glienicke Hunting Lodge, Grunewald Hunting Lodge, Kaiser Wilhelm Memorial Church, Church of St. Mary, Müggelberge TV Tower, Museum Island, St. Nicholas Church, Paul Löbe House, Peacock Island, Potsdamer Square, Pankow City Hall, Reichstag, Red City Hall, Bellevue Palace, Charlottenburg Palace, Köpenick Palace, Schönhausen Palace, Siegessäule (Victory Column), Church of St. Sophia, Berlin State Opera, St. Michael's Church, Zoo, Treptower Park, Zeughaus (Arsenal), Spandau Citadel

The Evangelical Lutheran Kaiser Wilhelm Memorial Church is located on Breitscheidplatz, at the starting point of the Kurfürstendamm.

Brandenburg Gate. At one time, the now-iconic Brandenburg Gate was just another gateway into the city. Its predecessor was built on the same spot between 1734 and 1737 as part of the construction of the Tariff Wall. During a later expansion of the city wall, Prussian king Friedrich Wilhelm II commissioned Carl Gotthard Langhans to build a new, more monumental Brandenburg Gate. Completed in 1791, the gate is a masterpiece of early neoclassical style. Sculptor Johann Gottfried Schadow cast its 5-metre-tall Quadriga (a chariot with four horses) in 1793. Standing tall on top of the arch, the victory chariot, driven by Irene, the goddess of peace, became an indelible symbol of Berlin.

A goddess of peace and victory. In 1806, Napoleon entered Berlin and had the Quadriga carried off to Paris, where it remained for eight years. He originally wanted it set on his own triumphal arch. Napoleon, however, was sent into exile before that could happen, and the Quadriga was eventually returned to Berlin. Irene, goddess of peace, was victorious once again. When the Tariff Wall was torn down in the 1860s, nearly all of the city gates went with it, but not the Brandenburg Gate. Unfortunately, the original Quadriga has not survived, and what we see on the Brandenburg Gate now is a copy. The original was almost completely destroyed by soldiers taking potshots at it in 1945 near the end of World War II. From August 1961 to December 1989 the Brandenburg Gate stood in the no man's land between the walls of a divided Berlin. When it was re-opened on 22 December 1989, a crowd of over 100,000 gathered at the gate to celebrate. Soon afterwards, the rest of the Berlin Wall came down.

Where was the Berlin Wall? Present-day Berlin is one of Europe's great metropolises, with theatres and museums everywhere, great universities and numerous monuments that celebrate Prussian, German and European history, art and culture. However, some visitors complain that they can't find the Berlin Wall. Locating the Berlin Wall, or even the places it once stood, is indeed a difficult task. Only a few short sections have been preserved at places such as Checkpoint Charlie and on Bernauer Street, where the fragments attract a great many sightseers. Built in 1961 and an important symbol of divided Germany until 1989, the detested Berlin Wall has been unceremoniously banished from the cityscape, systematic-

Below: The Victory Column at the "Great Star" in the Tiergarten district.

Right: The New Synagogue with its striking onion domes is on Oranienburger Street.

ally dismantled piece by piece and sold off all around the world.

The Ku'damm. When the Hohenzollerns laid out the Kurfürstendamm in the sixteenth century, they could not have foreseen that it would become Berlin's most popular thoroughfare and one of the best-known streets in the world. It only became a truly grand boulevard much later, between 1883 and 1886, when it was broadened to include a bridle path. The Ku'damm, as Berliners call it, runs for about 3.5 km from the Kaiser Wilhelm Memorial Church to the Hallensee and the residential areas of West Berlin. The eastern end of the Kurfürstendamm is livelier, with its department stores, boutiques and cafés. The western end is quieter, with many buildings dating to the end of the nineteenth century. Most of these are offices and galleries today.

Berlin's World Heritage Sites. Berlin is a truly international city. Museum Island, the northern tip of an island in the Spree River, was placed on the UNESCO World Cultural Heritage List in 1999. The very core of Berlin's cultural landscape, its architectural and cultural ensemble is unique to Berlin. The island is home to five world-class museums, including the Pergamon Museum with its amazing collection of archaeological treasures.

From the Berlin Zoo to the Victory Column. In addition to the extensive woodland areas in the western and south-eastern districts, Berlin is home to a number of large public parks. Nearly every street is tree-lined and Berlin proudly proclaims itself a green city. With a total land area of more than 5,500 hectares, Berlin's 2,500-odd public parks and green spaces offer a wide range of leisure activities along with ample space for simply relaxing beneath the trees and sky. The Tiergarten (zoo) is Berlin's largest park, and is located right in the heart of the city. Originally a large wooded area outside the city gates used by the Prussian nobility for hunting and riding, the Tiergarten today extends from Bahnhof Zoo to the Brandenburg Gate. The German parliament building (the Reichstag) and other government ministries are located nearby. Several large and important streets cut through the Tiergarten, including the east-west axis called the Straße des 17 Juni (Street of 17th June), commemorating a 1953 uprising against the Communist government in the former East Germany. All the streets in the Tiergarten meet at the intersection called the Großer Stern (Great Star), the site of another symbol of Berlin, the Siegessäule (Victory Column). The column has stood on that spot since 1939.

FAMOUS CITIZENS

* **Alexander von Humboldt** (1769–1859), naturalist and explorer
* **Walter Gropius** (1883–1969), architect
* **Marlene Dietrich** (1901–92), actress and singer
* **Konrad Zuse** (1910–95), inventor of the first functional computer
* **Hildegard Knef** (1925–2002), actress, singer and writer
* **Regine Hildebrandt** (1941–2001), biologist and politician
* **Angela Dorothea Merkel** (b. 1954), first female chancellor of Germany

POLAND

Warsaw

MODERN WARSAW OFFERS VISIBLE PROOF OF THE PROSPERITY THAT COMES WHEN A CITY FAMOUS FOR ITS HARDWORKING PEOPLE TAKES ADVANTAGE OF THE OPPORTUNITIES ARISING FROM THE REBIRTH OF DEMOCRACY AND THE DEVELOPMENT OF FREE MARKETS.

Increased investment in Warsaw is readily visible; the city has become a huge construction site with extensive redevelopment districts and special economic zones. More and more international firms and other organizations are choosing Warsaw as their base in Central Europe. Conveniently located, Warsaw offers a well-developed telecommunications network, economic growth and political stability.

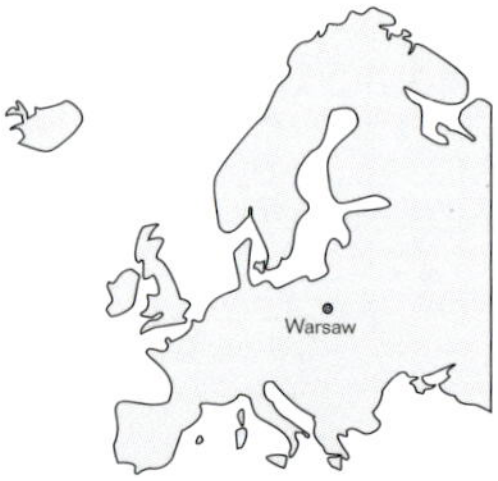

On the Vistula River. Warsaw was founded in the late thirteenth century on the site where the Imperial Palace stands today. For over three centuries, the city on the Vistula River flourished. It became politically important in 1596 when it was declared capital of Poland and royal residence of its king, Sigismund III. Warsaw remains the capital, but the country has gone through a great many changes since then. Following a series of disastrous wars and failed alliances, Poland was carved up by the European powers in 1772, 1793 and 1795. Warsaw was Prussian for a time and Russian after 1795. Warsaw became famous for its role in numerous rebellions against foreign rulers. Despite nearly constant unrest, the city continued to thrive. By 1918, Warsaw was part of Poland again.

The Old City of Warsaw is one of Poland's most popular tourist destinations. Despite its name, it is

FACTS

* **Name in the national language (Polish):** Warszawa
* **Population of Warsaw:** *circa* 1.7 million
* **Population of the metropolitan area:** *circa* 2.9 million
* **Places of interest:** The Barbican, Ship House (Renaissance-era town house), Jesuit Church, Cathedral of St. John, Imperial Palace, Palace of Culture, Lazienki Park, St. Mary's Church, Ostrogski Palace, Sigismund Column, St. Anna's Church

FAMOUS CITIZENS

* **Maria Skłodowska-Curie (Marie Curie)** (1867–1934), scientist and only recipient of Nobel Prizes in two sciences
* **Władysław Broniewski** (1897–1962), poet
* **Isaac Bashevis Singer** (1902–91), writer (1978 Nobel Prize)
* **Lech Kaczyński** (1949–2010), politician, president of Poland

King Sigismund III Wasa looks down on Market Square from on high.

actually quite new. Warsaw was devastated in World War II – nearly everything had to be completely rebuilt. Old plans and illustrations were used and every salvageable stone was put to use in the reconstruction, which was finished in 1953. Visitors to the cafés on Market Square, sampling Warsaw's famous wuzetka chocolate cake with whipped cream, might consider just how much effort went into recreating the view they are enjoying. The resolve of Warsaw's citizens to rebuild their beautiful city despite post-war deprivations has earned the city world-wide admiration; accomplishing so much under such difficult conditions is nothing short of a miracle.

Sigismund upon his throne. The oldest and most famous secular monument in Poland is the Sigismund Column, in the middle of Palace Square. In its centre, King Sigismund stands on a 22-metre-high perch with a tranquil expression, enjoying the admiring glances and comments of passers-by, and especially his city's continuing prosperity.

A gift from the Soviets. The Palace of Culture is the very first thing visitors see when leaving Warsaw's main train station. Built in just three years (1953–55), it was a gift to Poland from the Soviet Union. At 234 metres, it is the tallest building in Warsaw. Although many locals dislike its foreign origins and somewhat brutal architectural style, there is no question that the Palace of Culture plays a significant role in the city's life. Its houses theatres, cinemas, a casino, exhibition and conference halls, several museums, scientific institutions, businesses, cafés, restaurants and even sports facilities. The observation terrace on the 30th floor offers a stunning view of the city. The Palace of Culture has become a symbol of Warsaw, and its citizens are no longer trying to tear it down. In fact, the underground system leading to it, out of use since 1953, is currently being rebuilt.

Above: Restoration of the Imperial Palace in Warsaw was not completed until the 1970s.

Left: The Palace of Culture, a remnant of Soviet occupation.

ENGLAND

London

THERE IS THE UNITED KINGDOM, THERE IS ENGLAND AND THEN THERE IS LONDON. ALL THREE ARE RELATED, BUT STRICTLY SPEAKING, LONDON SEEMS TO BE A WORLD APART FROM THE REST OF BRITAIN, MARCHING TO ITS OWN UNIQUE RHYTHM.

Everything in London comes across as new and different. Throughout history, its people, fashions, trends and street life have always expressed the very essence of city life. Like New York, London is a city that never sleeps. Millions of tourists arrive in London every year, many of them already half in love with the city. You see them in the London Underground (the tube), on red double-decker buses and stepping into taxis. The new central London traffic zone, where private transport is essentially banned, makes the sights of London more navigable than ever before. It is also possible, and very pleasant, to walk through the city on foot, or to rent a bicycle along the Victoria Embankment on the Thames.

The first City of London. What is today London was once a small, rather insignificant settlement called Plowida, a name that means "settlement on the wide river". The Romans conquered the region in the first century and founded the fortified city of Londinium around 47 CE. The Roman city of London covered an area of approximately 1 km^2. The Romans built a bridge over the Thames, and used its banks as a shipping port for minerals and agricultural products. Londinium grew very quickly in the second century, when it became the

Right: The Thames Barrier is the biggest flood-control mechanism in the world.

Below: Lovely Greenwich Park is a UNESCO World Heritage Site.

commercial centre of the Roman province of Britannia Superior.

The Anglo-Saxon city. In 314, London became a bishop's see by order of Emperor Constantine. By that time, the Roman Empire was growing weak. Without imperial patronage, London settled into a long period of decline. By the time the Romans had officially departed from their colony of Britannia in 410, the city was essentially depopulated. After 150 years of near abandonment, the Anglo-Saxons arrived to take advantage of London's strategically advantageous position on the Thames. They did not settle there permanently, however, until 604, and even they chose not to rebuild within the ruins of the ancient fortified city, but somewhat further west. The new city, named Lundenvic ("London Harbour"), was declared the capital of the Kingdom of Essex. Its centre lay to the east of Trafalgar Square's present location.

The Norman invasion. The Normans defeated the Anglo-Saxons at the Battle of Hastings in 1066. After entering London, William the Conqueror had himself crowned king of Britain in Westminster Abbey, which had just been completed the previous year. All British monarchs ever since that time have been crowned there. In order to discourage any remaining Anglo-Saxon warriors from revolting, William had three fortresses built. Of the three – Baynard's Castle, Monfichet's Castle and the Tower of London – only the last survives today. In the interest of gaining popularity and ensuring domestic peace, William openly adopted the same rights, privileges and laws that had governed London during the Anglo-Saxon period.

A city in its prime. The sixteenth century was probably London's golden age. After the city of London annexed Westminster around 1600, it quickly became the centre of the British Empire. London was one of the most important European commercial cities on the North Sea, despite the fact that the city was located some 30 km away from the sea on the banks of the Thames estuary. During the late sixteenth century, London's cultural renaissance was in full swing. A great many theatres were built along the south bank of the Thames, the most famous of which was the Globe, where many of William Shakespeare's plays were first performed.

The New London. The Great Plague and Fire of 1665 and 1666 left London shaken to its very foundations. Over 70,000 people died of plague and nearly two-thirds of the city was consumed by flames. Architect Sir Christopher Wren was responsible for

FACTS

* **Population of London:** *circa* 7.4 million
* **Population of the metropolitan area:** *circa* 12.6 million
* **Places of interest:** Battersea Power Station, British Museum, Buckingham Palace, Canary Wharf, Coliseum, Crystal Palace Tower, Docklands, Globe Theatre, Greenwich Park, Hyde Park, Lambeth Palace, London Eye, London Palladium, Madame Tussaud's Wax Museum, Museum of London, National Gallery, National Theatre, Piccadilly Circus, Regent's Park, Royal Albert Hall, Royal Botanic Gardens, Royal Opera House, St. James's Palace, St. John's Church, St. Margaret's Church, St. Martin-in-the-Fields, St. Paul's Cathedral, Tate Gallery, Tower of London, Trafalgar Square, Victoria and Albert Museum, Westminster Abbey

The Tower Bridge is the icon of England's largest city.

rebuilding London's many destroyed churches, including St. Paul's Cathedral. The destruction of residential buildings in the city led many residents to settle outside the city walls in new districts that became London's first suburbs. Most aristocrats never returned to their city mansions, preferring to build townhouses in the now-prestigious West End.

Dickens' London. The nineteenth century saw the construction of many important buildings and squares, including Trafalgar Square, Westminster Palace and Big Ben, the Royal Albert Hall, the Victoria and Albert Museum, Tower Bridge and the University of London. Prosperous times, however, are often accompanied by a dark shadow. Millions of the less fortunate were forced to live in overpopulated, filthy slums and suburbs. This was the London immortalized by Charles Dickens in novels like *Oliver Twist* and *David Copperfield*. By the turn of the twentieth century, London was far and away the biggest city on Earth: a whopping 6.6 million people lived there in 1901. At the time, London was undoubtedly the most powerful city in the world.

The ravages of war. London was badly damaged during World War II. The German Luftwaffe thoroughly destroyed its once uniform cityscape of Georgian and Victorian buildings, leaving large parts of the city centre and most of the East End completely levelled. After the war, housing complexes were built cheaply and rapidly. London's docklands never recovered economically from the effects of World War II. Ship traffic was rerouted and the old piers and warehouses fell further into ruin, until city planners rediscovered the district in the 1980s. Redevelopment has made Docklands one of London's hottest commercial and residential locations.

A wonderland of things to see. There is a greater concentration of important sights and tourist attractions in London than anywhere else in Britain. Greenwich Park, Westminster Palace and Abbey, the Royal Botanic Gardens and the Tower of London are all on the UNESCO World Heritage List. Many of London's most popular museums offer free admission. Recent additions include British Airway's gigantic big wheel. Known as the London Eye, it is actually a slowly rotating observation platform from which most of the city can be seen. Madame Tussaud's Wax Museum, the changing of the guard at Buckingham Palace, a tour of the Tower of London, the Flower Market on Sundays, the bustle of Piccadilly Circus and Trafalgar Square ... the list is endless.

FAMOUS CITIZENS

* Daniel Defoe (1660–1731), writer
* Howard Carter (1874–1939), archaeologist and Egyptologist
* Charlie Chaplin (1889–1977), director, actor and comedian
* Alfred Hitchcock (1899–1980), movie director
* Sir Peter Ustinov (1921–2004), actor and director
* Queen Elizabeth II (b. 1926), Queen of the United Kingdom and the Commonwealth
* Sir Elton John (b. 1947), pop musician
* David Bowie (b. 1947), pop musician
* Daniel Day-Lewis (b. 1957), actor
* David Beckham (b. 1975), footballer

Westminster on the Thames is an impressive government complex built in neo-Gothic style.

The finest entertainment. Those eager for culture will find that the British capital is full of variety. While the mostly modern cultural facilities may look like nondescript concrete blocks from the outside, world-class performances are underway within. The Barbican Arts Centre is a case in point. Opinions about the exterior are divided; although it has its fans, it has also been described as an architect's nightmare. Still, there is no disagreement on the excellence of its presentations, which include performances by the Royal Shakespeare Company, the London Symphony Orchestra and the London Classical Orchestra. Visitors should not miss an opportunity to attend a performance here.

Breath of fresh air in the city. London does have a number of tranquil oases amidst the hectic activity of the city. London's numerous parks are popular destinations for those who like to stroll out in the open air. Hyde Park is located in west-central London. This spacious park was once a royal hunting ground, the scene of bloody duels and executions, as well as a venue for exciting horse races. During World War II, it was transformed into a gigantic potato field. Today it is a fresh-air getaway for sun worshippers, or for those who want to take a boat ride on the Serpentine, its sinuous lake. One corner of the park, near Marble Arch, is known as Speaker's Corner, where anyone can stand up and express his or her opinion before a more-or-less interested audience. In Regents Park, near London Zoo, the lovely Queen Mary Rose Gardens are a wonderful place to pause and reflect after a busy day of seeing the many wonderful sights of London. Finally, the ambitious tourist may want to take a double-decker bus or taxi north to Hampstead Heath, another vantage point that offers a magnificent view of the entire city.

Above: Anyone who has something to say can make a speech at Speaker's Corner in Hyde Park.

Left: An impressive view of the Thames, the Houses of Parliament and Big Ben from Lambeth Bridge.

BELGIUM

Brussels

OFTEN FEATURED IN THE MEDIA AS THE SEAT OF GOVERNMENT OF THE EUROPEAN UNION (EU), BRUSSELS IS MUCH MORE THAN A CITY OF BUREAUCRATS. IT IS A MEETING POINT FOR ALL THE DIVERSE CULTURES IN EUROPE, AND EXUDES A UNIQUE MULTICULTURAL ENERGY.

Brussels is not only the heart of the European Union. The Belgian capital is a lively and beautiful city in its own right, a town rich in history and full of places to see. Designated the cultural capital of Europe in 2000, Brussels is no mere town of faceless bureaucrats. It has its own story to tell.

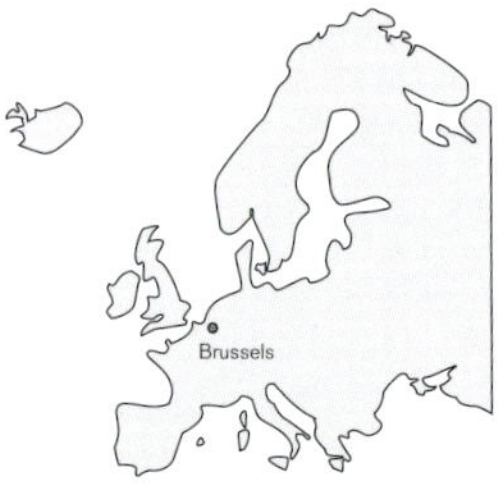

A fortress in the middle of a river. The name Brussels (Bruocsella) is first documented in 966. It means "chapel in a swamp", and likely refers to its location on the Senne River. The settlement itself had probably been founded between three and four hundred years earlier. The earliest fortification on Brussels Island dates back to around the end of the tenth century.

Central Brussels. The story of Grand Place (in French, or Grote Markt in Dutch), the town square located at the centre of Brussels, leads us on a trip through the city's history. Grand Place was created as a market and business square, but soon attracted the trade guilds and city administrators. They built magnificent guildhalls and government buildings as a testament to their power and affluence. Brussels became one of Europe's most important trading and financial centres during the High Middle Ages and would remain so until 1695, when French cannons bombarded the city for three days, levelling Grand

The Manneken Pis (nicknamed "Little Julian") dressed as the indomitable Gaul, Obelix, a much-loved cartoon character.

Place and reducing much of the city to soot and ashes. It was rebuilt fairly quickly, and the guildhalls that currently stand on Grand Place bear witness to the city's revival. Grand Place remains a favourite meeting place for residents and tourists alike. Many of its countless restaurants, cafés and taverns are open around the clock.

Brussels city hall. The Hôtel de Ville (Brussels city hall), completed in 1450, is an architectural jewel even among the grandiose guildhalls and buildings surrounding it. Its façade was one of the few structures to survive the French bombardment of 1695. With its 96-metre-tall tower topped by a gilded statue of St. Michael and the dragon, the Hôtel de Ville is Brussels' most recognizable landmark, visible from every part of the historic Old City.

A different kind of city emblem. Most visitors consider the statue called Manneken Pis (literally, "the boy peeing"), at the corner of the Rue de l'Etuve and Rue des Grands Charmes, to be the symbol of Brussels. Just who the little boy in this work by sculptor Heironimus Dusquesnoy is supposed to be remains an unsolved mystery. In any case, the brazen lad is certainly one of the city's main tourist attractions. Meanwhile, his female counterpart, the Jeanneken Pis, can be found at the end of a cul-de-sac called Impasse de la Fidélité just off La Grand Place. The citizens of Brussels have always been in favour of equal rights, and if that meant commissioning a statue of a similarly indisposed little girl, so be it. The statue was dedicated in 1987.

The giant molecule. The 102-metre-high Atomium is another symbol of Brussels. It began its existence as an exhibition hall built for the 1958 Worlds Fair. It represents a crystalline iron molecule, magnified 165 thousand million times. The tubes connecting the nine atomic particles are actually conduits containing escalators and walkways. Due to its use of futuristic materials and non-traditional design, it has long been considered both an architectural masterpiece and an impressive piece of civic monumental sculpture. Inside, the Atomium still houses the occasional exhibition on topics related to nuclear technology, aeronautics, astronomy and meteorology. Inside the uppermost sphere is a restaurant that affords a beautiful view of the entire city, weather permitting.

FACTS

* **Population of Brussels:** *circa* 142,850
* **Population of the metropolitan area:** *circa* 1 million
* **Places of interest:** Atomium, De Markten, Bourse (stock exchange), Brussels Park, St. Hubert Galleries (shopping arcade), Grand Place, Hôtel de Ville, Manneken and Jeanneken Pis, La Bécasse, Notre-Dame du Finistère Cathedral, Royal Palace, Victor Horta's townhouses, St. Catherine's Church and Square

FAMOUS CITIZENS

* **Jan Brueghel the Elder** (1568–1625), painter
* **Jacques Piccard** (1922–2008), Swiss deep-sea researcher and oceanographer
* **Jean Toots Thielemans** (b. 1922), jazz musician
* **Audrey Hepburn** (1929–93), actress

Centre: The Atomium is a gigantic and accurate representation of an iron molecule.

Bottom: Brussels also has a triumphal arch, at the entrance to the Parc du Cinquantenaire.

UKRAINE

Kiev

KIEV ORIGINATED ON THE HILLY GREEN BANKS OF THE DNIEPER RIVER. THE BEST VANTAGE POINT FOR THIS SUPERB CITY IS VLADIMIR HILL, WHERE KIEV'S PANORAMA OF GOLDEN CUPOLAS, CHURCHES AND CLOISTERS CAN BE SEEN IN ITS ENTIRETY.

Despite numerous invasions and devastating destruction, the Ukrainian capital of Kiev is still one of the most beautiful cities of Eastern Europe. The Communist period, which lasted barely seventy years, did it little harm. On the contrary, the new potentates of the post-WW II era built parks and created green spaces, along with the inevitable television tower found in every former Soviet city.

Cradle of the Slavs. The earliest mention of Kiev dates to the early sixth century. Three brothers founded it as a fortress, naming it the "City of Kyi" (Kyjiw) after the eldest brother. Over the course of many centuries, Kiev has been the administrative, political and religious centre for numerous different rulers and empires. One of these was the medieval state Kievan Rus, which included parts of what are now Russia, the Ukraine and Belarus. In light of this, Kiev has justifiably been called the cradle of the Slavs.

A Russian culture. Kiev was one of the great centres of medieval Europe in its ninth- and tenth-century golden age under the leadership of the grand dukes Sviatoslav, Vladimir and Yaroslav. Through its valuable commercial agreements with Constantinople, Kiev was always in close contact with the

Right: The Kiev Pechersk Lavra.

Below: St. Sophia Cathedral with its many cupolas and towers.

Byzantine Empire. This led, in 988, to the conversion of Kievan Rus to the Orthodox faith. This brought not only new sacred structures, but also an influx of Russian culture. This influence continued during the Middle Ages when nearly all of south-eastern Europe was under the yoke of the Mongol invasion (1240–1569). In 1667, Russia annexed Kiev, the "mother city of Russia", which in the meantime had been reduced to a simple provincial capital. Following its annexation, Kiev quickly made up for lost time, becoming the commercial and cultural centre of the Ukraine and, with the dissolution of the Soviet Union in 1991, the capital city of an independent Ukrainian state.

The cave cloister. Currently, Kiev is the undisputed centre of Ukrainian life, with its theatres and museums defining the cultural landscape. Kiev is also home to a number of sites that relate to its long history. The Old City includes buildings and other structures built over a period of 1,500 years. The greatest of these is probably the Kiev Pechersk Lavra (Monastery of the Assumption of the Holy Virgin), built in the year 1050 by immigrant monks who dug caves into the Dneiper escarpments. Eventually, the monastery was expanded to include a complex of churches and cloisters both above and below ground. This spiritual and cultural centre of the early Kieven Rus Empire is now a UNESCO World Heritage Site. In 1991, St. Sophia Cathedral was also added to the UNESCO World Heritage List. Begun in the eleventh century, the expansion and decoration of this exceptionally ornate church with its opulent frescos and mosaics was completed in the seventeenth century. The cathedral was a focal point of cultural and political life during the early years of the Russian State.

Kreschatik. In comparison to Kiev's many magnificently decorated historical façades, those along Kiev's main thoroughfare, the Khreschatyk, are no less impressive despite their more recent vintage. Completely destroyed during World War II and rebuilt since, many of the newer buildings, while conspicuously Stalinist in style, are somehow less staid, and perhaps more southern, than buildings from this period elsewhere in Eastern Europe. The street is lined with sidewalk cafés where young and old gather to share a drink and some conversation. Kiev's own particular variety of *joie de vivre* is most palpable along the Khreschatyk, and one even runs into the occasional tourist.

FACTS

*** Population of Kiev:**
circa 2.68 million

*** Population of the metropolitan area:**
circa 3 million

*** Places of interest:**
Old and New Botanical Gardens, St. Andrew's Cathedral, Holocaust Memorial at Babi Yar, Television Tower, Golden Gate, Hydropark, Cave Monastery, St. Michael's Church, Kreshtshatik, Mariyinsky Palace, Independence Square, St Sophia Cathedral

FAMOUS CITIZENS

*** Golda Meïr**
(1898–1978), Israeli politician who was born in Kiev

*** Vladimir Horowitz**
(1903–89), pianist

*** Zino Davidoff**
(1906–94), Ukrainian-Swiss entrepreneur

*** Milla Jovovich**
(b. 1975), actress

CZECH REPUBLIC

Prague

THE CAPITAL OF THE CZECH REPUBLIC IS ONE OF THE MOST IMPORTANT HISTORICAL PRESERVATION AREAS IN CENTRAL EUROPE. PRAGUE'S ONE-OF-A-KIND CITY CENTRE HAS BEEN A UNESCO WORLD CULTURAL AND NATURAL HERITAGE SITE SINCE 1992.

Prague is a great city for romantics. Traces of the city's history are found on nearly every corner. A stroll through the Old City past Powder Tower (1475), the old town hall and other equally marvellous baroque architectural treasures leads to the Charles Bridge, one of the most photographed in the world.

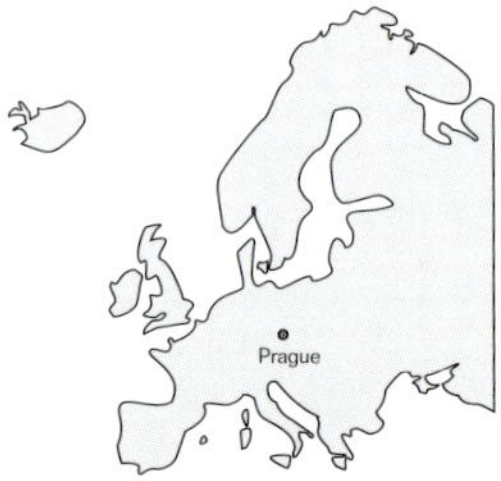

Prague Castle was erected on the Hradshin River by a landowner named Premysl sometime around 870, and Prague soon became the seat of the House of Premysl. Vratislav I, the first Bohemian king, moved the royal residence to Vysehrad Castle in 1085, probably due to a power struggle with his brother, Bishop Jaromir. Prague Castle remained the seat of the bishops of Prague for many years. The Cathedral of St. Vitus, another early structure, is also located on the castle grounds.

Prague expands. Protected by the two castles, an influx of German and Jewish merchants and local craftsmen led to rapid expansion on both sides of the Moldau River. The largest fortified area was near the already ancient Prague Castle. Prague received its city charter in 1234 from King Wenceslas I, who made it his primary residence. Shortly thereafter, the "New Town" districts of Malá Strana and Hradshin were founded. The fourteenth century brought yet more prosperity to Prague. In 1348, the first university in

FACTS

*** Name in the national language (Czech):** Praha

*** Population of Prague:** *circa* 1.18 million

*** Places of interest:** Old City, Antonin Dvorák Museum, Bedrich Smetana Museum, Lapidarium Sculpture Museum, Lobkowitz Palace, National Museum, National Theatre, Black Light Theatre, State Opera, Estates Theatre, Villa Bertramka, Wenceslas Square

FAMOUS CITIZENS

*** Antonin Dvorák** (1841–1904), composer

*** Rainer Maria Rilke** (1875–1926), poet

*** Franz Kafka** (1883–1924), writer

*** Egon Erwin Kisch** (1936–2011), reporter and journalist

*** Václav Havel** (b. 1936), writer and politician

*** Madeleine Albright (Marie Jana Korbelova)** (b. 1937), US politician born in Prague

The world-famous town hall (built in 1338) graces the entrance to the Old City. Tyn Church is in the background on the opposite side of the square.

central Europe was founded here, Charles University, named after Emperor Charles IV.

In the fifteenth and sixteenth centuries, Prague was ravaged by two religious wars. The Hussite Wars (1419–37) and the Thirty Years' War (1618–48) left deep scars. The events that set off both of these conflicts took place in Prague. These include the famous "defenestrations", in which Catholic office holders and dignitaries were thrown out of windows by dissenters, the first time by Hussites, followers of rebel reformer Jan Hus, and later by Protestants, setting off the Thirty Years' War. The victims of the first defenestration did not fall far, but landed in the arms of a mob waiting outside to lynch them. The second time was from an upper storey, but the Catholics were saved because they fell into a heap of manure. From the Catholic point of view, divine intervention prevailed. The two long, debilitating wars killed hundreds of thousands, setting back development for generations. Like other afflicted cities, Prague lost most of its international prominence during this time.

Prague Spring. In 1945, Prague became the capital of the Soviet Socialist Republic of Czechoslovakia. Communist leadership precipitated a deep-seated financial crisis: the Soviet central planning bureau contributed to nearly complete economic stagnation. In the spring of 1968, public criticism grew and much of the population became increasingly radicalized. Street demonstrations of the "Prague Spring" were news all over the world. Ultimately, power struggles within the ruling party led to the invasion of Prague by Warsaw Pact troops on 21 August 1968, and the brief period of expression was ruthlessly terminated. It would be 1989 before Prague separated itself from Russian control, and in 1993 was named capital of an independent Czech Republic.

Above: The quaint streets of Hradshin invite a stroll.

Left: Prague's romantic bridges on the Moldau as dusk approaches.

FRANCE

Paris

PARIS IS FAMOUS AS THE CITY OF LOVE, ARTISTS AND THE ART OF LIVING. ROMANTICS AND DREAMERS EVERYWHERE CELEBRATE ITS BREATHTAKING ARCHITECTURE, BOHEMIAN CULTURE, SEINE PROMENADES AND, MOST OF ALL, THE *JOIE DE VIVRE* OF ITS CITIZENS.

Few who visit Paris leave disappointed, but Paris can also be experienced from different, unexpected angles. Try leaving preconceived notions about the city behind and instead of making a beeline for the major tourist sights, drift along the city's grand boulevards, turning down the occasional side street, or stopping for a drink in a small, unremarkable café. If you happen to see the top of the Eiffel Tower or the steeples of Notre Dame Cathedral along the way, so much the better.

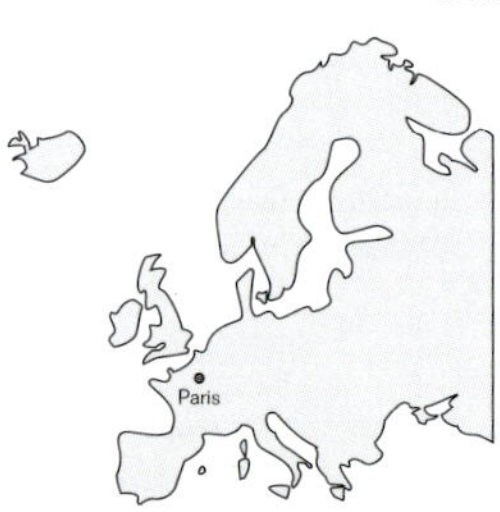

Where did the Eiffel Tower get its name? The now-famous name is in fact the region of Germany (the Eifel, in the Rheinland) whence the famous architect Gustave Eiffel's grandfather emigrated to France. He thought Boenickhausen was too difficult for French tongues to pronounce. The Eiffel Tower built by his grandson, Gustave, opened the 1889 World Exhibition in Paris. It was intended to stand for twenty years, but tourists loved it and paid good money to climb it, and it became important as one of Europe's first long-distance radio towers. In the end, the Eiffel Tower was simply too good a thing to demolish. Today, between 10,000 and 25,000 tourists visit *La Tour Eiffel* every day, each of them willing to queue for an hour or more to ascend it. It can take another hour or longer to move from the ticket window to

Right: The basilica of Montmartre resembles a mosque.

Below: The grandiose yet elegant Notre-Dame Cathedral, seen here from the banks of the Seine.

the uppermost viewing platform. The view of Paris from its heights is well worth their time and effort.

Early history. A Celtic-Gallic tribe built the settlement of Lutuhezi on the Île de la Cité in 200 BCE. Romans called this tribe the "Parisii". As many know from the Asterix comics, Julius Caesar conquered all of what is now France in 50 BCE. Lutuhezi was renamed Lutetia and became capital of the Roman province of Gaul. After the fall of the Roman Empire, Lutetia was renamed Paris by Clovis I, king of the Franks. In 508, he made it the capital of his Franconian Empire, and thus de facto of all of France.

Medieval flowering. Paris has seen the good and the bad. Vikings regularly plundered the city throughout the ninth and tenth centuries, burning it to the ground on several occasions. The French kings rebuilt the city more beautifully after each disaster. Paris' first golden age took place during the medieval period, when the city began its cultural ascent, which has never really ended. A number of important medieval buildings survived and are some of Paris' most popular attractions, including La Sainte Chapelle, the Louvre, the Sorbonne and Notre-Dame Cathedral.

The Hunchback's domain. Notre-Dame is one of Europe's most important examples of Gothic architecture. As is true of many of Europe's cathedrals, construction was drawn out over several centuries, from 1163 until 1345. Its massive interior space, overlooked by its famous rose windows, can accommodate over 6,000 people. Visitors who are fit can climb the stairs inside the north tower of the western façades and get eye-to-eye with the terrifying gargoyles perched along the roof while enjoying the magnificent view. Notre-Dame is also where Victor Hugo's fictional bell-ringer, Quasimodo, fought for the favour and life of the beautiful Esmeralda. Famously portrayed in films by actors including Lon Chaney, Charles Laughton and Anthony Hopkins, Quasimodo has become a part of popular culture to the extent that many visitors to Notre-Dame assume there is a statue of Hugo's hunchback somewhere on the premises. There isn't, but Notre-Dame's bell, located in the south tower of the west facade, can be reached via a staircase.

The dream of the Sun King. During the seventeenth century, King Louis XIV (1643–1715) began the most ambitious building campaign ever undertaken in the city. His greatest legacy is Versailles Palace, located in the suburb of that name west of Paris. Guarded by the famous musketeers, the Sun King turned his father's old hunting lodge into a magnificent palace and park grounds. Completed in 1698, it

FACTS

*** Population of Paris:**
circa 2.13 million

*** Population of the metropolitan area:**
circa 11.56 million

*** Places of interest:**
Arc de Triomphe, Arènes de Lutèce (Roman Amphitheatre), Champs Élysées, The Bastille, Bois de Boulogne, Pompidou Centre, Comédie Française, Paris Disneyland, Les Invalides, Eiffel Tower, Élysée Palace, Fontainebleau,Tuileries Garden, Luxembourg Garden, Paris Lido (most famous of the Paris cabarets), Louvre, Musée d'Orsay, Notre-Dame Cathedral, Opéra National de Paris, Luxembourg Palace, Imperial Palace, Panthéon, Place de la Concorde, Place d'Étoile, Pont Neuf, Sacre Coeur, Saint Denis, Saint Eustache, Sainte Chapelle, Saint Sulpice, The Sorbonne, Versailles

The Louvre's central courtyard acquired a glass pyramid during the 1980s. The Arc de Triomphe is visible in the background.

remains an immensely popular attraction today. It is said that the extravagant Sun King emptied the national treasury to fund his architectural marvels, bringing France to the verge of bankruptcy. In fact, the king's finance minister, Colbert, had everything under control. Contracts were made public, open to bidding and subject to review, and estimated costs were strictly adhered to. Labour costs were reduced by using soldiers in times of peace to do much of the work. In today's terms, Colbert paid about $200 million in construction costs for Versailles, or as little as 2–3 per cent of state spending at the time. Understood as 3 per cent of the current working budget of France, the palace would have cost some $5 billion.

Long live the Revolution! The wastefulness and debauchery of the French kings ultimately led to an outpouring of public rage on 14 July 1789, when the citizens of Paris stormed the Bastille, the state prison for political prisoners. The French Revolution began, ran its course, and soon began to consume its own leaders. Paris collapsed into chaos. The noble goals of the early Revolution were quickly replaced by a reign of terror in which over 17,000 heads rolled, literally, due to the implementation of the guillotine, which swiftly and efficiently decapitated the condemned. Most of the original leaders of the Revolution lost their heads in this fashion. The end finally arrived in the form of a young Corsican general named Napoleon Bonaparte. He took control in 1799, bringing peace to the badly shaken capital. His legacy includes French civil law, known as the *Code Napoléon,* and monuments including the massive, neoclassical Arc de Triomphe.

The Louvre began as a sixteenth-century imperial palace, and was first utilized as a museum in 1793. In the 1980s, a 21-metre-tall glass pyramid designed by architect I. M. Pei was added to the museum's courtyard to serve as an entrance to the Paris catacombs and other exhibition spaces. The modern design was initially declared a flop, but has since developed a large following. Groups of art lovers crowd into the Louvre's myriad galleries filled with masterpieces of painting, sculpture and antiquities. Among its most famous works are the *Mona Lisa*, the *Venus de Milo* and *Nike of Samothrace*. Most recently, Dan Brown's novel *The Da Vinci Code*, parts of which are set in the Louvre, has brought a whole new influx of visitors to the museum.

FAMOUS CITIZENS

* Cyrano de Bergerac (1619–55), writer
* Molière (1622–73), actor and playwright, France's greatest comedy writer
* Voltaire (1694–1778), writer and Enlightenment philosopher
* Alexandre Dumas, *fils* (1824–95), writer
* Émile Zola (1840–1902), writer
* Edith Piaf (1915–63), cabaret singer
* Charles Aznavour (b. 1924), cabaret singer and actor
* Brigitte Bardot (b. 1934), actress and environmental activist

The Eiffel Tower remains the unmistakable icon of Paris.

A small gift. The Third French Republic was still young when it gave the Statue of Liberty to the United States in 1885. This symbolic act strengthened the republic, which was seen as nothing more than an interim solution by its many opponents. Sculptor Frédéric Bartholdi designed the statue, while Gustave Eiffel contributed his expertise to the design of its cast iron and steel frame. The statue was finished in France in July 1884. For test purposes, Bartholdi conducted a trial assembly of the statue outside Paris, using temporary rivets to attach the copper plates to Eiffel's scaffolding. The entire statue was then disassembled into 350 individual parts, packed in 214 boxes and shipped to New York, where it arrived on 17 June 1885 aboard the French frigate *Isère*. Bartholdi's original working scale model of the Statue of Liberty, standing only 2 metres tall, can be seen today in the Jardin du Luxembourg, one of the most popular parks in the Latin Quarter of Paris.

A shopper's paradise. Paris has long been a mecca for shoppers. Visitors thrill to the selection of high-fashion clothing available at Paris' many designer shops and department stores. Whether traditionally elegant and up-market, or conceptually and stylistically daring, fashionable shoes, dresses, designer ensembles and haute couture are all readily available in Paris. London and New York may now have comparable fashion industries, but the boutiques in Paris are much more venerable. Names like Dior, Givenchy and Yves St. Laurent ensure that Paris is not only the city of romance, but also the centre of the fashion world. Whether or not designer clothes are within one's budget, a shopping excursion to the Galleries Lafayette on Boulevard Hausmann is a must for every visitor. The side streets branching off the Champs Élysées are another shopper's paradise, with something for everyone, much like Paris itself.

Above: Luxembourg Palace surrounded by its beautiful park.

Left: Louis XIV, the Sun King, built Versailles as an eternal monument to the glory of his reign.

AUSTRIA

Vienna

LOCATED IN THE VERY HEART OF EUROPE, VIENNA IS BOTH A LIVELY MODERN METROPOLIS AND A CITY KNOWN FOR ITS COFFEE HOUSES, HISTORIC DISTRICTS, LOVELY PARKS, ELEGANT SQUARES AND ROMANTIC COURTYARDS.

Vienna means café culture, music and wine. Where else can one so contentedly spend all day sitting in a café, reading the newspaper, sipping a Viennese coffee or a glass or two of wine?

Where the torrent rushes. Roman Vindobona, founded in the year 15 CE, was completely destroyed by the Germanic migrations of the fourth and fifth centuries. With the Roman legions long gone, only a small settlement remained. The name Vindobona is likely a version of the Celtic "Vedunia", which means "torrent", a reference to the settlement's location on the banks of the snow-fed Danube River.

Vienna was a city of dubious repute at the end of the twelfth century. Its ruler, Duke Leopold V, was complicit in the abduction of the English king, Richard Lionheart, on his way home from the Crusades. The two nobles had clashed during the Third Crusade. Forced to stop in Vienna, Richard was recognized and arrested. An enormous ransom was paid for his release, roughly twenty-five tons of silver, a huge sum for those days. The duke used the silver to found a mint, the vast profits from which enabled him to expand the city and build new fortification walls. Although Emperor Henry VI had given his blessing to the duke's illicit activities, the pope had not, and in 1194 Leopold V was excommunicated.

FACTS

* Population of Vienna: *circa* 1.63 million
* Population of the metropolitan area: *circa* 1.87 million
* Places of interest: Burgtheatre, Gasometre City, Hofburg, Hundertwasser House Museum, Millennium Tower, Museum Quarter, Liechtenstein Palace, Vienna State Opera, St. Stephen's Cathedral, Theatre an der Wien, Theatre in der Josefstadt, Wotruba Church

FAMOUS CITIZENS

* **Ignaz Bösendorfer** (1796–1859), piano maker
* **Johann Nestroy** (1801–62), dramatician and satirist
* **Johann Strauss, the younger** (1825–99), composer of well-known waltzes
* **Friedensreich Hundertwasser** (1928–2000), artist and architect
* **Romy Schneider** (1938–1982), actress
* **Niki Lauda** (b. 1949), racing driver

St. Stephen's Cathedral is the primary symbol of Vienna.

In the shadow of St. Stephen. The first version of Vienna's cathedral was completed in 1147 as a small parish church, and was actually too large for the tiny population of Vienna at that time. The city would not become important for another decade, after it was named capital of the Duchy of Austria. A hundred years later, the original church was replaced by one built in the Romanesque style. Its façade, known as the Roman Towers, was preserved when construction of a Gothic church began in 1340. In 1359, Duke Rudolf IV laid the cornerstone for the soaring Gothic nave, which was completed in 1474. Vienna's early dukes had not been successful in elevating the town to a bishop's see, which was necessary for St. Stephen's to be declared a cathedral; it had always been simply a church within the diocese of Passau. It did not become the seat of a bishop, and thus formally a cathedral, until 1469. St. Stephen's has undergone many changes since then. As tastes changed, the interior and exterior were altered to reflect the times. Recent restoration has uncovered traces of older versions of Vienna's beloved "Steffl", as the church is known locally.

Baroque building boom. The sixteenth century was very much focused on rebuilding Vienna's fortifications, which had been damaged during the Turkish siege of 1529. Work was not quite finished when the Turks returned in 1684. They were stopped just outside Vienna, the gateway to Europe, and never reached that far again. Bombardment from Turkish positions in what is today the Wienerwald ("Vienna Woods") left the city badly damaged in the wake of the Turkish retreat. Rebuilding Vienna brought a large number of baroque architects to the city. The most outstanding buildings from that era are noble and royal residences, including the Schönbrunn, Liechtenstein, Schwarzenberg and Belvedere palaces.

Above: The Prater with its famous big wheel, a popular Viennese destination.

Left: The Vienna Rathaus (city hall) was completed in 1883.

SLOVAKIA

Bratislava

THOUGH BRATISLAVA IS ONE OF THE SMALLEST OF THE FAMOUS CITIES ALONG THE DANUBE, IT HAS PLAYED A ROLE IN EUROPEAN HISTORY. PRIOR TO WORLD WAR I, THE CITY'S NAME HAD BEEN PRESSBURG FROM ITS FOUNDING IN THE THIRTEENTH CENTURY.

The capital of Slovakia lies halfway between her two much larger sister cities of Vienna and Budapest. Bratislava has always been a melting pot of the peoples and cultures of the Pannonian Plain. In the morning one might speak Slovakian with labourers and domestic help, Hungarian with businessmen in the afternoon and German at home in the evening or on a visit to Vienna. With the end of socialism and Slovakia's independence in 1993, the social stratification, resentments and prejudices of the past have dissipated. Today, the people of Bratislava are living and working together in peace.

The Celts were the region's first settlers, building a fortified settlement on the Slovakian shore of the Danube around 125 BCE. They did not get to enjoy this beautiful spot for long; the Romans arrived soon afterward and made life very difficult for them. The Celtic tribes fled. The Romans remained in the Bratislava area for 500 years, before they too were displaced, this time by invading hordes of Huns, Slavs and Avars from the east. For an extended period after the Romans' departure, no one was really in control of this section of the Danube, which was racked by dissension and disagreement among the conquerors. In the end, Bratislava ended up being formed from a combination of Hungarian, Austrian

When it isn't market day, Bratislava's Market Square is a quiet place to linger.

FACTS

*** Official name until 1919:** Presporek or Pressburg

*** Name in English:** Bratislava

*** Population of Bratislava:** *circa* 425,150

*** Places of interest:** Old Town Hall, Franciscan Church, Bratislava Castle, St. Martin's Cathedral, St. Michael's Gate, National Gallery, Grassalkovic Palace, Philharmonic Hall, Primate's Palace

FAMOUS CITIZENS

*** Georg Raphael Donner** (1692–1741), Austrian sculptor

*** Imre Esterhazy de Galantha** (1722–92), bishop of Esztergom

*** Johann Nepomuk Hummel** (1778–1837), composer

*** Alexander Dubček** (1921–92), politician

*** Hugo Portisch** (b. 1927), Austrian journalist

Centre: Entrance to the Primate's Palace.

Bottom: The Cathedral of St. Martin is the most important sacred building in Bratislava.

and Morovian influences. Political control passed back and forth between many rulers.

Visiting a café. There are many wonderful places to see in Bratislava. The beautiful Old City, completely restored in recent years, is an absolute must. It is one big pedestrian zone, and this is where most of the city's historical buildings and monuments can be found. As is characteristic of the imperial and royal cities of the "dual monarchy" of Austria and Hungary, there are cafés everywhere. Bratislava has preserved café culture in its purest form, with delicious pastries and luscious drinks. Haus Mayer, a café on the main square, still advertises itself as purveyor to the imperial and royal court, a title only awarded to establishments that met the highest standards. The square in the city centre also contains the Roland Statue and Fountain, which stand near the old town hall, today the Bratislava City Museum. The town hall, begun in the fourteenth century, is one of the oldest secular buildings in all of Slovakia.

The palace of the archbishops. Leaving the town hall through its back door, one stands opposite the neoclassical Primate's Palace, the former residence of the archbishops of the Holy See of Pressburg. A bishop's residence stood on this spot as early as 1370. The neoclassical style of its successor was in vogue in 1780–81 when it was designed and built. It is considered the masterpiece of its architect, Melchior Hefele. Austria's aristocracy associates the Bratislava Primate's Palace with the ignominious 1805 Treaty of Pressburg, which forced Austria to give up Dalmatia and its beloved Tyrol following defeat by Napoleon at the Battle of Austerlitz.

A castle and St. Martin's. The symbol of Bratislava sits high on a hill, where, in typical Central European style, an impressive castle stands. Today it is the Slovakian National Museum, but Bratislava Castle was once the seat of kings. Looking out over Bratislava from the castle, church spires are everywhere to be seen. St. Martin's Cathedral is the most important of the city's many sacred structures. The kings and queens of Hungary, as well as several Habsburg emperors and their queens, were crowned here from 1563 to 1830, including Empress Maria Theresa. The three-aisled church was built with a tower 85 metres high so that it could serve as part of the city's defence system. St. Martin's also has several smaller chapels dedicated to St. Anna, St. Sophie and St. John.

GERMANY

Munich

MUNICH IS FULL OF SHADED BEER GARDENS, MAGNIFICENT PUBLIC PARKS AND BUILDINGS WITH ORNATE STUCCO FAÇADE. TRADITION AND MODERNISM RUB SHOULDERS IN MUNICH AS IN NO OTHER GERMAN CITY.

The small-town charm of many Munich districts stands in great contrast with the hectic pace of big city life on the Marienplatz or along the pavements of Maximilian Street. Quite aside from the famed Oktoberfest held each autumn, this city on the Isar River offers visitors a wealth of architectural treasures. During the course of the last century, Munich has become one of Germany's most important media and commercial centres. Munich's unique combination of laptops and lederhosen have made the city one of the most popular business and tourism destinations in Europe.

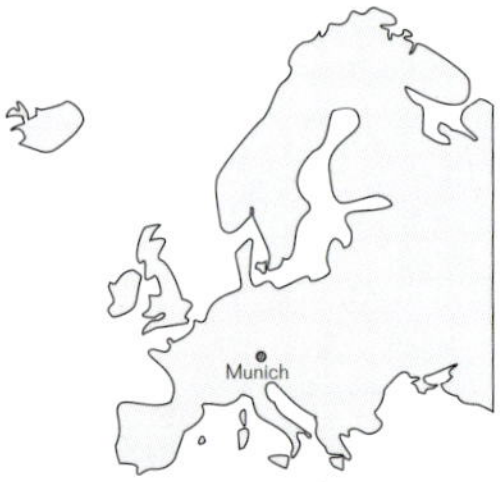

From Petersbergl to Munich. Monks settled on the Isar in the eighth century, building Tegernsee Monastery at the place they called Petersbergl. The crypt of the church of St. Peter, Munich's oldest, dates back to the early Middle Ages. In the twelfth century, Heinrich the Lion, Duke of Saxony and Bavaria, built the city of Munich around St. Peter's. Under the command of this powerful duke, Munich became an important city. It was the official residence of the Bavarian dukes from 1255 and named the capital city of Bavaria in 1506.

A square for football celebrations. Just as Munich is the heart of Bavaria, the Marienplatz is the heart of the city, the most popular and best known of the

Right: Bavarian dukes and kings resided in Schloss Nymphenburg.

Below: The FC Bayern München football team plays in Allianz Arena.

many squares in Munich. The new city hall is on the north side of the square, with the old city hall, the Rathaus, on its eastern side. St. Peter's is just a few steps away. The famous and beloved Bayern München football team has traditionally celebrated its championship titles on the Marienplatz with thousands of enthusiastic fans.

Munich conjures up images of Oktoberfest, the Hofbräuhaus, shady beer gardens and people wearing lederhosen and dirndl. All of these images are accurate, but Munich is more than simply a bastion of Bavarian traditions. The city is one of Germany's most important publishing and television centres, for example. Many publishing houses, radio and television stations, film-production companies and music studios have headquarters in the media city of Munich. As a result, Munich is home to more actors, artists, television producers and celebrities than any other German city.

Summer residence of the Bavarian monarchs. The celebrities of the past, the Bavarian dukes, princes and kings, also resided in Munich. Their legacy has left the city with a number of fascinating historical attractions. There are so many to choose from, visitors may have a difficult time deciding which of the many sights to visit first. Nymphenburg Palace and its park should be near the top of the list. The former summer residence of the Bavarian rulers, Schloss Nymphenburg is one of the most popular tourist destinations in Bavaria today. Its elaborate interior furnishings, including King Ludwig I's almost surreally ornate "Gallery of Beauties", should not be missed.

Symbol of Munich. The twin towers of Munich's most famous symbol, the Frauenkirche (Cathedral of Our Lady), are 99 metres tall. Duke Sigismund laid the cornerstone of Munich's most beloved church on 9 February 1468. Today the Frauenkirche is officially the Cathedral Church of the Archbishops of Munich and Freisling. Its towers, which can be seen for many kilometres, is in part because the city administration prohibits the construction of any building within Munich's central ring higher than 99 metres. New construction of taller buildings further away from the centre has been permitted in the past, but is currently under review. Only the south tower of the Frauenkirche can be climbed. It offers a unique view of Munich, its surroundings and the nearby Alps, which on clear days appear to be close enough to reach out and touch.

FACTS

*** Population of Munich:** *circa* 1.28 million

*** Population of the metropolitan area:** *circa* 2.6 million

*** Places of interest:** Alte Pinakothek (Museum), Bavarian State Opera, Deutsches Museum, English Garden, Feldherrnhalle, Frauenkirche, Friedensengel, Church of the Holy Ghost, Hofgarten, Lenbachhaus Museum, St. Michael's Church, Münchner Residenz, Neue Pinakothek, Prinzregententheatre, Nymphenburg Palace, Theatre am Gärtnerplatz, Theatiner Church, Hellabrunn Zoo, Viktualienmarkt

FAMOUS CITIZENS

*** King Ludwig II of Bavaria** (1845–86), "Mad King Ludwig", built Neuschwanstein Castle

*** Richard Strauss** (1864–1949), composer

*** Franz Beckenbauer** (b. 1945), footballer

HUNGARY

Budapest

THE HEART OF HUNGARY BEATS IN BUDAPEST. MAGNIFICENT TURN-OF-THE-CENTURY ART NOVEAU ARCHITECTURE, DECADENT TURKISH BATHS AND LUXURIOUS HOTELS ARE WAITING TO BE REDISCOVERED.

The location of Budapest has to be among the most beautiful in the world. According to Hungarians, no place on Earth is as lovely as the wide reaches of the Puszta region on the banks of the great Danube River. The river winds its way like a silver thread through the city, dividing the hilly, sleepy banks of Buda from the flat, metropolitan Pest, all against the backdrop of a romantic castle perched on top of a hill.

Two cities, one commercial, one political. The Roman city of Aquincum, founded in the first century, was the first settlement in the area of what is now Budapest. Traces of that provincial capital have recently been excavated in what is today the Old Buda district. After the Roman Empire fell in the fourth century, most of the residents packed up and left, leaving Aquincum deserted. The first Magyar tribes coming into the region settled near Old Buda around 896. Buda and Pest came into being around that time. Many trade routes met here, with the Pest side of the river, a better port due to its level terrain, becoming more and more commercial over time. Buda, on the opposite bank, became a political and religious centre. Bela IV built Buda Castle there in 1241, and its latest manifestation, a baroque palace, still towers over the city. Buda became the permanent residence

FACTS

*** Population of Budapest:** *circa* 1.7 million

*** Places of interest:** Aquincum, Buda Fortress District, Corvinus University, Fisherman's Bastion, Gellértberg, Heroes Square, Chain Bridge, Imperial Fortress, St. Matthew's Church, Margaret Bridge, National Gallery, Parliament, Sándor Palace

FAMOUS CITIZENS

*** Empress Maria Theresia** (1717–80), Queen of Hungary and Bohemia, Archduchess of Austria

*** Theodor Herzl** (1806–1904), writer, publicist and journalist

*** Paul Almásy** (1906–2003), photographer

*** Sir Georg Solti** (1913–97), born Georg Stein, conductor

*** Ephraim Kishon** (1924–2005), born Ferenc Hoffmann, Israeli satirist, journalist and stage director

The Gellert Hotel stands on the Pest side of the Danube banks, beyond Freedom Bridge. It houses a beautiful indoor swimming pool.

of the Hungarian crown in 1361, remaining so until 1536.

Turkish baths. The Ottoman Turks conquered much of Hungary during the fifteenth and sixteenth centuries. Buda became the seat of the Turkish governors in 1541, while Pest declined in importance. The new Islamic rulers converted the churches into mosques, and also built a great many Turkish baths. Budapest never lost its Turkish bath tradition. Tourists and locals alike frequent famous establishments like the Király, Rác and Rudash baths.

Budapest under the Habsburgs. The Habsburgs regained control of Hungary at the end of the seventeenth century. At first, little changed for the residents of Buda and Pest. In 1723, Pest once again became the regional administrative seat and the city began to develop rapidly. The unification of Buda and Pest first took place in 1872, originally as Pest-Buda. The city's underground system, sewage systems, electric lighting, bridges and horse paths also date from this period, in which Budapest experienced an unprecedented building boom. After World War I, Budapest became the capital of the independent kingdom of Hungary.

Destruction. After World War II, however, the centre of Budapest had to be rebuilt almost in its entirety. Siege by the Russian army and house-to-house combat wreaked havoc on the city. It took Soviet troops more than 102 days to capture Budapest, with the German army and Hungarians defending their positions at a terrible cost. Every bridge across the Danube was blown up, and most of the city destroyed.

Budapest is a Western-oriented metropolis today, attracting tourists in droves with its endless charm. The Fisherman's Bastion monument in the Buda district offers one of the best views of the city.

Above: The Chain Bridge over the Danube.

Left: The neo-Gothic parliament buildings lie directly across the Danube from the banks of Buda.

SWITZERLAND

Zurich

ONE OF EUROPE'S MOST PICTURESQUE CITIES IS NESTLED IN THE SWISS ALPS ON THE SHORES OF LAKE ZURICH. ONE OF THE LARGEST BANKING CENTRES IN THE WORLD, BILLIONS OF DOLLARS ARE TRANSFERRED DAILY WITH THE MERE CLICK OF A MOUSE.

Zurich is not only a city of bankers and financiers. The city is lively, tolerant, open-minded and multicultural. Zurich's heart can be found in its Old City on the Limmat River, between the shore of Lake Zurich and Central Square. Zurich's world-famous Bahnhofstrasse, the main thoroughfare of its stylish banking and shopping district, runs from one end of the Old City to the other. The street has been called "the shop window of Switzerland".

Roman remains. A second-century tombstone discovered on the Lindenhof, a small natural hill in the centre of the Old City, is the earliest physical evidence of settlement of the city area. Zurich was the site of the Roman trade city of Turicum, which may have replaced a still earlier Celtic settlement. The ancient name is unusual and may go back to the predecessors of the Romans, the Helvetians. Zurich is the Germanic version of the Latin name, and was first used in the ninth century.

Lindenhof. Lindenhof, the centre of ancient Turicum, was a hill on an island between the Sihl and Limmat rivers. This ancient mound contains the remains of a Roman trade post and some later fortifications. This remnant of what was once a way station along the heavily travelled route between Germany

The Landesmuseum (National Museum) is devoted to Swiss cultural history.

FACTS

* **Population of Zürich:** *circa* 366,800
* **Population of the metropolitan area:** *circa* 1.1 million
* **Places of interest:** St. Augustine Church, Belvoir Park, Fraumünster (Church of Our Lady), Großmünster, Hardturm Stadium, Liebfrauenkirche, Bellerive Museum, Pestalozzi Monument, Predigerkirche, Swiss Landesmuseum, Sechseläutenwiese, St. Peter's Church, Zurich Tonhalle, Wasserkirche (Water Church)

FAMOUS CITIZENS

* **Huldrych Zwingli** (1484–1531), church reformer
* **Johanna Spyri** (1827–1901), author of *Heidi*
* **Max Bircher-Benner** (1867–1939), naturopath, inventor of Swiss Müesli
* **Hermann Rorschach** (1884–1922), psychiatrist

and Rome is now a peaceful, urban oasis, famous for its chess players. The view from the top of the Lindenhof is superb, offering a veritable panorama of the Old Town with the Limmat River flowing below.

Chocolate! The old parade ground on the opposite bank of the Limmat is where the world-famous Confiserie Sprüngli, a sweet shop founded in 1836, can be found. The finest chocolates have been sold and sampled here for many generations. This elegant sweet shop is still one of the best in all of Switzerland, stocking everything a connoisseur's heart could possibly desire. Its handmade pralines and truffles are much more than simple treats – each chocolate creation is an edible treasure.

The parade ground (Paradeplatz) is the most expensive property on the board in the Swiss version of Monopoly. Its fame and glamour are relatively recent developments; during the seventeenth century, the area was Zurich's designated pig market. It wasn't until 1870 that the area was paved over for military exercises and received its current name.

Big spenders only. The parade ground lies more or less at the centre of Zurich's shopping district along its world-famous Bahnhofstrasse. This thoroughfare, just under a mile long, runs from the main train station to the shore of Lake Zurich. It does not take long to spend a fortune here. Anyone who wants to rent an office or purchase a home in this district must have a great deal of money in the bank, preferably in a numbered Swiss bank account. The legendary banking district is famous for having the most expensive rents and property prices in the world. The main train station in Zurich, dedicated in 1871, is located on Central Square at the Bahnhofstrasse's north end. A beautiful structure with unique architectural details, it goes without saying that the train station also has an extensive, exclusive shopping mall beneath it.

Zurich's Old Town. Most of the interesting sights in Zurich, including the elegant shops and businesses of the Bahnhofstrasse and the Old City, are spread across both banks of the Limmat River between the train station and the shores of Lake Zurich. The mouth of the Limmat on Lake Zurich is the location of the city's baroque town hall and a number of impressive churches, including the Großmünster, Fraumünster and Zurich's oldest church, St. Peter's, famous for having the largest clock face in Europe.

Centre: The Fraumünster and St. Peter's tower above the left bank of the Limmat River.

Bottom: A sculpture of a lion watches over the entrance to the Zurich Stock Exchange.

ITALY

Venice

IN THE EARLY MORNING LIGHT, GONDOLAS TIED TO WOODEN STAKES ROCK GENTLY ON THE GRAND CANAL. AT DAWN, VENICE IS A PEACEFUL CITY ON A LAGOON, A UNIQUE LAND- AND SEASCAPE OF ALMOST UNIMAGINABLE BEAUTY.

Ten million visitors a year come to experience this unique city on the Adriatic. Venice is first on the UNESCO list of cultural monuments worthy of protection. The historic city centre is scattered across several islands in the middle of a lagoon. Just how many islands are there? Only geographers know for sure. Most sources count 118 islands, joined by over 400 bridges and traversed by 177 of Venice's famous canals.

Escape to the lagoon. Venice was founded in 453, when the people who lived in the region fled into the lagoon to escape the invading Huns. Later, they fled the Lombards the same way, seeking shelter on sandbanks and islets. The largest island is the Rialto. Near it are the islands of Luprio, Gemine, Mendicola, Ombriola, Olivolo and Spinalunga. With space at a premium, buildings were extended out into the water. Dense grids of elm and larch trunks were rammed into the swampy ground to serve as scaffolding and pilings for new construction.

A powerhouse of European trade. Venice was once subordinate to the Byzantine Empire under the Bishop of Ravenna, and was so in 1456, when the conquest of Constantinople by the Ottoman Turks changed everything. De facto, however, Venice had long operated as an independent republic. The doges,

Right: San Giorgio Maggiore is on an island in the Venetian lagoon.

Below: Venice's main waterway, the Grand Canal, with the Rialto Bridge in the background.

its elite elected rulers, had established the local Venetian government on the Rialto as early as 811. With the collapse of the Byzantine Empire, however, the lagoon city seized the opportunity by taking over the empire's former role as the leading economic power in the Mediterranean.

The winds of fortune. Disputes with other nations were commonplace during the fifteenth century. Venice and the emerging Republic of Genoa were often at war, frequently with each other. There was a great deal of competition for supremacy in trade in the Mediterranean region, particularly in the Aegean Sea near the coast of Turkey and Greece. Over the course of the following century, the Iberian states, England and the Netherlands all attempted to build empires based on naval power and trade. Venice, which for a time was the undisputed power in the Mediterranean, began to lose its grip on the leading position around this time as the centre of world trade began to shift away from the Old World towards the New. The economic prosperity of the Spanish and British colonies in the Western hemisphere overwhelmed trade with the East, and Venice's profits and prosperity declined.

A city of brigands? The residents of the lagoon city conducted not only the honourable kind of business. Whenever it was necessary, that is, whenever it was profitable, Venetians were more than happy to take up weapons and take what they wanted. The city has always been famous for its pirates and it was Venetians who stole the mortal remains of St. Mark from Alexandria and took them back home. The Cathedral of San Marco was then built to house them. And what about Enrico Dandolo? In 1201, the 95-year-old Venetian doge set out for Jerusalem to drive the "heathen Arabs" out of Jerusalem. Instead, in 1204, still on the way to the Holy Land, his army decided to plunder Constantinople first. Roman Catholics unscrupulously killed the city's Orthodox Christians, slaughtering thousands in order to get their hands on their great wealth. The Crusader sack of Constantinople helped make Venice a world power, and an immeasurably wealthy one.

The end of the Republic. The proud history of what the Venetians refer to as *La Serenissima*, which means "the most serene", came to an end on 14 May 1797 when Napoleon's troops marched into Venice. The city did not remain under French control for long. Not long afterwards, France ceded the entire Veneto region and Friuli to Austria as part of the Treaty of Campo Formio. Venice's days as an independent republic, however, were finally over.

FACTS

* **Name in the national language (Italian):** Venezia
* **Population of Venice:** *circa* 280,000
* **Places of interest:** Ca' d'Oro, Ca' Foscari, Fasetti, Loredan, Palazzo Corner Spinelli, Palazzo dei Camerlenghi, Palazzo Ducale, Palazzo Grassi, Residence of the Patriarchs, Rialto Bridge, San Giorgio Maggiore, San Marco Cathedral, Church of Santa Maria della Salute

FAMOUS CITIZENS

* **Giovanni Bellini** (1430–1516), painter
* **Titian (Tiziano Vecelli)** (1488/90–1576), artist, diplomat
* **Antonio Vivaldi** (1678–1741), composer
* **Giacomo Casanova** (1725–98), world traveller, writer and famous lover
* **Ludovico Manin** (1725–1802), the last doge

SERBIA

Belgrade

BELGRADE IS ONE OF THE OLDEST CITIES IN EUROPE, LOOKING BACK ON 7,000 YEARS OF CONTINUOUS HABITATION. IN THE FOURTH CENTURY, A ROMAN EMPEROR WAS BORN IN THIS CITY AT THE CONFLUENCE OF THE DANUBE AND SAVA RIVERS.

Following a long period of socialist rule as part of the multinational republic of Yugoslavia, which was followed by a decade of the Balkan War, this Serbian capital is finally getting the chance to explore the peaceful, Mediterranean side of its personality. River promenades invite visitors to stroll and stop for a coffee or espresso along the way. No longer the grey, soulless city of the Cold War period, Belgrade is today all dressed up and ready to go.

Celtic city fathers. The founders of Belgrade were probably immigrant Celts. Archaeological finds confirm their presence here from around 279 BCE. Their city was called Singidun. As was so often the case throughout Europe, the Celts were driven out by the Romans, who conquered the territory around what is now Belgrade in the first century.

Serbian Belgrade. The Slavs didn't arrive in the region until the sixth century. They renamed the old Roman city Beograd, or "White Fortress". Bulgarians, Byzantines, Hungarians and Serbs took turns ruling Beograd until 1521, when the Ottoman Turks under the leadership of Suleyman the Magnificent invaded and conquered the city. Although its majority Serbian residents repeatedly took up arms to expel them, the Turks remained in power in Belgrade until

FACTS

✲ Name in the national language (Serbian): Beograd

✲ Population of Belgrade: *circa* 1.7 million

✲ Population of the metropolitan area: *circa* 2 million

✲ Places of interest: Old City, Cathedral of the Archangel Michael, Kalemegdan (Belgrade Fortress), Knez Mihailova Street, Konak (Residence of Princess Ljubica), National Museum, Nikola Tesla Museum, Skadarlija Street, Cathedral of St. Sava, White Fort

FAMOUS CITIZENS

✲ Jovianus Flavius Claudius (331–364), Roman emperor

✲ Anica Dobra (b. 1963), actress

The walls of Belgrade Castle combine architectural elements of many different eras into a single, powerful fortified complex.

1867. Following the decline of Ottoman rule in Europe, the Principality of Serbia was declared in 1882, with Belgrade as its capital city.

The city takes a pounding. Belgrade retained its capital-city status through two world wars. Today, most of the damage visitors see is from NATO air strikes during the 1999 Kosovo War. The city along the Danube and Sava rivers is perhaps not as inviting as it might be right now. It still has charm, however, and is well on its way towards regaining its former status in the Balkans.

Kalemegdan Fortress. Belgrade's Old City is located on top of a rocky spur on the Danube where it meets the cliffs of the Sava River. The symbol of Belgrade, Kalemegdan Castle towers above the landscape. Two thousand years ago, this is where the Romans built their fortified settlement. Goths, Huns, Avars and Slavs all stormed its walls and tore them down. Later, Byzantine rulers began a fortress here as well. The Serbian despot Stefan Lazarevic strengthened its massive fortifications into one of the largest castles in Europe. However, in 1521, the Turks were able to surmount these monumental walls with little difficulty. During a brief period in the eighteenth century when the castle was in Austrian hands, the Kalemegdan was expanded again. It mattered little: the Turks re-took the Kalemegdan a few years later.

Republic Square in the Old City is the heart of Belgrade. The pedestrian zones of Knez Mihailova and Tschika Ljubina streets run parallel all the way to Kalemegdan. Knez Mihailova is one of Belgrade's oldest city districts, standing where the Ancient Celtic settlement of Singidun probably had its centre. It is full of important monuments and buildings from all periods, including blocks of working-class housing dating to the 1970s.

Above: The National Museum exhibits many articles from the early history of the region.

Left: Fishermen in Belgrade Harbour.

PRINCIPALITY OF MONACO

Monaco

CHATEAU GRIMALDI LOOKS OUT OVER THE PICTURESQUE OLD CITY OF MONACO WITH ITS TWISTING LANES AND SHADED SQUARES. PARTS OF THIS IMPOSING FORTRESS DATE BACK TO THE FOURTEENTH CENTURY.

Tiny, the only sovereign state in the world smaller than the Principality of Monaco is the Vatican. Monaco has two very different faces. Monacoville occupies a rocky peninsula jutting out into the sea, while across the harbour lies the chic district of Monte Carlo. The harbour itself and its adjacent commercial district, entirely filled with modern office buildings and apartments, lies between Monacoville and Monte Carlo. The spacious, luxurious yachts of the rich and famous are anchored here year-round.

The tenth of June. Greek settlers gave the place its name in the fifth century BCE to honour their god and hero, Heracles Monoikos, or Heracles the Hermit– he who lives alone. The Ligurians built the first fortress on the cliffs, which are today known as the Rock of Monaco, in 1215. They had received the harbour as part of a fiefdom from Holy Roman Emperor Henry VI. In 1309, the oldest parts of the Chateau Grimalidi were constructed on the same spot.

Grimaldi's cliffs. The civil war between the Genoese Guelph and Ghibelline factions in the struggle between the popes and Holy Roman emperors had long-term implications for Monaco. The Doria and Spinola families in the Ghibelline faction and Guelph supporters from the Fieschi and Grimaldi families

The cornerstone of Chateau Grimaldi was laid in 1309. Most of the present structure was built in the 17th century.

FACTS

✻ Population of Monaco: *circa* 32,000

✻ Places of interest: St. Nicholas Cathedral, Grand Casino, La Chapelle de la Miséricorde, Napoleon Memorial Museum, Museum of Prehistoric Anthropology, Chapel of the Visitation Museum, National Doll Museum, Oceanographic Museum and Aquarium, Saint Charles, Monaco Zoo

FAMOUS CITIZENS

✻ Louis Chiron (1899–1979), Grand Prix driver and champion of the sport

✻ Grace Patricia Kelly (1929–82), Princess Gracia Patricia

✻ Boris Becker (b.1967), professional tennis player, lives here

traded control of the rock back and forth until the late thirteenth century, when the Grimaldis were exiled. Their response was to try to conquer Monaco by attacking the old Genoese fortifications. The founding of the Monégasque House of Grimaldi dates to this first, failed attempt. Although the Grimaldis were not able to occupy and control "their" principality until 1419, once firmly ensconced, they never lost it. Genoa's last attempt at a reconquest was in 1507, when its forces besieged the cliffs for one hundred days. Unsuccessful, they never tried again.

The first casino. For centuries, the princes and princesses of the House of Grimaldi ably steered their ship of state through the tides of European history. Changing alliances, wars and the French Revolution all plagued the tiny country. Monaco was bled dry by each passing army and navy. It fell to Prince Charles III (1856–89) to get the ailing nation back on track. In order to create a new revenue source to supplement the slowly improving tourist trade, he founded the Société des Bains de Mer. Its goal was to build a gambling casino, which it did, in magnificent belle-époque style. The casino flourished from 1863 onwards and became famous worldwide. The casino was so successful that the monarchy was able to abolish direct taxation in 1869. Profits were reinvested in hotels, spas, elegant promenades and cultural facilities like the Monaco Opera. The casino district is named Monte Carlo in honour of the prince.

Gentility meets Hollywood. Monaco's leisure industry and casino kept the principality wealthy, but it was the 1956 wedding between Prince Rainier III and Hollywood star Grace Kelly that gave Monaco its glitter and chic. Known for her cool, aristocratic presence in films like *To Catch a Thief*, Princess Grace made Monaco an international stomping ground for the rich and famous.

Motor sports. Monte Carlo is not the capital of Monaco, but a city and government district with casinos, beaches and the social set. The city of Monaco itself is really a city-state. The principality is famously home to the annual Monte Carlo Rally and the even more venerable Formula One series Monaco Grand Prix. Considered one of the most challenging racecourses in the world, the famed Circuit de Monaco runs from Monte Carlo through the harbour district and back. A tight track with narrow stretches and sharp turns, the course record is just over a minute.

Centre: The Monte Carlo Casino.

Bottom: Yachts in Monaco Harbour.

FRANCE

Marseille

MARSEILLE HAS ALWAYS BEEN FRANCE'S MOST IMPORTANT MEDITERRANEAN PORT. IT IS ALSO KNOWN AS THE GATEWAY TO AFRICA BECAUSE OF THE FERRIES THAT TRAVEL FROM THE HARBOUR SOUTHWARDS TO TUNIS EVERY DAY.

The city is plagued by the noise of traffic, suffocating in fumes, and fighting against social woes and high unemployment. Drug dealers and the Mafia run the show to a large extent – Marseille is not known as "the Chicago of France" for nothing. Despite all of this, Marseille is still a very beautiful city, with streets like the grand boulevard of La Canebière that teem with life.

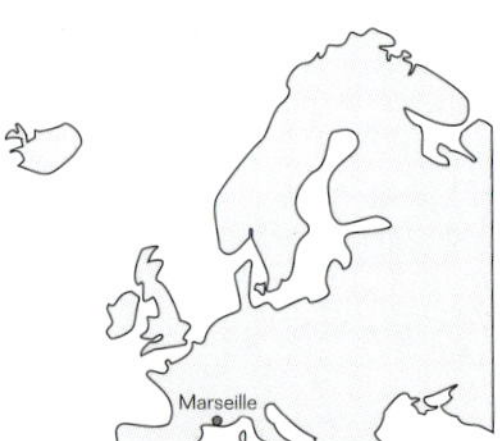

A dot on the map. More than 2,500 years ago, Greek merchants founded the town they called Massilia at the mouth of the Rhône River, where the Vieux Port (old harbour) lies today. The coastline was ideal for a harbour, but its distance away from the centre of power and influence of the Greek Empire kept its growth in check. Into the beginning of the medieval period, the town of Marseille occupied only the relatively small area between the new and old harbours.

The Marseillaise. The city awakened at last with the outbreak of the French Revolution. Surprisingly, it first came to the notice of the rest of France through music. In spring of 1792, the *Chant de Guerre de l'Arme du Rhin* ("Battle Hymn of the Rhein Army"), with text and melody written by a certain Lieutenant General Rouget de Lisle, became a popular marching song in Marseille. In May, a group

Right: The Old Harbour.

Below: A bird's-eye view of Marseille with its famous island prison, Château d'If.

of men from Marseille who wanted to join the revolution in Paris marched into the capital city singing the song. The song was soon heard everywhere, and the "Marseillaise" was famous all over France. It was proclaimed the French national anthem in 1879.

Marseille Harbour. Marseille Harbour, the "southern Europort", is France's most important tanker port. The petroleum-storage facilities and oil refineries in Laveral and along the Étang de Berre, connected to the harbour by means of a system of canals, are among the most extensive in Europe. The harbour is responsible for Marseille's commercial success, attracting a host of related industries. Metal-processing factories, car-assembly plants, and the tool and die industry are prominent. Finally, Marseille also has the Old Harbour district with its famous main artery, La Canebière, which is the city's most important tourist attraction.

The Count of Monte Cristo. Today, there are only yachts, fishing and motorboats in the old harbour where the seventeenth-century forts of St. Nicholas and St. Jean once framed a forest of wooden ship masts. The harbour still has its famous island, the one that has been a tourist attraction ever since the publication of Alexandre Dumas the Elder's novel, *The Count of Monte Cristo*. The Île d'If, one of four small islands near the harbour, was once home to an infamous prison where the novel's protagonist, Edmond Dantes, spent fourteen years. The character may have been fictional, but Marseille's island prison, one of the most feared in all of France, was all too real. It was only fitting that in 1961, a native of Marseille, Louis Jourdan, played the role of Edmond Dantes in the fifth movie version of the classic novel.

Gateway to Africa. The Marseille souk is not far from the harbour. The streets near the Rue d'Aubagne have long functioned as the traditional marketplace of the people from the North African Maghreb countries who make their home here. The wonderful variety of Moroccan, Tunisian and Algerian goods on display, animated exchanges in Arabic and a lively, almost hectic pace lend an exotic atmosphere to this old French harbour city.

FACTS

* **Population of Marseille:** *circa* 900,000
* **Population of the metropolitan area:** *circa* 1.2 million
* **Places of interest:** Major Cathedral, Chaine de l'Etoile, Château d'If, Saint Jean Fort, Saint Nicolas Fort, Marseille Stock Exchange, Museum of Fine Arts, Natural History Museum, Museum of Old Marseille, Cathedrals of Notre Dame de la Garde and Notre Dame des Accoules, Longchamp Palace, Panier Quarter (Old Harbour), Saint Victor, Saint Vincent de Paul

FAMOUS CITIZENS

* **Éliane Browne-Bartoli** (1917–44), French Resistance fighter
* **Louis Jourdan** (b.1919), actor
* **Jean-Pierre Rampal** (1922–2000), flautist
* **Maurice Béjart** (b.1927), choreographer

BULGARIA

Sofia

AS EASTERN EUROPE OPENS UP, IT OFFERS IMPRESSIVE BIG CITIES BUT ALSO SMALLER, JEWEL-LIKE PLACES THAT ONE SIMPLY MUST SEE. THE BULGARIAN CAPITAL OF SOFIA IS UNDOUBTEDLY SUCH A GEM.

The centre of Sofia is bustling and loud, but not the least bit unpleasant as a result. Like Paris, Sofia dominates the cultural life of an entire country. In Bulgaria, where different ethnic groups occupy physically separate parts of the country, everything truly comes together only in Sofia. Although it is not diverse as a city like Istanbul, Sofia has long been a city where Europe and the Orient meet.

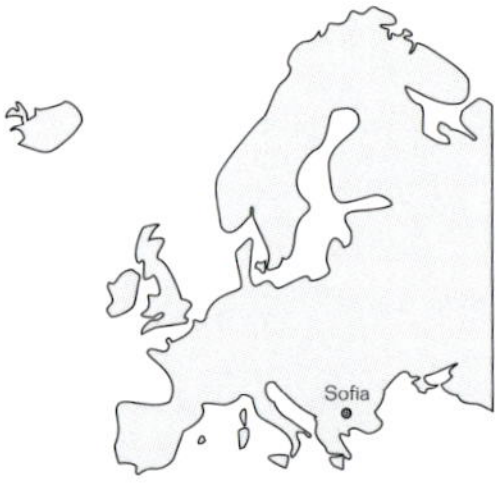

The city beneath the city. Sofia has a history that goes back nearly three thousand years. A Thracian tribe, the Serdi, arrived at the edge of Vitosha Mountain in the western part of modern-day Bulgaria in the seventh century BCE. They founded Serdica, literally "the city of the Serdi". The Thracians dominated the fortunes of the Balkans for nearly four hundred years. Then Roman legions arrived and easily conquered Serdica, making it their provincial capital. The remains of the Roman and Thracian cities are still there, buried beneath a metre of earth below Sofia's modern buildings. The remains of the old town hall lie underneath the Sheraton Hotel, for example, and an early Christian basilica was excavated beneath the foundations of the National History Museum. The Roman baths beneath the Rila Hotel can be viewed today.

FACTS

* **Population of Sofia:** *circa* 1.14 million

* **Places of interest:** Alexander Nevsky Cathedral, Archaeological Museum, National Gallery of Art, Ivan Vasov National Theatre, Natural History Museum, St. George Rotunda, St. Nedelja Church, Church of St. Petka of the Saddlers

FAMOUS CITIZENS

* **Georgi Markow** (1929–78), writer

* **Christo and Jeanne-Claude** (b.1935), installation artists

* **Tzvetan Todorov** (b.1939), philosopher

A monument to Tsar Alexander II of Russia stands in front of the National Assembly. The symbol of Sofia, the Alexander Nevsky Cathedral, is nearby.

St. Sofia. As Rome dissolved in chaos during the fifth century, Byzantium took over control of the Balkan territories. Soon after, the first invading tribes arrived. The Bulgars, possibly Central Asians related to the Huns, quickly mixed with the local population of Slavs. They renamed the ancient city Sredets and founded the first Bulgarian Empire around it. At the end of the twelfth century, during the second Bulgarian empire, Sredets grew into an important mercantile centre. The city received its current name in 1386, just a few years before the Turkish conquest, in honour of its patron saint, Sofia. Her relics are housed in the ninth-century basilica of that name.

Sofia comes to terms with Europe. The third Bulgarian Empire was founded in 1879 as the Ottoman Empire weakened. Sofia was now the capital of a free Bulgarian nation. The somewhat Near Eastern provincial capital was quickly transformed into a European metropolis. Visitors can still stroll through the many streets and parks laid out during Bulgaria's late nineteenth/early twentieth-century heyday. Sofia has a number of well-preserved urban developments built entirely in the Art Nouveau style.

Around the cathedral. The Alexander Nevsky Cathedral on the square of the same name is the symbol of Sofia's Old City. It was built to commemorate Bulgaria's liberation during the Russo-Turkish War (1877–78). St. Sofia, the red-brick basilica of the city's patron saint, stands nearby. The Presidential Palace and a number of government buildings make up much of the rest of the city, with many now turned into museums. The National Gallery of Art is housed in the magnificent Palace of the Tsars, the former seat of the Russian Consul. Sofia's famous hot mineral springs are another reason to visit. Once spread throughout the Old City, most of those that remain are now in the districts of Bankia and Kniazevo.

Above: St. George Church, directly behind the Sheraton Hotel, is the oldest intact structure in Sofia.

Left: The Banya Basi Mosque is a remnant of over 400 years of Turkish rule in Sofia.

ITALY

Rome

ROME'S FAMOUS *LA DOLCE VITA* ("THE SWEET LIFE") STEMS FROM THE INCREDIBLE CONTRASTS THAT CHARACTERIZE THE INIMITABLE ETERNAL CITY: JOY AND MELANCHOLY, BEAUTY AND DECAY, ELEGANCE AND INFORMALITY AND MUCH MORE.

Just how Rome gained this distinction remains unclear. Cynics might claim that the only thing "eternal" in Rome is the chaos on the streets as well as its long history of political disarray, of course. The epithet has much more to do with the city's more than 2,500 years of continuous occupation and leading role in the development of Western culture. "Eternal" also refers to Rome's amazing ability to survive, despite barbarian raids, invasions, occupations and plagues. What other city can lay claim to a renaissance like Rome's after a thousand years of decline? Finally, the term has a religious subtext, for Rome is also the city of the pope, the head of the Roman Catholic Church for all eternity.

The fall of Romulus. Rome is the only ancient European city of the classical age for which scholars have identified a very precise date of founding, specifically, 21 April 753 BCE. Modern research has called this date into question. Archaeologists have found still older remains on the Palatine Hill, dating to around 1000 BCE. Rome's historians said that the city was named after Romulus, who founded the city with his twin brother Remus. The legend of Romulus and Remus, however, developed long after the founding of Rome, meaning Romulus may have received his name because of the city, not vice versa.

Right: The Piazza del Popolo, the People's Plaza.

Below: The Colosseum, symbol of Ancient Rome, was once the largest arena on Earth.

Entertainment for the masses. Romulus and Remus certainly did not create what we today think of as Ancient Rome. The glorious period of Roman architecture began shortly before the birth of Christ. The Roman Forum is earlier, but monumental building in stone did not really gain momentum until the reign of Emperor Augustus. Rome's biggest construction boom took place after the Great Fire in 64, the one almost certainly not started by a pyromaniac emperor named Nero, in spite of the rumours. Nero actually blamed the fire on the early Christians in the city, and they have got their revenge ever since by accusing him in return. The Colosseum is one of the splendours of the post-Nero period, built by the emperors Vespasian and Titus. The Colosseum could seat 5,000 spectators gathered in Rome's most magnificent arena for gladiatorial games and other entertainment spectacles. The audience sat in well-upholstered chairs, or on soft pillows, and there was an ancient version of a stadium's retractable roof, a sailcloth awning called a 'velarium', to shade them from the sun.

Decline and fall. In the fourth century, Christianity took root in the very place where Christians had been persecuted and crucified. By this time, barbarians besieged the Roman Empire from all sides. Fear and panic pervaded every corner of the realm. At first, as had happened after the Great Fire, the Christians were blamed for Rome's precipitous decline. Many of the late emperors, such as the merciless Diocletian, had them hunted down and executed. That changed under Emperor Constantine, who tolerated Christians even before converting to the religion himself, though he was only baptized on his deathbed. Constantine's decision to move the capital of the empire east to Byzantium was the final blow that made the collapse of the city of Rome inevitable. Constantine's new city, first re-named "New Rome" and later Constantinople, cut into Rome's exclusive access to Mediterranean ports and markets. With its economy in shambles and barbarians literally at the gates, Rome fell, able to muster only a small force to defend its shrinking population.

Pilgrimage to Rome. Only about 20,000 people lived in Rome in the eighth century, down from a population of over a million. It was the Frankish king Pippin III who ensured Rome's future importance by making the city the capital of the Papal States in the eighth century. It would remain so until 1871. The Holy Roman emperors were all crowned in Rome, and the pope had his seat there. Its many reliquaries and other Christian shrines and monuments made

FACTS

* **Population of Rome:** *circa* 2.55 million
* **Population of the metropolitan area:** *circa* 3.6 million
* **Places of interest:** Caracalla Mineral Springs, Castel Sant'Angelo, Roman Forum, Colosseum, Concert Park, St. John Lateran, Basilica of Maxentius, Capitoline Museums, Roman National Museum, Palazzo Farnese, Palazzo Venezia, Pantheon, St. Peter's, Piazza Navona, San Pietro in Vincoli, St. Paul's Outside the Walls, Sistine Chapel, Tempietto, Trastevere, Vatican Museums, Villa Farnesina,Villa Giulia

Looking up at the Onofrio Cloister on Gianicolo, formerly the Janiculum, one of the Seven Hills of Rome.

Rome a popular pilgrimage destination, which it remains for Roman Catholics to this day.

Indescribable Rome. There are cities that cannot be described in words, and Rome is undoubtedly one of them. The city's long and eventful history is tangible on every street corner. Buildings from the first millennium stand alongside modern, glass-walled palaces. Rome is also dirty and loud. It is almost certainly the noisiest Italian city, and probably always has been. It is still nearly impossible for visitors to tear themselves away. Rome once ruled the entire Western world. The empire's influence can be seen throughout Europe, in every monumental building, arched bridge and plumb-straight road through the countryside. It all began in Rome.

Fascinating Rome. Rome is more than just a collection of ancient ruins and the Vatican, though both are UNESCO World Heritage Sites. Every city is more than just its historic structures. Modern Romans have a unique, joyful approach to life. It takes some time to get to know Rome, more than a week, let alone a weekend, and even after a great many trips, it is likely that visitors have sampled no more than a small piece of the Roman *torta* ("cake"). This is precisely what makes Rome so exciting, and why some people come here again and again. While the ancient city of Rome is the primarily attraction for some, "later" monuments such as St. Peter's Basilica, the famous Trevi Fountain and the Spanish Steps that have led to the Spanish Embassy since 1647, are also popular attractions. No one should leave Rome without seeing them. St. Peter's Basilica alone, the second largest church in Christendom, is the product of some of the most brilliant artists the world has known (Bramante, Michelangelo, Bernini and more) and contains a nearly overwhelming number of artistic treasures.

The gridlocked city. The Roman districts of Trastevere and San Lorenzo are the heart of modern-day Rome. The streets are always packed, day and night. The cafés and trattorias are crowded all day, all year round, not just in the evenings or on mild summer nights. Rome has long been on the verge of traffic paralysis, particularly during the morning and afternoon rush hours. Thousands upon thousands of Romans try to get around the city by moped or motorcycle instead. Those who prefer to walk take their lives in their hands outside the pedestrian

FAMOUS CITIZENS

* Lucretia Borgia (1480–1519), Italian princess
* Maria Montessori (1870–1952), physician and educator
* Enrico Fermi (1901–54), Nobel-Prize winning physicist
* Sergio Leone (1929–89), film director
* Sophia Loren (b. 1934), film star
* Cecilia Bartoli (b. 1966), opera singer
* Max Biaggi (b. 1971), motorcycle racer

There is always a lively atmosphere around the Spanish Steps. The church of Trinità dei Monti forms the background.

zones. In spite of everything, there are fewer serious problems than one would expect. While accidents do occur, they are no more frequent in Rome than in other European capitals.

La dolce vita. As a shopping mecca, Rome is almost comparable to Paris. Although the main fashion centre of Italy is the northern city of Milan, Rome still has a finger on the pulse of the fashion world, and designer boutiques abound. Via Condotti and Via Giubbonari are the most chic in Rome. Tired after all that sightseeing and shopping? In Rome, there is always a café, trattoria or park nearby where one can sit down and relax. You will need to restore your strength, perhaps with a pastry or strong cup of espresso, while the Ponte Garibaldi or Santa Maria Maggiore (Rome's oldest church) should not be missed. Wander by the Trevi Fountain again. Swedish movie star Anita Ekberg bathed there *au naturel* in Fellini's 1959 cult film *La Dolce Vita*. Every now and then, someone jumps in to recreate the scene.

The view from the hill. For more than a few people, an unforgettable evening in Rome begins on one of the city's Seven Hills. Young couples may plan a romantic rendezvous on the Gianicolo, the hill dedicated to the two-faced Roman god Janus. The hill's ancient name was Janiculum, after the sanctuary to the god located here. The long climb to the top over a series of switchbacks from Viale Trastevere is definitely worth the effort. The church of San Pietro in Montorio (St. Peter in Montorio) stands at the top. It was built in the ninth century on the exact spot where, according to legend, St. Peter was crucified. The Gianicolo provides an amazing view of Rome with the lovely Alban Hills in the background. The American Academy in Rome, founded in 1913, is located on the hill, as are several other foreign research institutions.

Above: Via Condotti is Rome's fashion street with big-name boutiques.

Left: Castel Sant'Angelo was originally built as Emperor Hadrian's mausoleum (117–138 CE), then turned into a medieval fortress and later a 15th-century duke's castle.

SPAIN

Barcelona

LOCATED ON THE MEDITERRANEAN COAST BETWEEN THE NOYA AND LLOBREGAT RIVERS, THE CAPITAL OF CATALONIA IS A VIBRANT AND EXCITING CITY. ANTONI GAUDÍ'S FANTASTIC ARCHITECTURAL WORKS ARE AMONG BARCELONA'S UNIQUELY MAGICAL ATTRACTIONS.

Multicultural influences are what make Barcelona the most cosmopolitan of Spain's big cities. The development sparked by Barcelona's hosting of the 1992 Summer Olympics has further added to the city's appeal. Its famous beach has been upgraded, its public transport system expanded, and its Olympic village redeveloped into housing that has attracted worldwide attention. Barcelona has always been a city on the go, constantly reinventing itself. New projects are continually under way, altering the cityscape and adding new dimensions to the character of Barcelona.

From Barcino to Eixample. According to legend, it was the Cartheginian Hannibal's father, Hamilcar Barca, who founded the city some 2,200 years ago, naming it Barcino after his family. When Carthage fell in 146 BCE, the small walled city of Barcino was incorporated into the Roman Empire. After the fall of the empire, Barcelona came under the influence of Visigoths, Moors and Christians in turn. Traces of the city's eventful past, one that led to frequent clashes between diametrically opposed cultures, can be found throughout Barcelona. There are well-preserved buildings dating from the Gothic period through to the fanciful modernism of native Catalan Antoni Gaudí's amazing buildings.

Barcelona would be unimaginable without the Sagrada Familia Basilica. This unique sacred building, still under construction, attracts visitors from around the world with what will be a total of 18 ornate towers. Its sculptural surfaces and organic façades are signatures of Gaudí's work. There has never been another architectural imagination like his.

FACTS

* Population of Barcelona: *circa* 1.57 million
* Population of the metropolitan area: *circa* 3 million
* Places of interest: Gothic Quarter, Casa Batlló, Casa Milà, Eixample, El Liceu, Hospital de Sant Pau, Columbus Statue, The Cathedral, La Ciutadella Park, La Sagrada Família, Joan Miró Museum, National Museum of Catalonian Art, Picasso Museum, Palace of Catalan Music, Güell Park and Palace

FAMOUS CITIZENS

* Antoni Gaudí (1852–1926), architect
* Joan Miró (1893–1983), artist
* Montserrat Caballé (b.1933), opera singer
* José Carreras (b.1946), tenor
* Pau Gasol (b.1980), NBA basketball player

The Old City. The Ciutat Vella, or Old City, is the historic centre of Barcelona. Barcelona began as a small village, surrounded by a massive fortification wall. During the city's golden age in the fourteenth and fifteenth centuries, its population increased exponentially. Its many impressive Gothic buildings, medieval squares and winding streets date to that period. In the nineteenth century, Barcelona was the site of the World Exhibition in 1888.

Culture and culinary delights. Las Ramblas is probably the city's most famous boulevard. This street runs through the entire Old City, beginning at Placa Catalunya (Catalunya Square) and continuing down to the harbour. The wide pedestrian zone in the middle of Las Ramblas is the perfect spot to meet people, or to observe busy vendors and street artists. A rich store of architectural and cultural delights, including the Liceu Opera House, Columbus Monument and the Maritime Museum, are found all along the 2-km length of this avenue. Its culinary delights may be an even bigger attraction. The enticing covered market La Boqueria offers everything a discerning palate could wish for.

Gaudí's city. Antoni Gaudí was one of Spain's most famous architects working in the Art Nouveau style. Among his works are the Casa Batlló and the Casa Milà (also called La Pedrera) on the Passeig de Gràcia, another of Barcelona's magnificent boulevards. In his design for Park Güell, a commission from the textile manufacturer, fantastic architectural elements are integrated into a richly landscaped hilltop garden.

Sagrada Familia. In 1882, he took over the design and project management of Barcelona's basilica church, Sagrada Familia (Holy Family), which had been started some time earlier. He worked on it for over forty years, eventually devoting himself solely to this project. Unfortunately, Sagrada Familia remains unfinished to this day, despite Gaudí having spent nearly his entire personal fortune on the project. He spent his last years living in a small house near the building site. He died on 7 June 1926 after being hit by a tram on his way to the church. His shabby appearance led to him being taken to a hospital for the poor, where he received inadequate treatment and died shortly thereafter. Since Gaudí worked only loosely from plans, it has been difficult to continue his vision, but progress is being made.

Centre: The old harbour jetty with the Mare Magnum Complex have become magnets for visitors.

Bottom: The Casa Batlló is one of many buildings in Barcelona designed by Antoni Gaudí.

SPAIN

Madrid

COMPARED TO ROME OR PARIS, MADRID'S HISTORY IS LESS EXTENSIVE AND LACKS THE VERVE OF ITS CATALAN COMPETITOR, BARCELONA. BUT MADRID BEGUILES WITH A WIDE ARRAY OF ATTRACTIONS CATERING TO EVERY KIND OF TOURIST, YOUNG AND OLD.

Madrid is both exciting and irrepressible, and often romantic and charming as well. It is also fast-paced and a bit dangerous. Visitors of all generations from all over the world gather to meet at Madrid's Puerto del Sol, the square at the heart of the city centre.

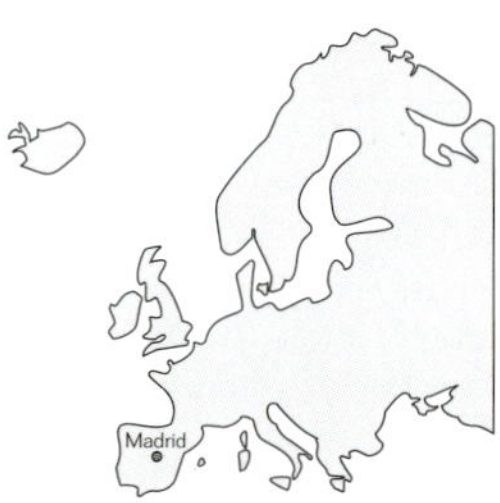

A young metropolis. Mohammed I, the Emir of Córdoba, came here to build a fort in 852. He hoped it would secure his frontiers. The Moorish prince surely knew that, sooner or later, the Castilians would attack, which is exactly what happened. It would be 1083 before Alonso VI of Castile conquered the Arab fortress. He then abandoned both the fortress and the budding city developing around it, moving his capital to nearby Toledo. The Habsburg emperor Charles V was the first important monarch to take an interest in reviving the area by commissioning a number of important public buildings, and in 1558, the royal residence was relocated from Toledo to Madrid; the parliament followed in 1561. Madrid had become the capital of imperial Spain practically overnight. All it took was a little help from the Austrian Holy Roman emperor.

Residents of Madrid still call their Old City centre "el Madrid de los Austrias", after the Habsburgs. The area around the Plaza Mayor (Main Square), framed

FACTS

✻ Population of Madrid: *circa* 3.15 million

✻ Places of interest: Capilla del Obispo (Bishop's Chapel), Casa Cisneros, Casa de la Villa (City Hall), Vicente Calderón Stadium, Santiago Bernabéu Stadium, La Almudena Cathedral, Thyssen-Bornemisza Museum, Palacio de Comunicaciones (now a museum), Imperial Palace, Parque del Retiro (Retiro Park), The Prado, Prado Plaza, Plaza Mayor, Alcalá Gate, Puerta del Sol, Toledo Gate, Basilica of St. Francis the Great, Cathedral of San Isidro the Royal, Church of St. Nicholas, Royal Theatre, Torre de Madrid, Torre Puerta de Europa

FAMOUS CITIZENS

✻ Lope de Vega (1562–1635), poet

✻ José Ortega y Gasset (1883–1955), philosopher

✻ Andrés Segovia (1893–1987), classical guitarist

✻ Plácido Domingo (b. 1941) and **✻ Julio Iglesisas** (b. 1943), singers

The Prado, one of the most famous museums in the world, houses Spain's largest collection of art.

by more than one hundred arches, lies in the heart of the Habsburg city. A bronze statue of King Philip III of Spain sitting high upon his steed dominates the middle of the plaza, which he himself had commissioned. Dedicated in 1620, it was completely renovated after a fire in 1790. For hundreds of years this was the site of bullfights, theatrical performances, canonizations and the *auto de fe*, a ritual penance enacted publicly during the Spanish Inquisition of 1478–1834. As many as 50,000 spectators could attend. The Habsburg monarchs and nobles reserved the balcony of the Casa de la Panadería (Baker's House) so that they might have the best view of events taking place in the Plaza Major.

Spain's fairy-tale castle. The imposing Royal Palace of Philip V is a pearl of Spanish architecture. The work of Madrid architect Ventura Rodríguez, its design is based on the traditional Spanish prototype of the alcázar, or fortress. The stolid granite and limestone structure consists of four wings built around a square courtyard. Today, the less opulent Zarzuela Palace is the residence of the current king of Spain, Juan Carlos, and the 3,000-room Royal Palace is only used for official functions.

A wall of widely varying façades line Gran Vía Boulevard connecting Calle de Alcalá with the Plaza de España. This cosmopolitan, commercial boulevard and entertainment district was built straight through a maze of old lanes. The round towers of the Metropolis and Grassy insurance buildings at the entrance to the Gran Vía are symbols of the modern Madrid. The closer one gets to the Plaza de España, the more international in design, and less Spanish, the buildings become. The Telefónica at No 28 is perhaps the least typically Spanish building in the city, despite the fact that it is a government building housing the Spanish telephone company.

Above: The Gran Vía is Madrid's great shopping boulevard.

Left: The Plaza Mayor was once the heart of Madrid, but today it is mainly tourists who visit the square.

PORTUGAL

Lisbon

LISBON EXHIBITS THE SPLENDOUR OF A CITY THAT WAS ONCE A GREAT CENTRE OF WORLD EXPLORATION. ITS CULTURE REFLECTS A CAREFREE RHYTHM, A TENDENCY TOWARDS MELANCHOLY AND WORLD-WEARINESS, ALL ENVELOPED IN A HAUNTING AIR OF DECADENCE.

In addition to its spiritual complexity, Lisbon is also quite simply one of the most beautiful cities on Earth. The elegant "white city" of legends is located on the bank of the Tagus River, spread over the seven hills of its original foundation. The quicker pace of modern life has seemingly only enhanced her beauty. Castle battlements and ornate, towering churches are found right alongside soaring, modern bank and insurance buildings constructed of steel and glass. American-style shopping centres have sprung up everywhere amidst a sea of red-tiled roofs.

City of Odysseus? Greeks, Phoenicians, Carthaginians, Romans and, indeed, all the movers and shakers of the ancient world were drawn here because of the magnificent natural harbour of the city they called Alis Ubbo ("lovely bay"). The origins of the city remain obscure. Perhaps it actually was the Greek hero Odysseus who sailed here and founded a Greek colony, as some legends say.

The Age of Discovery. The Moors conquered what was then the Visigothic city of Lisbon in 715, and the city flourished under Muslim rule. Portuguese king Alfonso I led the reconquest of the city in 1147, and in 1260 Lisbon became a royal city. In the fourteenth and fifteenth centuries, the Age of Discovery

Right: View over the red rooftops of Lisbon's Old City.

Below: The Hieronymites Monastery (Mosteiro dos Jerónimos) in Belém has been a UNESCO World Heritage Site since 1983.

brought unanticipated prosperity to the city with its fine harbour. Lisbon soon became one of the most important ports in Europe.

The great earthquake. The catastrophic earthquake of 1755, one of the strongest ever to hit a European city, left Lisbon utterly destroyed. Counted among history's worst natural disasters, the quake rated over 9 on the Richter scale and resulted in more than 100,000 deaths. Uncontrollable fires and a powerful tidal wave followed, reducing what was left of Lisbon to soot and ashes. The city never did recover its former grandeur, even after rebuilding, as if the psyche of Lisbon was irrevocably shaken. Its self-confidence as Portugal's seat of colonial power disappeared. As the rest of the country sank into poverty, so did the "white city".

Modern awakening. In the present-day capital, the fatalistic longing for the past that is often said to characterize the Portuguese is barely perceptible.

The transformation of Lisbon into one of Europe's modern, international cities continues apace. As the 1994 European Cultural Capital, and again during EXPO 98, funding poured into Lisbon permitting redevelopment on a scale that had not been experienced since the great earthquake of 1755. Expenditures to modernize the city centre for these events totalled billions of dollars. Despite improvements downtown, conditions outside the city are comparable to what one would expect in the Third World rather than in a member state of the European Union. An extensive ring of slums surrounds Lisbon, the legacy of a backward-looking former colonial power that did little to improve its own country, and granted its colonies independence as late as 1975.

UNESCO World Heritage Site. The most outstanding attraction in Lisbon is the Hieronymites Monastery, also known as the Mosteiro dos Jerónimos, located in the western suburb of Belém. Scale, harmony and beauty coalesce to make this former monastery of the Order of Jerome one of the most exquisite architectural monuments in the world. Construction began in 1500, during the reign of King Dom Manuel. One of the true masterpieces here is the south portal, a towering and ornately detailed entryway artfully carved from stone by the most important master builder of that period, João de Castilho. The interior is impressive in its Gothic simplicity and engineering skill. Its transept vault is not supported by piers, making it seem as if it is floating in the air. The sarcophagi of national heroes, including Dom Manuel I, Vasco da Gama and Fernando Pessoa are found in the monastery as well.

FACTS

* **Population of Lisbon:** *circa* 517,800
* **Population of the metropolitan area:** *circa* 2.68 million
* **Places of interest:** Alfama District, Águas Livres Aqueduct, Bairro Alto Quarter, Castelo da São Jorge, Carmo Convent and Museum, Discovery Monument, Elevador de Santa Justa, Miradouros, Hieronymites Monastery, Lisbon Oceanarium, Queluz Palace, 25 April Bridge, São Roque Church, Sé Catedral, Belém Tower, Vasco da Gama Tower

FAMOUS CITIZENS

* **Francisco de Almeida** (1450–1510), mariner
* **Manuel do Nascimento** (1734–1819), lyric poet
* **Amália Rodrigues** (1920–99), Fado singer
* **Jorge Sampaio** (b. 1939), former Portuguese president

GREECE

Athens

THE ROCKY ACROPOLIS OF ATHENS WAS FIRST SETTLED OVER A MILLENNIUM BEFORE THE FIRST MYCENAEAN PALACE WAS BUILT IN THE FOURTEENTH CENTURY BCE. ATHENS HAS BEEN A BEACON OF WESTERN CULTURE FOR OVER 2,000 YEARS.

It was a Venetian shell that blew up Turkish munitions stored inside the Parthenon in 1687, destroying most of the ancient temple and large parts of the rest of the buildings remaining on the Acropolis as well. Reassembled, most of the buildings can still be appreciated today. Would so many tourists climb the steep hill otherwise? Once on top, the panorama of the ancient and modern city is simply stunning.

The Acropolis. The marble buildings on the Acropolis of Athens, on the UNESCO List of World Heritage Sites since 1987, were built between 467 to 406 BCE in the aftermath of the Persian Wars. This was the golden age of Athens. The Propylaeum (gateway to the Acropolis), the Erechtheion, Nike Temple and the Parthenon bear witness to the city's power, wealth and glory. The Parthenon once housed a colossal gold and ivory statue of the goddess Athena. Long destroyed, only copies of the original are available today. A scale copy of the head of the statue can be seen in the Louvre in Paris.

A long decline. When the Romans conquered Athens in 86 BCE, the city could already look back on an eventful, thousand-year history. Athens remained an intellectual centre even after the Romans took political control, but the world's first democratic city

An excursion to the Plaka offers many opportunities to stop for refreshment before climbing up to the Acropolis.

FACTS

*** Name in the national language (Greek):** Athinai

*** Population of Athens:** *circa* 729,000

*** Population of the metropolitan area:** *circa* 3.75 million

*** Places of interest:** Acropolis, Agora, Acropolis Museum, National Archaeological Museum, Athens Trilogy (Academy-University-Library), Byzantine Museum, Theatre of Dionysus, Hadrian's Library, Kerameikos Archaeological Museum, Daphni Monastery, Mt. Lykavettos, Odeon of Herodes Atticus, Olympieion, Plaka, Temple of Zeus

FAMOUS CITIZENS

*** Socrates** (469 – 399 BCE), philosopher

*** Stavros Niarchos** (1909 – 96), Greek shipping magnate

*** Arianna Huffington** (b. 1950) journalist

no longer governed itself. Its international stature had declined to the nothing. In the medieval period, Athens continued to be a pawn of foreign interests. A bishop's see since the ninth century, the city had seen countless rulers come and go by the time it was conquered by the Ottoman Turks in 1456. The Parthenon, already transformed from a pagan temple to a church by the Orthodox patriarchate, was re-dedicated as a mosque.

A return to the light. Early nineteenth-century Athens was a small town with 300 houses and 1,000 residents. In 1834, following the Wars of Independence against the Turks, it became the capital of Greece and seat of the monarchy. The first Greek king, Otto I (r.1832–62), had to be imported from the German House of Wittelsbach. He expanded Athens and commissioned numerous neoclassical government and administrative buildings. Athens was finally awakening from her long slumber.

Ancient Athens. It would be unreasonable to reduce Athens to the Acropolis alone. There is an ample pedestrian zone around its rocky base in the neighbourhood known as the Plaka. Narrow lanes and steep stairways of the village-like Plaka can be navigated entirely on foot. There are no large buildings here, just modest houses, small and usually made of render-covered wood. Unfortunately, tourism dominates this area more and more every year. It is still great fun to wander around, particularly in the evening, when the sidewalk tavernas serve souvlaki accompanied by new wine drawn from a barrel.

The Ancient Athenian Agora is located behind Monastiraki Square, north-west of the Acropolis. The Agora was Ancient Athens' centre of commerce, art and philosophy. The Hephaistos Temple, one of the best preserved in Greece, is also here. Built between 449 and 444 BCE on a terrace, it was dedicated to the god of blacksmiths, metallurgists and fire because so many craftsmen plied those trades there.

Still more culture. The Roman Odeon of Herodes Atticus, a large second-century amphitheatre, lies on the southern hillside of the Acropolis. Because of its wonderful acoustics, it is still used today for Athenian summer festivals, where concerts, lectures, musicals and dramas are presented. The broad, round amphitheatre can accommodate up to 5,000 spectators. Attending a performance in an ancient theatre is an experience not to be missed.

Centre: Luciano Pavarotti has performed in the Odeon of Herodes Atticus.

Bottom: The Olympic Stadium was renovated for the 2004 Olympics.

Many, but not all, of the major Central and South American cities were founded during the era of European colonization. They are infused with a unique energy, particularly when salsa or samba music is involved. Other cities are bastions of Latin American finance and banking, where glass and steel towers stand side by side with the remains of a more distant historical past.

CENTRAL AND SOUTH
AMERICA

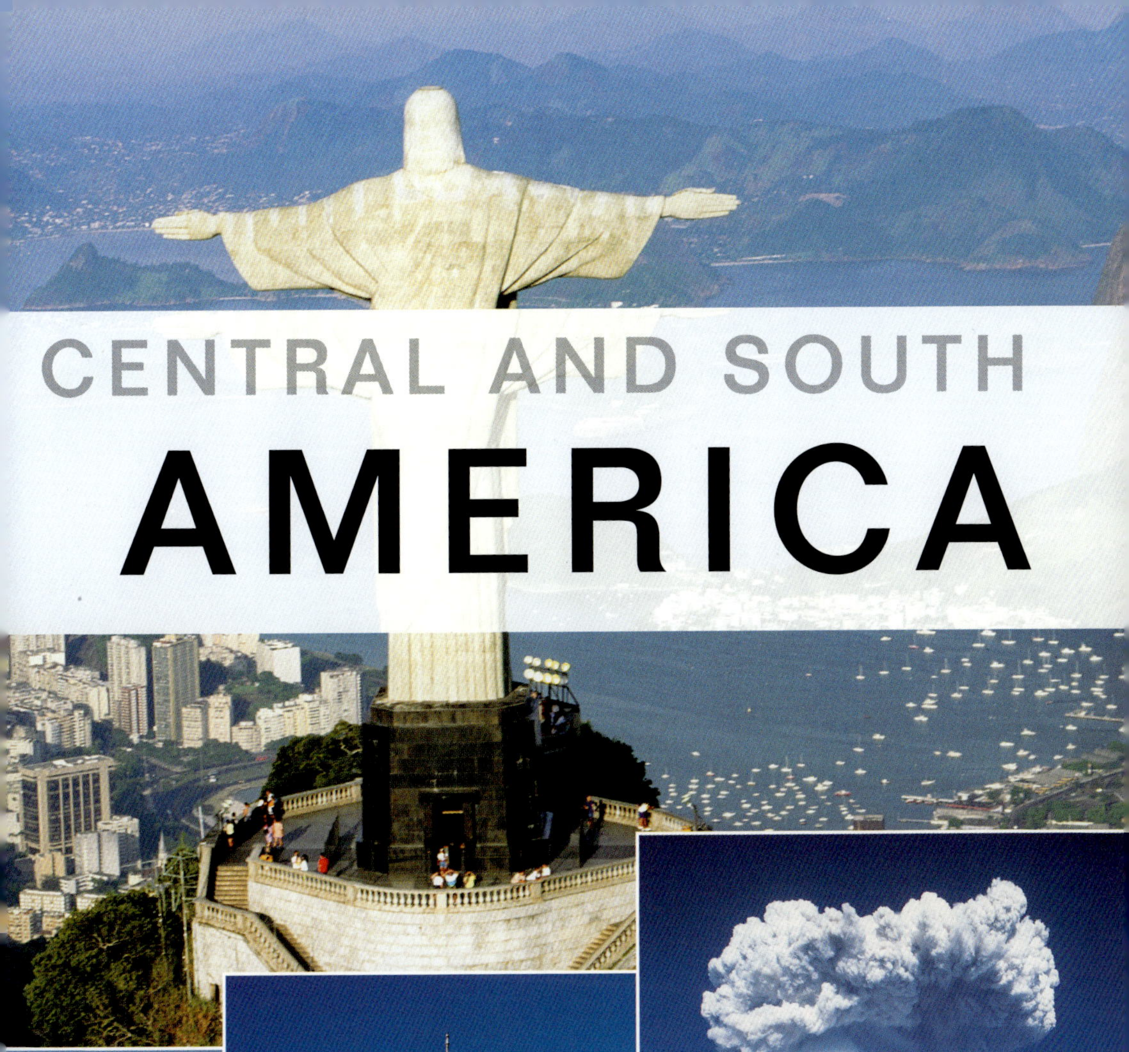

CUBA

Havana

SADLY, HAVANA'S DIVA-LIKE SPLENDOUR IS BEING CHIPPED AWAY BY THE RAVAGES OF TIME. UNESCO HAS DECLARED OLD HAVANA A WORLD HERITAGE SITE AND FUNDS HAVE BEGUN TO FLOW INTO PROJECTS ALL OVER THE CITY, BUT WORK HAS ONLY JUST BEGUN.

Havana is a grid-plan city, making it easy to navigate its broad avenues and side streets, originally lined with splendid churches and mansions of the city's former aristocracy. They have suffered greatly from neglect, and many are now crumbling and decrepit. For three hundred years, urban life in the Cuban capital took place *intramuros*, or "within the city walls". Then, in the early nineteenth century, a building boom began. Havana's city walls were pulled down to facilitate city planning and road building between the old Intramuros Plaza and the newer Extramuros Plaza.

Gateway to the New World. The city of Havana was founded in 1515 where the Cuban capital stands today. Its naturally protected harbour began operation slightly later, in 1519. Havana's central Caribbean location was a boon to the city's development. All the important trade routes to and from Mexico and Peru passed through here. Havana was named the capital of the Cuban colony in 1607 and unofficially proclaimed the gateway to the New World. Although its population would remain in check for a century or more, its progress as a commercial and political centre was continuous and uninterrupted.

Hemingway's Cuba. In the early twentieth century, American Prohibition brought tourism of a sort to

Cathedral Square is the heart of Havana. The bells of San Cristóbal de La Habana still ring out.

FACTS

* **Name in the national language (Spanish):** San Cristóbal de La Habana
* **Population of Havana:** *circa* 2.2 million
* **Places of interest:** Real Fuerza Castle, Central Havana, Cathedral, Castle of San Carlos de la Cabaña, Malecon, Miramar, Museum of the Revolution, Plaza de Armas, Plaza Martí, Prado

FAMOUS CITIZENS

* **José Martí** (1853–95), national poet
* **Juan Almeida** (b. 1927), revolutionary and politician
* **Andy Garcia** (b. 1956), American actor
* **Gloria Estefan** (b. 1957), pop diva

Havana for the first time. The Caribbean metropolis, especially the Vedado district, where the 142-metre-tall memorial to national hero José Martí stands, became a jet-set stomping ground where everyone could enjoy a bottle of rum, an aromatic cigar and a little salsa dancing. Ernest Hemingway was drawn to Havana, and many of his novels were written here. He was locally famous for downing a glass or two and smoking a thick Havana cigar. The long Cuban party ended on New Year's Eve in 1959, when rebels under the command of Fidel Castro marched into the city. There are still nightclubs in modern-day Havana, once again attracting thousands of visitors.

La Habana Vieja (Old Havana) was declared a UNESCO World Heritage Site in 1982. Some of its loveliest buildings were converted into museums. Visitors looking for culture will find that the city has churches, palaces, castles, monuments and markets. Cathedral Plaza is a popular attraction and one of the most beautiful squares in the city. The steeples of the Cathedral of San Cristóbal de La Habana dominate the look of the square. Not far from the square is the 1588 Real Fuerza Castle, the oldest surviving colonial fortress in the New World. The Plaza de Armas, its streets lined with swaying royal palms, has been the Cuban centre of power and government for four hundred years. The majestic Capitanes Generales Palace, home of the National Museum, is on the west side of this plaza. It is one of the grandest buildings in Cuba.

Cigars. Central Havana functioned as the red-light district of the city prior to the Revolution; currently, one might rather say it glows in pale pastels. Visitors tend to avoid this area as a rule, most preferring to stick to the comforts of the Vedado district and the famous attractions of Old Havana. There is nevertheless a great deal to see in central Havana. The district is dominated by the monumental El Capitolio Nacional, built as a more ornate twin of the US Capitol in Washington, DC as if to mock capitalism. Havana's oldest cigar factory is located on the west side of the Capitolio. The approximately 400 people employed here continue to roll cigars the old-fashioned way, by hand.

Centre: The Museum of the Revolution was once the Presidential Palace.

Bottom: Cuba at night with a view of the Hotel Nacional.

MEXICO

Mexico City

ENDLESS LINES OF VEHICLES WIND THEIR WAY ALONG THE BROAD AVENUES, FILLING THE AIR WITH EXHAUST. MEXICO CITY APPEARS UNCONCERNED. AT FIRST GLANCE, VISITORS MAY BE OVERWHELMED BY MEXICO CITY'S NOISE, DIRT AND CHAOS, BUT LOOK AGAIN.

Mexico City is the largest metropolis on the American continent and it is still growing. Despite the problems that inevitably accompany unrestrained growth, there are superb architectural treasures hidden behind the rather dull facades of this huge city. No other Latin American city boasts as many baroque churches, monasteries and colonial palaces. It also has a number of acclaimed modern buildings, some of which are decorated with monumental paintings by the famous Mexican muralists, and world-class museums house still more art and treasure.

The eagle, the snake and the cactus. In 1325, the Aztecs, who called themselves the Méxica, migrated into what is now central Mexico, where they founded their capital city, Tenochtitlán. They had chosen the site well, with a little help. According to legend, the Aztecs received a vision that told them to wander until they found an eagle perched on a cactus with a snake in its talons. In the Valley of México at an elevation of more than 2,000 metres they came upon this very scene in a swampy area scattered with lakes and islands. From a strategic standpoint, the location was ideal. They colonized the islands in the middle of a shallow lake, which protected their settlement well. The wandering Méxica had finally settled down.

FACTS

*** Name in the national language (Spanish):** La Ciudad de México

*** Population of Mexico City:** *circa* 8.66 million

*** Population of the metropolitan area:** *circa* 22.1 million

*** Places of interest:** Alameda Park, Casa Azul, Chapultepec Park, Cholula, Corrida Plaza México, Iztaccíhuatl and Popocatépetl Volcanoes, Museum of Modern Art, National Museum of Anthropology, National Museum of Art, Palace of Fine Arts (opera house), Postal Palace Museum, Paseo de la Reforma Avenue, Templo Mayor, Teotihuacán, Xochimilco Park, Zócalo

Constitution Square, also called the Zócalo, is the heart of the city. The monumental Cathedral of Mexico City rises up behind it.

Later, they built dams and causeways between the islands, which developed into a complex hydraulic system with canals, drawbridges and sluices. Tenochtitlán grew in size to cover more than 13 km^2. The Aztecs ultimately conquered the entire high valley by force of arms, and soon controlled nearly all of modern-day Mexico, as well as other parts of Central America.

Hernán Cortés. The precipitious fall of the Aztec Empire began in 1519 when Hernán Cortés landed on the Gulf Coast of Mexico with just a few men. What Cortés achieved is incredible. With a small force, a few horses and indomitable will, not to mention a good dose of brutality and recklessness, he subdued an entire empire. His total command consisted of 500 Spanish soldiers, 16 mounted fighters, 6 cannons and 400 Indian mercenaries. The Aztec population he confronted numbered in the hundreds of thousands.

On 8 November 1519 the Aztecs' fate was sealed. The Aztec ruler Montezuma II received Cortés unarmed, possbily because he thought Cortés was the god Quetzalcoatl. This was an invitation to disaster. The Spaniards quickly took Montezuma hostage and massacred the assembled priests and nobles. The Aztecs were at first able to push back the interlopers and force them to retreat. Unfortunately, this only postponed their demise by a few years. In 1521, Cortés moved in with fresh troops, completely overwhelming the Aztec forces. The Spanish rulers then built their own city with churches and palaces on the foundations of the old one. Most of the lake was drained, as more and more land was needed. Tenochtitlán disappeared under a Spanish city. Parts of it, such as the Templo Mayor, have since been excavated by archaeologists and are on view again after hundreds of years of obscurity.

Above: The Aztec Templo Mayor, or Great Temple, lies directly behind the cathedral.

Left: The National Palace on the Zócalo (Constitution Square) stands at a right angle to the cathedral.

The Xochimilco Water Gardens, a lush recreation area, are about 20 km south of the city centre.

Decades of fighting. By 1821, Mexicans had been fighting their war of independence against the Spaniards for six long years. Three hundred years after the decimation of the Aztecs, they finally succeeded. What followed was not peace, but a century of non-stop civil war. The United States of America took advantage of Mexico's instability, grabbing land in the north of the country: Texas, Arizona and large parts of California were lost. Emperor Napoleon III of France entered the fray in 1864, naming his brother, Archduke Maximilian, emperor of Mexico. Unsupported by Napoleon in the end, Maximilian was executed by firing squad in 1867. Benito Juarez, Mexican folk hero and leader of the resistance, stood by and watched.

A difficult ascent. After the many long years of fighting finally came to an end, Mexico City began to grow and prosper. Under President Porfirio Díaz (1870–1911) an enormous building campaign was soon under way. Industrialization was prioritized and Mexico City's rise to the status of one of Latin America's most important cities began. The population had grown to 750,000 by the outbreak of the Mexican Revolution in 1910. All the same, the living conditions in Mexico City were poor at best, in part due to the swampy topography that had so attracted the Aztecs. The revolution had changed little for millions of the desperate poor. While tens of thousands of rural peasants migrated to the rapidly industrializing capital in search of work and a better life, most made the trip in vain. The problems Mexico City experienced as a result of a century of uncontrolled growth are still in evidence today.

Adding and subtracting. Currently, Mexico City is defined by the contrasts between the new and old, the rich and poor. A glittering and glamorous megacity dazzles visitors at night, but the smog, noise and crowds of the following morning are the rudest of awakenings. Where are the palaces that eighteenth-century German explorer Alexander von Humboldt wrote about so lyrically? Where have they hidden the amazing history and unique architecture of this city? Fragments of Mexico City's history are indeed there to be seen, many startlingly juxtaposed. The Aztec Templo Mayor is located directly behind the cathedral, for example, and the Government Palace was built next to an ancient Aztec ball court. There's a baroque church on the Plaza de las Tres Culturas (Square of Three Cultures) on the other side. The Basilica of the Virgin of Guadalupe lies on Tepeyac

Right: Market days are a regular occurrence in Alameda Central Park.

Below: Paseo de la Reforma Avenue, with the Independence Monument, is the city's main artery.

Hill, where it is said the Aztec goddess Tonantzín was once worshipped.

Mural painting. Ancient walls can also be found in the Centro Histórico of the Old City. They have been on the UNESCO World Heritage List since 1987, along with the Xochimilco Water Gardens. Life on the streets and lanes of the Old City follows a more leisurely pace than Mexico City's teeming downtown business districts. Visitors who escape to the hidden corners of the metropolis are especially fortunate, for they get to know Mexico City in a completely new and surprisingly vivid way. The famous early twentieth-century murals, the work of a number of Mexican artists, can be found everywhere, on courtyard walls and along staircases. Of special interest are the paintings in the National Palace, the seat of the Mexican president. Between 1929 and 1935, Diego Rivera, the acknowledged master of this style of mural painting, painted a famous mural cycle on the history of Mexico that can still be seen in the palace.

From the Zócalo to the modern city. The heart of the city is Constitution Square Plaza, called the Zócalo by locals. Montezuma's Imperial Palace once stood here. The baroque cathedral, the Municipal Palace and the National Palace form three of its four sides. Also close to the Zócalo is Calle Moneda, lined with colonial buildings and palaces built with red tezontle stone. This is also where La Santísima Church and the baroque Archbishop's Palace are located. Despite his short reign and conspicuous lack of success, Emperor Maximilian did leave a legacy behind. It was he who laid out the city's main traffic artery, the Paseo de la Reforma. This splendid broad boulevard once led from the Old City to the site of Chapultepec Palace, Maximilian's summer residence. Today it follows the same route overlooked by the city's modern skyscrapers.

Theaters and museums. Mexico City has a great many theatres. One of the best known is the Palacio de Bellas Artes, which opened on the east side of Alameda Central Park in 1934. Diego Rivera's omnipresent murals are also found here, along with those of his fellow mural painters. The city is also rich in museums. Mexico City's museums are among the most renowned in the world. The Museum of Modern Art, with works by Rivera and his wife, Frida Kahlo, as well as the National Museum of Anthropology are popular attractions. The national art collection housed in the Rufino Tamayo Museum includes the works of the great masters Miró, Dalí and Picasso.

FAMOUS CITIZENS

* **Porfirio Díaz** (1830–1915), ruled Mexico from 1876–1880 and 1884–1911
* **Charles Seeger** (1886–1979), US-American composer
* **Frida Kahlo** (1907–54) and **Diego Rivera** (1886–1957), painters
* **Octavio Paz** (1914–98), writer
* **Vicente Fox** (b. 1942), politician
* **Ernesto Canto** (b. 1959), athlete and Olympic champion

VENEZUELA

Caracas

WHEN CONQUISTADOR ALONSO DE OJEDA SAW THE WOODEN PILE DWELLINGS IN LAKE MARACAIBO, THEY REMINDED HIM OF A FAMOUS ITALIAN CITY. IN ITS HONOUR, HE NAMED THE PLACE VENEZUELA, SPANISH FOR "LITTLE VENICE". CARACAS IS ITS CAPITAL CITY.

The first Europeans to take an interest in the future site of Caracas were the Welsers, a German banking family from Augsburg. Supported by land grants from Charles V, the Habsburg Holy Roman Emperor, the Welsers funded a colonization expedition that took place from 1529 to 1556. Led by Ambrosius Ehinger, who would be Venezuela's first colonial governor, the enterprise met with some initial success. Charles V, however, revoked the Welsers' charter rights in 1559 on account of their "usurious dealings". Without a regular source of funds, the German colonies, never very populous, disintegrated. Ambrosius Ehinger was not among the departing Europeans. He had been killed by a poisoned arrow in 1531.

Simón Bolívar. The area was all but deserted until Spanish conquistador Diego de Losada arrived and officially founded the city of Santiago de León de Caracas in 1567. By the mid-eighteenth century, cacao exports had made Caracas one of the most prosperous cities in South America. Its wealth and potential are the most likely reasons why Spain fought so hard to hold onto the country in the face of the fierce fight for independence led by Caracas' greatest son, the renowned revolutionary Simón Bolívar. Venezuelans had to fight for an entire decade

Right: The capitol, home of the Venezuelan Congress.

Below: Bolívar Plaza with the equestrian statue of Simón Bolívar.

before finally gaining their freedom from Spain in 1821. Colombia, Panama, Ecuador and Venezuela banded together and were renamed the Republic of Gran Colombia. The union lasted until 1831, when Colombia seceded. Venezuela became an independent country with Caracas as its capital.

Further turmoil. On 26 March 1812, while still in the midst of the war of independence, the citizens of Caracas were confronted with yet another battle when a catastrophic earthquake destroyed the city. It was rebuilt quickly, but the process of recovery, while steady, was much slower.

The great oil rush. Oil was discovered near Caracas in 1917, giving the city an economic boost it badly needed. Its population doubled overnight, and construction of buildings and infrastructure suitable for a large city began in earnest. A legacy of that oil wealth is the 1950s'-era Centro Simón Bolívar with its two striking towers. Once the tallest building in Caracas, they have since been surpassed by the surrounding high-rises and skyscrapers of the Parque Central district.

Historic sites. Once one of the wealthiest Spanish colonial cities in South America, Caracas is now the industrial and economic centre of Venezuela. Throughout the oil boom and recent period of immense growth, Caracas has managed to preserve its historic roots. Most of the colonial-era buildings have fallen prey to recurrent earthquakes, but Simón Bolívar Plaza with its equestrian bronze statue of Venezuela's national hero, "El Libertador", remains the centre and focal point of Caracas. The cathedral, with its magnificent gilded altar, is not far from there. Originally built in 1614, it was later renovated in the baroque style. Next to the cathedral is La Casa Amarilla ("Yellow House"), the seat of the archbishop.

The University City. The Central University of Venezuela, founded in 1725, is located near the golden-domed capitol building and the heavily frequented tomb of Simón Bolívar. Eighty-seven buildings comprise the university area today, most of which were built as part of the extensive renovations and rebuilding carried out during the 1940s and 1960s under the direction of the Venezuelan architect Carlos Raúl Villanueva. A masterpiece of city planning, the virtuoso use of concrete and contemporary design in this undertaking were acclaimed, and emulated, all over the world. In the year 2000, twenty-five years after Villanueva's death, the first "university city" was added to the UNESCO List of World Heritage Sites.

FACTS

* **Population of Caracas:** *circa* 1.82 million
* **Population of the metropolitan area:** *circa* 5.72 million
* **Places of interest:** Arch of the Federation, Caracas Cathedral, Municipal Council Building, The National Capitol, National Gallery of Art & Fine Arts Museum, Church of San Francisco, Caracas Mosque, Museum of Contemporary Art, Sacred Museum of Caracas, Government Palace, National Pantheon, El Ávila National Park, Bolívar Plaza

FAMOUS CITIZENS

* **Alonso de Ojeda** (*circa* 1465–1515), Spanish explorer of noble Bulgarian parentage
* **Francisco de Miranda** (1750–1816), freedom fighter
* **Hugo Chávez** (b. 1954), president

COLOMBIA

Bogotá

COLOMBIA'S CAPITAL CITY LIES ON A PLATEAU AT AN ELEVATION OF OVER 2,500 METRES ABOVE SEA LEVEL. THIS CITY OF MILLIONS HUGS THE SLOPES OF THE HILLS RUNNING BETWEEN THE MOUNTAINS OF GUADALUPE AND MONTSERRAT.

It was an irresistable legend, and a good dose of greed, that led to the founding of Bogotá. Long before the Spaniards arrived, since before the period of the Inca Empire, the Muisca people had lived on the Andean plateau of Sabana de Bogotá. Their primary settlement, Bacatá, fell victim to the onrush of European invaders in search of the riches of the legendary El Dorado. The conquistador Gonzalo Jiménez de Quesada founded Santa Fe de Bogotá upon the remains of the Muisca settlement on 6 August 1538. The avaricious European adventurers then used their new city as a base from which they could set out to find the legendary city of gold and gems.

The legend of the Muiscas. The region was understood to be the gateway to El Dorado because of nearby Guatavita Lake, which lay about 30 km to the north-east. There, according to legend, the Chibchas, a tribe of the Muisca nation, bathed their chieftains in gold dust, after which they would jump or be thrown into the lake. The gold dust would wash off and sink to the bottom, or so the story went. The myth of a city of El Dorado seems to originate with the Chibcha people themselves, but no one has ever found it. In the end, once the Spaniards realized that the natives were trading with emeralds and

The neoclassical cathedral on Bolívar Plaza is the focal point of La Candelaria, the Old City.

FACTS

* Population of Bogotá: *circa* 7.19 million

* Population of the metropolitan area: *circa* 8.25 million

* Places of interest: Sagrario Chapel, National Capitol, Cathedral, Guatavita Lake, La Candelaria, Santa Clara Monastery, Museum of Colonial Art, Gold Museum, Simón Bolívar Metropolitan Park, National Park, Bolívar Plaza, Salt Cathedral in Zipaquirá, Tequendama Falls

FAMOUS CITIZENS

* Gabriel García Márquez (b. 1928), author

* Álvaro Uribe Vélez (b. 1952), president of the Republic of Colombia

* Andrés Pastrana Arango (b. 1954), politician

* John Leguizamo (b. 1964), actor

* Juan Pablo Montoya (b. 1975), racing driver

other fine gems, finding the city of gold became somewhat less urgent. The gem mines would suffice to attract fortune seekers to the Sabana de Bogotá.

A Republic is born. Bogotá quickly became an important trading centre in Spain's colonial empire. With the founding of the Viceroyalty of New Granada in 1717, it became the capital of most of the area that comprises modern-day Colombia. Adventurers from all over the world visited the city, and some settled there, while others continued on in search of El Dorado or emeralds. Those who stayed developed into an influential class of Colombians of Spanish and European descent. At the turn of the nineteenth century, they began their fight for independence. Colombia broke away from the colonial empire in 1819, with Bogotá as the capital of the New Republic of Gran Colombia, a federation that also included Ecuador and Venezuela, both of which became separate independent republics in 1830 as well as Panama.

The grid-plan city of Bogotá presents a picture not unlike other contemporary Latin American cities. It includes a unique assembly of buildings from the early colonial era, as well as baroque-style churches and towering skyscrapers. There is a popular bullfighting arena in the midst of it all, something like the Roman Colosseum. The sequentially numbered streets off Caracas Avenue and the main shopping boulevard of Séptima become increasingly prestigious as the numbers increase. From 100th Street onwards, the districts are pleasantly upper middle-class. Further down, the city's worst slums dominate the landscape.

La Candelaria (the Old City). Despite the rapid pace of new construction throughout the city, Bogotá's historical buildings are still on view everywhere, especially near Bolivar Plaza in the district called La Candelaria. Its many churches define the district architecturally. They include the Church of San Francisco and the neoclassical Bogotá Cathedral. Sagrario Chapel, the National Capitol and the National Palace are also located on or near the plaza. Most of the remaining colonial-era buildings are now museums or libraries. The Gold Museum (Museo del Oro) is an absolute must for every visitor to the city. It houses 38,000 articles from the golden age of the Inca Empire and Muisca nation. El Dorado has been found at last.

Centre: Guatavita Lake, source of the legend of El Dorado.

Bottom: View of the rooftops in the courtyards of La Candelaria.

ECUADOR

Quito

QUITO IS BY FAR THE MOST SPANISH CITY IN THE NEW WORLD. THE CAPITAL OF ECUADOR CURRENTLY FINDS ITSELF IN A TRANSITIONAL PHASE, NEITHER COLONIAL NOR MODERN. NEW BUILDINGS ARE BEING CONSTRUCTED IN THE MIDST OF THE OLD COLONIAL CITY.

Volcanoes, some active and some not, form a majestic backdrop for Quito. Within its magnificent natural setting, the city's colourful markets are the focus of urban life. The full range of diverse peoples in multicultural Ecuador are all there, buying, selling or simply watching the world go by. Quito Old City, including its many churches and monasteries, is a UNESCO World Heritage Site.

The search for El Dorado. The Inca Empire conquered Quito not long before the first Spaniards arrived. The Quitu people, who gave the city its name, were able to hold the Incas at bay for a long time but were subjugated in the early sixteenth century. When the Europeans arrived in 1534, the Inca inhabitants of Quito burned the city to the ground to keep the Spaniards from controlling what had been an important provincial capital. Conquistador Sebastián de Belalcázar simply rebuilt the city in the same spot. This new city, which he named San Francisco de Quito, was the starting point for some of the most spectacular, if misbegotten, adventures in the New World, including the search for the legendary Land of Cinnamon and, of course, the ongoing search for El Dorado. While neither was ever found, explorers did discover the route down the Amazon River, altering the fate of South America forever.

FACTS

*** Population of Quito:** *circa* 1.84 million

*** Places of interest:** Old Quito, Cathedral, San Augustín Convent, Ejido Park, El Panecillo Hill, Basilica, La Ronda Street, Mariscal Artisanal Market, San Francisco Monastery, City Museum, National Museum of the Central Bank, Independence Plaza, San Francisco Plaza, San Francisco Church, Telerifico Cable Car, Vivarium Exhibition

FAMOUS CITIZENS

*** Manuela Sáenz** (1797–1856), female freedom fighter and early feminist

*** José María Velasco Ibarra** (1893–1979), president of Ecuador

*** José Ayala-Lasso** (b. 1932), diplomat and politician

*** Rodrigo Borja Cerallos** (b. 1935), politician

The cathedral stands on the edge of Independence Plaza, and the Government Palace is to its right.

Monks and missionaries followed the Spanish conquistadores, and Quito became the centre for Catholic missions to the Indians. Soon Quito had more than thirty churches and monastic orders; it was even described as the "baroque jewel of the Andes". The most remarkable architectural masterpiece is the Church of San Francisco. The largest Spanish colonial building in the Americas, it was home to a famous art school where Indians were encouraged to express their faith in painting, sculpture and illumination; it is still in operation. The sheer number of colonial churches in baroque and mannerist style makes Quito a unique open-air museum of sacred architecture rivalling many European towns in quality and diversity.

The first World Heritage Site. Old Quito, the colonial core of the modern Ecuadorian capital, was the first city included on the UNESCO List of World Heritage Sites, in 1978. Visitors should not miss the wonderful Jesuit Church of La Compania with its gilded high altar, but there are also homes, streets and squares from the same period that deserve attention. Quito's Renaissance, baroque and classical architectural styles, particularly in domestic and administrative buildings, also include elements of the Mudéjar style, a late fusion of Moorish and Gothic elements found otherwise only in southern Spain.

The spectacular location of this equatorial city framed by glaciated volcanoes contains hidden dangers. Some of the volcanoes are still active, including Cotopaxi, Cayambe, Antisana and Illiniza. Earthquakes and catastrophic ash falls have afflicted Quito in the past, and still do today. Most of the city lies at the foot of the active Pichincha volcano. Since 2005, visitors can ride a funicular railway 4,000 metres up the slope of the mountain. From the observation deck at the top, near the crater, the views of the city and surrounding mountains are simply majestic.

Above: Quito Plaza is a popular gathering place.

Left: The Pichincha volcano again drew attention on the morning of 7 October 1999.

PERU

Lima

LIMA IS A CITY OF CONTRASTS. DESOLATE INDUSTRIAL DISTRICTS ARE RIGHT NEXT DOOR TO POSH RESIDENTIAL AREAS, AND DARK, RUBBISH-FILLED ALLEYWAYS MERGE INTO BAROQUE SQUARES AND BROAD BOULEVARDS LINED WITH SLEEK SKYSCRAPERS.

Located on a broad, 15-km-wide plateau, Lima has a remarkably temperate, dry climate given its nearly equatorial latitude. In this geographical transition zone between the Pacific and the foothills of the Andes, breezes generated by the cold-water Peru Current keep the city cool. Although the skies over the Peruvian capital are uniformly smoggy grey and overcast, there is little precipitation because the plateau lies in the arid rain shadow of the Andes Mountains.

The first university in the Americas. Spanish conquistador Francisco Pizarro (*circa*1476–1541) founded Lima on 18 January 1535, naming it Ciudad de los Reyes ("City of the Kings"). It would actually become the seat of Spain's viceroys. The site was well chosen. The valley on both sides of the Rimac River was fertile, and the location was strategically advantageous for the military actions Pizarro planned to take against the remnants of the Inca Empire in the Andes. Lima began as a small settlement for a handful of conquistadores, and began to expand only after the Benedictine monks settled here. The monks founded the University of San Marcos as early as 1551; it was the very first university in the Americas.

The wealth of the viceroy's city. Lima quickly became the religious, commercial and political centre

Right: The cathedral is in the heart of the Old City.

Below: The Archbishops Palace.

of the Spanish colonies in South America and a secure Spanish foothold on the South American continent. Gold and silver mined in the Andes were the foundation of the city's wealth. Some of those riches are still visible today in Lima's many superb colonial buildings, which are survivors of numerous earthquakes. Among the most visited are the cathedral, where Francisco Pizarro is buried, the church and monastery of San Francisco, and the church of Santo Domingo.

The beginning of a new era. At the start of the nineteenth century, the independence movement that swept South America finally hit the Peruvian capital. Rebels under the command of José de San Martín (1778–1850) conquered Lima in 1820, declaring Peru an independent republic. Lima was named the capital and has remained so ever since.

A colourful mix of peoples. In the nineteenth century, Chinese railway workers arrived in Peru by the thousands to help build the first South American railway line, which began operations in 1854. Lima's population did not reach one million, however, until the first half of the twentieth century. Immediately before and after World War II, the population grew through the influx of immigrants, many of them refugees, from all over the world. Post-1950, most of the city's population gains were due to rural migration, primarily of settled native peoples. This is how Lima's multicultural society came into being, one that has endured and contributes to its present cosmopolitan atmosphere.

Then and now. The once-flourishing colonial city has become a somewhat unmanageable metropolis in which what remained of Lima's natural setting has been completely covered over by asphalt, steel and concrete. Lima has a thoroughly attractive city centre and fashionable suburbs, including San Isidro and Miraflores. Most of Lima's financial and commercial activities, along with its best hotels and most prosperous citizens, are found there. Lima's historic city centre, its Old City, has been listed on the UNESCO List of World Heritage Sites since 1991. It is full of wonderful examples of Spanish colonial architecture. This is particularly true of the area around the Plaza Mayor (Main Square), formerly known as the Plaza de Armas. The city hall, Peruvian Presidential Palace, Archbishop's Palace and the cathedral are all there, lined up picture-perfect around the square.

FACTS

*** Population of Lima:** *circa* 6.87 million

*** Population of the metropolitan area:** *circa* 7.36 million

*** Places of interest:** Rafael Larco Herrera Archaeological Museum, San Pedro Basilica, Aliaga House, Church of San Francisco, Huaca Pucllana Restaurant, Church of San Pedro, Lima Cathedral, Jesuit Church of La Compañía, Municipalidad, Museum of the Inquisition, National Museum, Gold Museum, Archbishops Palace, Government Palace, Torre Tagle Palace, Central Park, Kennedy Park, Plaza de Acho, Plaza Mayor

FAMOUS CITIZENS

*** Alberto Fujimori** (b. 1938), politician

*** Álvaro Vargas Llosa** (b. 1966), author

*** Claudio Pizarro** (b. 1978), footballer

BRAZIL

Rio de Janeiro

THE SILHOUETTE OF SUGARLOAF MOUNTAIN IS RIO DE JANEIRO'S MOST RECOGNIZABLE LANDMARK, BUT ITS MOST TREASURED SYMBOL IS THE STATUE OF CHRIST ON TOP OF THE CORCOVADO. COPACABANA'S BEACHES ARE A CATWALK FOR EROTIC SWIMWEAR.

Rio de Janeiro lies within the Tijuca Massif, a river-indented mountain range with lushly forested slopes. Rio sprawls elegantly over the hillsides, its urban areas bordered by thick jungles, scenic bays and sun-drenched, palm-lined beaches. Visitors have little choice but to experience the full spectrum of life in Rio. Immense luxury can define one side of a street, while the grim struggle for survival dominates the other. Rich or poor, the people of Rio de Janeiro, known as Cariocas, have a spirited zest for life.

Carioca, or "white man's house". Sailors on a Portuguese caravel sighted Sugar Loaf and Corcovado from afar on 1 January 1502. They gave the place the name Rio de Janeiro (January River), based on the false assumption that this was a river delta. Later expeditions ascertained that it was not a river, but a saltwater bay, the shores of which were inhabited by Tamoyo Indians. When the first European house was built on the coast very close to what is now the city centre, the Indians called it the *carioca,* or "house of the white man". This is how the residents of Rio de Janeiro came to be called Cariocas.

Delays in founding. The coastal section around Rio de Janeiro was not rich in precious metals, so Lisbon did not consider it worth much effort. Pirates

FACTS

* **Population of Rio de Janeiro:** *circa* 6 million
* **Population of the metropolitan area:** *circa* 11.7 million
* **Places of interest:** Metropolitan Cathedral, Christ the Redeemer Statue, Copacabana, Corcovado cable car, O Bodinho (funicular tramway), Candelária Church, Santo Antônio Church and Convent, Ipanema, Hélio Oiticia Cultural Centre, São Bento Monastery, Museum of Contemporary Art, National Museum, Imperial Palace, Tijuca National Park, Quinta da Boa Vista, Municipal Theater, Sugarloaf Mountain

The giant Christ the Redeemer statue on Corcovado Mountain stretches its arms wide over Rio de Janeiro.

and buccaneers were the first to come here regularly, mainly to trade with the Indians on behalf of the French crown. Many of the bay islands were colonized in the process. Only then did Lisbon become concerned. Piracy was a serious threat. A contingent of soldiers under the command of a governor general was sent directly to Rio to drive out the squatters. The governor laid the cornerstone for the city of São Sebastião do Rio de Janeiro (St. Sebastian of Rio de Janeiro) on 1 March 1565, but it was two years before the pirates and their French patrons were completely driven out of Brazil.

Sugar. Portuguese settlers, called Sesmarias, were specialists in the cultivation of sugar cane. During the entire colonial period, this product brought more income to the Portuguese crown than gold from the hinterland. Many African slaves were brought across the Atlantic by the Portuguese colonial rulers to grow and process the crop. These slaves are the roots of Afro-Brazilian culture. Rio de Janeiro expanded steadily until 1750. Its streets were paved and expanded, and its fortifications strengthened. A new canal brought water from the Carioca River to a public fountain on Carioca Plaza in the city centre.

The Kingdom of Brazil. Not long afterwards, the French once again intervened in Brazil's destiny. When Napoleon Bonaparte conquered Portugal, the Portuguese royal family fled to Rio, arriving in 1808. Seven years later, King Dom João VI pronounced the city to be the capital of the joint Kingdom of Portugal and Brazil. The designation did not last for long, however. Following Napoleon's defeat, the monarch left Rio and returned to Lisbon, leaving behind his son Pedro as governor. It was he who, with his father's permission, declared Brazil an independent monarchy in 1822. Rio de Janeiro was named the capital of the new kingdom.

Above: The Municipal Theatre is an almost exact replica of the Paris Opéra.

Left: Parade of the samba school through the Sambódromo, a 6,000-seat parade venue, during the Brazilian Carnival.

Deep blue sea and white sands define Rio de Janeiro's world-famous Copacabana. Sugarloaf beckons in the background.

The city modernized. In the nineteenth century, Rio's development accelerated primarily due to extensive investment in infrastructure and public transport. Horse-drawn trams were introduced, and wherever the trams travelled, progress and prosperity soon followed. Rio was soon the most modern metropolis in South America. The building of the Estrada de Ferro Central do Brasil, the main railway connecting Rio de Janeiro, São Paolo and Minas Gerais, made further contributions to its development. The construction sector took off. A large percentage of the private homes, public buildings, monasteries and churches currently in use in the city were built during this period.

Renovation. At the beginning of the twentieth century, an almost entirely new city plan was imposed by Mayor Pereira Passos. Brazil was now a republic, not a kingdom, and its capital needed to keep up with the times. Boulevards and avenues were built, among them the Avenida Central, later renamed Avenida Rio Branco, between Passeio Público Park and the harbour on Mauá Plaza. This boulevard, very much the cultural, political and commercial focal point of the city, runs right through the centre of Rio. Plaza Floriano, one of Rio's most impressive plazas, lies at the south end of the avenue, as do the cafés, bars and cinemas of the Cinelândia district to its south. In order to implement Pereira Passos' plans, most of the earlier colonial buildings were sacrificed to the wrecking ball. The National Historical Museum, dedicated to the history of Brazil, is one of very few surviving structures from Rio's early days. The municipal theatre (Teátro Municipal), dedicated in 1909 and strongly modelled after the Paris Opéra, is right nearby. Marble arcades and ornate bronze detail adorn this stylish building. The Café do Teátro, on the ground floor of Assírio Hall, is decorated with a famous series of mosaics. The long panels are copies of the Ancient Mesopotamian glazed-tile figures from the cities of Susa and Babylon.

Samba. The Roaring Twenties gave the city's arts scene a boost. It was during those years that Rio de Janeiro became a city of music, dance and pure, unadulterated high spirits. Rio's Carnival was born and, along with it, its now ubiquitous samba schools. Today they still compete against each other during Carnival, attracting thousands of tourists and even greater numbers of enthusiastic locals.

Right: On most game days, Maracana Stadium is filled to capacity with 103,000 spectators.

Below: View of chic Leblon over the rooftops of Rocinha Favela.

Christ stretches out his arms. The following decade, in contrast, the 1930s, was more focused on political matters. The strongman of the new, authoritarian national government was named Getulio Vargas. His initial success at winning increased rights and protections for wage earners brought people from all over Brazil into Rio de Janeiro, all hoping to find work. Within a short time, all existing housing was occupied. Poorer sections of town were demolished and high-rise housing developments were erected. The 1930s brought yet another change to Rio de Janeiro, for it was then that the 38-metre-tall statue of Christ was erected on Corcovado Mountain. Fifty years beforehand, a rail track had been built up to an observation deck located just below the summit. The city finally had a worthy symbol, and visitors, a magnificent view.

James Bond. In 1913, a steep tramway was built to the top of the 394-metre-high Sugarloaf (Pão de Açúcar in Portuguese), the mountain that stands on a peninsula in Guanabara Bay. The Pão de Açúcar tramway served as a set for the 1979 James Bond film *Moonraker*, starring Roger Moore.The film introduced a new generation of people around the world to the wonders of Rio de Janeiro, and visitors flocked to the city.

Over 20 km of beautiful beaches. The famous beaches of Copacabana, Ipanema and Leblon are all located due south of Sugarloaf. In Rio, the beaches are where the good times roll. There is a famous nightclub in New York named after one of the beaches (Copacabana) and a classic song composed by Brazilian Antonio Carlos Jobim about another ("The Girl from Ipanema"). Leblon is thus – undeservedly – the only one of these three districts without an international reputation. Locals, however, know that it is by far the best place for viewing the colourful processions of the samba schools during Carnival.

Fla-Flu. Rio would not be Rio without a good dose of football mania. Two of the four major football teams from Rio, Flamengo and Fluminense, have been at the top of Brazil's elite league for years. Fluminense was Rio's first team, founded in 1902. Flamengo, which was originally a rowing club, followed in 1911. It famously poached former Fluminense players by offering them higher salaries, a practice which it continues to this day. This, along with the consistent high quality of both teams, has contributed to the eternal Fla-Flu rivalry. Maracana Stadium, the second largest in the world, is where these great teams battle it out on the field.

FAMOUS CITIZENS

* **Heitor Villa-Lobos** (1887–1959), composer and conductor
* **João Havelange** (b. 1916), football official, IOC member
* **Antonio Carlos Jobim** (1927–94), bossa nova composer and singer
* **Paulo Coelho** (b. 1947), best-selling author
* **Nelson Piquet** (b. 1952), Formula 1 racing driver
* **Ronaldo Luís Nazário de Lima** (b. 1976), football superstar

BRAZIL

São Paulo

SÃO PAULO MEANS COFFEE, SOME OF THE WORLD'S BEST. THE SURROUNDING COUNTRYSIDE IS FILLED WITH HUGE COFFEE PLANTATIONS. EVERYTHING IN SÃO PAULO IS BIGGER AND BETTER THAN IN THE REST OF BRAZIL, SADLY, INCLUDING ITS LEVEL OF POVERTY.

São Paolo is the engine of Brazil, the economic pulse of the country. The active Brazilian stock market is based here, drawing a skilled and ambitious workforce with incomes double the national average. São Paolo seduces visitors one moment, and shocks them the next. Poverty exists side by side with extreme wealth. The city is just under 80 km long and 40 km wide. Skyscrapers stretch as far as the eye can see, as do endless traffic jams and sidewalks crowded with people scurrying in all directions.

The history of São Paolo is as old as colonial Brazil. In 1545, Jesuits selected this high plateau with fertile soil and adequate precipitation to fulfil their Apostolate, bold missionary work based on that of St. Paul. The religious infrastructure they founded, including churches, schools and hospitals, led to the city officially founded in 1711 being named São Paolo ("St. Paul") in his honour. Its advantageous location along a mountain pass in the Serra do Mar range gave the city direct coastal access, ensuring its importance as a trade port for inland resources.

Gold and coffee. Bold Portuguese conquistoradores, called *bandeirantes*, penetrated ever deeper into the continent via São Paulo, enabling Portugal to expand its territory further into the country's interior. When

The Cathedral of São Paulo is one of the last remaining witnesses to the colonial period.

FACTS

✱ Population of São Paulo: *circa* 10 million

✱ Population of the metropolitan area: *circa* 19 million

✱ Places of interest: Se Cathedral, Metropolitan Cathedral, Ibirapuera Park, Our Lady of Light Church, Mirante do Vale Building, Museum of Contemporary Art, Museum of Sacred Art, Presépio Napolitano, Solar da Marquesa de Santos, Municipal Theatre, Velodrome

FAMOUS CITIZENS

✱ Oscar Niemeyer (b. 1907), architect

✱ Roberto Burle Marx (1909–94), landscape architect

✱ Archbishop Paulo Evaristo Arns (b. 1921), liberation theologian

✱ Ayrton Senna (1960–94) and **✱ Rubens Barichello** (b. 1972), Formula 1 racing drivers

Centre: Paulista Avenue.

Bottom: A monument to the European discoverer of Brazil, Pedro Alvares Cabral.

bandeirantes discovered the lands' abundant natural resources, they settled down and began to exploit them. One of them was gold; the states Minas Gerais and Mato Grosso became synonymous with the gold rush. Prospectors and shady figures from all over the world, and African slaves they brought, stopped in São Paulo on their way to the gold mines. From 1850 on, more and more of those people decided to stay in São Paulo. One reason was the increased importance of coffee, the crop best suited to the local environment. Once coffee farming took off, São Paulo's prosperity and growth skyrocketed almost overnight.

Architecturally speaking, the city began to shoot into the sky in the 1920s. The old core of the city was unceremoniously razed and rebuilt, only the great cathedral surviving. After World War II, a large wave of immigration led the city to burst at the seams, expanding outwards in concentric rings. This development is still visible on the ride from the airport to the city centre. On this initial, involuntary sightseeing tour, one passes through a 20-km corridor of industrial complexes, working-class subdivisions and slums. São Paulo's slums are the infamous *favelas*, where shelters are constructed out of salvaged bricks, wood, tin and cardboard.

A sea of skyscrapers. At the top of São Paolo's highest building, the Edificio Itália, is a restaurant offering a panoramic view of this metropolis of millions, with high-rises as far as one can see. Built on hilly terrain with great variations in elevation, they rise and fall in waves like a steel-concrete-and-glass sea. Towards the north-west, if it is visible through the smog, the view culminates in the Serra da Cantareira mountain range, site of a wildlife refuge and one of the city's most important water reservoirs.

The gardens. At street level one can practically suffocate among all the people, cars, buses, dust and yet more people pushing to and fro along busy pavements and squares. It is time to head for the *jardins* ("gardens"). These are not actual gardens, but chic shopping promenades and entertainment districts where prosperity and luxury are on display. São Paolo's signature boulevard, Paulista Avenue, is the king of all the other "gardens". It is also the financial centre of Brazil, home of the stock market. There are, however, a few Italian villas in neo-renaissance style located right in the midst of the office towers that are worth seeing.

CHILE

Santiago de Chile

ONE'S FIRST IMPRESSION OF THE CHILEAN CAPITAL IS THAT OF TRANQUIL PROSPERITY. THERE'S NOTHING FANCY OR PRETENTIOUS ABOUT SANTIAGO, A GRID-PLAN CITY WITH NEAT ROWS OF HOUSES, CLEAN PAVEMENT AND BARELY NOTICEABLE TRAFFIC.

Spacious parks, modern shopping centres and nearly universal cleanliness are not commonly associated with the urban sprawl characteristic of so many South American megacities. Santiago is different, and all the more attractive for being so. Its historic sights are all located near the Plaza de Armas in the centre of town. When the guard changes at the Presidential Palace, German brass-band music accompanies it.

The city on the Mapocho River. The Spanish founded Santiago de Nueva Extramadura with great fanfare on Santa Lucía Hill on 12 February 1541. Conquistador Pedro de Valdivia, once an officer under the command of Francisco Pizarro, chose the locale because it was easily defensible. The Mapocho River surrounded the hill on three sides, protecting it against invaders.

Moving towards independence. Chile, and Santiago along with it, was part of the Viceroyalty of Peru until 1778. All Chilean trade was conducted by way of Callao, the main Peruvian port. This arrangement, as well as steady plundering by English pirates and endless fighting with the Araucan native peoples, kept Chile the poorest of all the Spanish overseas possessions. By the beginning of the nineteenth century, the Chilean desire for independence could

Right: Constitution Plaza with the Presidential Palace.

Below: The equestrian statue of Pedro de Valdivia on Plaza de Armas.

no longer be quelched, and after bloody fighting, Chile finally became an independent state on 12 February 1818, exactly 277 years after the founding of the city. The leader of the Chilean revolt, Bernardo O'Higgins (1776–1842), is still honoured today as a national hero.

Wealth and prosperity. The discovery of saltpetre in the rich mineral deposits of Antofagasta, about 65 km north of Santiago, gave the local economy the boost it so urgently needed. Investment capital began to flow and the city became prosperous, or rather, its upper classes did. In the 1930s, Santiago was well on its way to becoming a modern, industrialized metropolis.The government district of Barrio Cívico, home to Chile's many ministries and other public institutions, was constructed near La Moneda (the former mint) and the Presidential Palace. Immigration of people from the northern and southern reaches of Chile hoping to share in the wealth had doubled the city's population by the end of World War II.

The Plaza de Armas. The traditional heart of contemporary Santiago de Chile is the Plaza de Armas with its neoclassical cathedral and equestrian monument to Valdivia, the city's founder. The central market and its many fish restaurants can be reached by means of one of Santiago's many pedestrian zones. Few buildings from the Spanish colonial period have survived in their original condition. Casa Colorado, a late nineteenth-century structure, is one of the oldest. The Presidential Palace on Constitution Plaza was witness to the tragic events of 1973. On 11 September, Chile's beloved President Salvador Allende was killed here in the course of a military coup led by the dictator Augusto Pinochet.

Smog over Santiago. Anyone looking for even greater peace and quiet might enjoy a visit to Cerro Santa Lucía (Santa Lucía Hill), the place where the city was founded. Today the site is graced with a small park. The hill offers a lovely view of the Old City of Santiago. If you continue to climb higher, up to Cerro San Cristóbal at an elevation of 860 metres, you will find yourself in Santiago's shopping district. From there, ideally, one should have a good view of the entire valley and cordillera, but in reality smog usually interferes. In order to get the smog under control, cars may only drive on even or odd days, according to their licence-plate numbers. In response, most wealthy Chileans treat themselves to several cars so that they can drive around the city "legally" every day.

FACTS

* **Population of Santiago de Chile:** *circa* 5 million
* **Population of the metropolitan area:** *circa* 6.5 million
* **Places of interest:** City Cathedral, Casa Colorada, Cerro San Cristóbal, Cerro Santa Lucía, Church of San Francisco, Central Market, Chilean Museum of Pre-Columbian Art, National Museum of Fine Arts, La Moneda Palace, Paseo Ahumada, Plaza de Armas, Posada del Corregidor

FAMOUS CITIZENS

* **José Miguel Carrera** (1785–1821), national hero and politician
* **Isabel Allende** (b. 1942 in Peru), writer and politician
* **Michelle Bachelet** (b. 1951), current and first female President of Chile
* **Horatio Sanz** (b. 1969), comedian

ARGENTINA

Buenos Aires

BETWEEN THE ATLANTIC AND THE ANDES, NORTH OF TIERRA DEL FUEGO AND SOUTH OF THE WATERFALLS OF IGUAZÚ LIES BUENOS AIRES, SOUTH AMERICA'S MOST EUROPEAN CITY AND, OF COURSE, THE UNDISPUTED WORLD CAPITAL OF THE TANGO.

Jorge Luis Borges, Argentina's greatest poet, once said, "Buenos Aires is as eternal as air and water." That may be, but this city on the Río de la Plata got off to a slow start – the Spanish conquistadores had to found it twice. The first time was in 1536, when Don Pedro de Mendoza declared the new settlement Ciudad de Nuestra Señora Santa María del Buen Ayre (City of St. Mary, Our Lady of Good Air). The town was abandoned in 1541 after a series of attacks by local tribes, but Juan de Garay founded it again in 1580. **The second attempt** by Europeans was more successful. Juan de Garay changed the city's already prodigious name slightly, calling it Ciudad de la Santísima Trinidad y Puerto Santa María de los Buenos Aires (City of the Holy Trinity and Port of St. Mary of the Fair Winds). Still, the colonial administration's mandate that all goods from Argentina pass through Lima on the way to Europe kept the city from advancing. Ever inventive, Argentinian merchants smuggled their way out of the situation whenever they could. Buenos Aires was finally declared an open port in the late eighteenth century. The city flourished, becoming capital of the Viceroyalty of La Plata and, in 1880, of Argentina. **Buenos Aires** is intimately connected to the Perón family. Although it was her husband, Juan, who was

FACTS

✱ Population of Buenos Aires: *circa* 2.75 million

✱ Population of the metropolitan area: *circa* 11.55 million

✱ Places of interest: Bolsa de Comercio (Stock Exchange), Cabildo, Casa Rosada, La Boca (Port District), Cathedral, Enrique Larreta Museum of Spanish Art, MALBA (Buenos Aires Museum of Latin American Art), Museum of Modern Art, National Museum of Fine Arts, Obelisk, Palace of Congress, Reconquista Park, St. Ignatius of Loyola Church, Teatro Colón

FAMOUS CITIZENS

✱ Jorge Luis Borges (1899–1986), writer

✱ Daniel Barenboim (b. 1942), pianist and conductor

✱ Guillermo Vilas (b. 1952) and **✱ Gabriela Sabatini** (b. 1970) professional tennis players

president, many more people remember Eva Perón, more popularly known as Evita. Active on behalf of her country's poor, her life was immortalized in the Andrew Lloyd Webber musical of that name. Its most famous song, "Don't Cry for Me, Argentina", was a hit around the world. Her grave in Recoleta Cemetery attracts many visitors; indeed, it is practically a pilgrimage site. Tens of thousands visit it annually.

In the heart of the city. The old, historical core of the city is concentrated in the area of the Plaza de Mayo (May Plaza), a spacious oval with important buildings like the cathedral, La Casa Rosada (seat of government) and city hall. The residents of Buenos Aires, called Porteños, gather on the Plaza de Mayo for protests and demonstrations. They always have. In May 1810, the first steps towards independence from Spain began here. In commemoration of that first demonstration, the Pirámide de Mayo was erected in the middle of the plaza. To this day, the Plaza de Mayo symbolizes the unhealed wounds of the dictatorship of the years 1976 to 1983. Many who demonstrated here during those years were tortured and executed by the military junta.

Traffic noise and perfect acoustics. The Avenue of the 9th of July, where all of Buenos Aires' major traffic arteries merge, is very grand. Pedestrians running for dear life are as much a part of the daily morning picture as the newspaper salesmen shouting out the headlines of the day. A 67-m-high obelisk towers over this grand boulevard. It was erected as a memorial to the first city of Buenos Aires, the one founded by Mendoza. Just two corners away is the Teatro Colón, a world-famous opera house known for its perfect acoustics. Its walls have reverberated with the sound of Placido Domingo's arias, and indeed, most of the world's best musicians and singers have performed here.

La Casa Rosada (Presidential Palace) stands on Plaza de Mayo, the historic core of Buenos Aires.

Above: Buenos Aires is the world's capital of tango.

Left: The Teatro Colón is not far from the Avenue of the 9th of July.

Grid-plan cities designed on a drawing board – this image applies to quite a number of North American cities. The prototypical North American city is the US and DC built from the ground up based on a commissioned city plan. Straightforward street plans do have their advantages. They certainly help visitors get oriented, even in a megacity like New York.

NORTH AMERICA

CANADA

Vancouver

VANCOUVER IS BEAUTIFULLY SITUATED AT THE MOUTH OF THE FRASER RIVER ALONG A NARROW STRETCH OF COASTLINE IN CANADA'S FAR WEST. WAVES CRASH ON ITS PACIFIC SHORE AGAINST THE MAGNIFICENT BACKDROP OF THE COASTAL MOUNTAINS.

Grouse Mountain is only fifteen minutes by aerial tramway from central Vancouver. Observation decks at the top of the mountain provide terrific views of the city and the ocean, with Vancouver Island behind it. As long as the inland fog is held in check, the view extends to include a number of coastal mountain chains. When Vancouver hosted the 21st Winter Olympic Games in February 2010, they seldom have had such an impressive natural setting.

Built on timber. In the beginning, Vancouver was just a trading post whose main importance was to the timber industry. Two sawmills, the 1863 Moddyville Saw Mill and the 1865 Stamp's Mill, formed the core of what would later become Vancouver. Granville Township was established around them in 1870. At the time it was better known as Gastown, after "Gassy" Jack Deighton, a local saloon owner who liked to "gas", or talk, a lot. Today, a statue of Mr Deighton stands on the exact spot where his saloon once stood. Not far from here lies Granville's most famous symbol, the Steam Clock, which is still in use.

A change of name. The Canadian Pacific Railway reached Vancouver in 1885, bringing progress to the city. Vancouver Island, named after George

Right: Science World, once part of the 1986 Vancouver Expo, is located on False Creek.

Below: Vancouver's rise began with the timber trade.

Vancouver, the British officer who first explored it in 1791, was well known in the rest of Canada, too. Few had heard of the coastal mill town of Granville, an unimportant place nicknamed after a saloon. The railway magnates therefore suggested that Granville change its name to Vancouver. On 6 April 1886, Vancouver was declared the new name of the town, which was the final stop on the important Canadian Pacific Railway, and bound for glory.

The Gold Rush of 1858 and the building of the railway brought many Chinese immigrants to Vancouver, so many, in fact, that Vancouver's Chinatown is the second largest in the Americas today. In terms of physical size, it is actually just a few square blocks. Visitors turn a corner and are suddenly right there in the middle of it. The only thing overtly non-Chinese in this part of town is the currency. As is the case in Chinatowns everywhere, all the store signs are written in Chinese. Nearby is Dr Sun Yat-Sen Park, which has a typically Asian design. Chinese landscape architects were imported to construct a characteristic Chinese park for the 1986 Vancouver Expo. The park features a lake and water lilies, numerous footpaths and bridges, and groves of bamboo abound. This peaceful oasis is pierced by the sound of loudly cawing crows, a common bird in British Columbia's coastal region.

What a view. Like every other city of millions, Vancouver has its share of skyscrapers. The Harbour Centre Tower, Vancouver's tallest building, is the modern symbol of the city. Neil Armstrong, the first man to set foot on the moon, was on hand to dedicate the 177-metre-tall tower in 1977. An observation deck called the Lookout, which is also the visitors' information centre, provides a marvellous 360-degree panorama of the city and its environs.

Northern film industry. For some years, Vancouver has been the Hollywood of the north. The city currently holds the number two spot, behind Los Angeles, for film and television production. Many US production companies come to Vancouver to film their movies and television series. This is due in part to the more favourable labour conditions and advantageous exchange rate in Canada. Another attraction is British Columbia's stunning natural beauty. The city of Vancouver is remarkably diverse in terms of its architecture, ideal for filmmakers. Clever production designers can easily transform Vancouver into New York, Seattle, Boston or any other North American city. *Stargate* was filmed here, rather than in Wyoming, for example, and *MacGyver's* houseboat was not anchored off Los Angeles, but in Vancouver Bay.

FACTS

* **Population of Vancouver:** ca. 550,000
* **Population of the metropolitan area:** *circa* 2.16 million
* **Places of interest:** Capilano Suspension Bridge, Chinatown, Dr Sun Yat-Sen Classical Chinese Garden, Gastown, Granville Island, Grouse Mountain, Lions Gate Bridge, Little Italy, Robson Street, Science World British Columbia, Stanley Park, Vancouver Aquarium

FAMOUS CITIZENS

* **James Doohan** (1920–2005), actor ("Scotty" from Star Trek)
* **David McTaggart** (1932–2001), Greenpeace activist
* **Bryan Adams** (b. 1959), rock musician
* **Michael J. Fox** (b. 1961), actor

USA

Seattle

SEATTLE'S SETTING ALONE WOULD QUALIFY IT AS ONE OF THE LOVELIEST CITIES IN THE UNITED STATES. NUMEROUS LAKES AND GREEN SPACES IN THE CITY EMPHASIZE THE MAJESTY OF THE CASCADE MOUNTAINS AND MOUNT RAINIER IN THE BACKGROUND.

Green is the most prevalent colour in Seattle; it is not called "The Emerald City" without reason. The incorporation of natural border features such as hills and waterways into the city plan encouraged the development of distinct and varied neighbourhoods, each with its own special charm.

Denny's city. Before the arrival of the first Europeans, the peaceful Duwamish tribe inhabited the area around what is today Seattle. New Yorker David Denny led the first group of settlers to the Pacific North-west in 1851. Denny realized right away that the area was perfectly suited for an ocean harbour. He staked his claim at Alki Point, in what is today West Seattle. After an especially windy and rainy winter, the group moved its permanent settlement to Elliott Bay and christened it Seattle, after Chief Seattle of the Duwamish tribe. We know little about him, except that he must have left a lasting impression on the first settlers. The official founding and naming of the city took place in the following year, 1869.

The story of the women. At first Seattle failed to thrive, in part because almost all the people who lived there were unmarried men. Finally, one of the founding fathers made a trip back east with the goal of convincing unmarried women to come to Seattle.

The icon of Seattle is, without a doubt, the soaring Space Needle.

FACTS

*** Population of Seattle:** *circa* 571,500

*** Places of interest:** Burke Museum of Natural History and Culture, Frye Art Museum, Key Arena, Klondike Gold Rush National Historic Park and Museum, Maritime Heritage Museum, Monorail, Museum of Flight, Pioneer Square, Science Center, Seattle Aquarium, Seattle Art Museum, Smith Tower, Space Needle, Waterfall Garden Park, Waterfront, Woodland Park Zoo

FAMOUS CITIZENS

*** Judy Collins** (b. 1939), folk singer

*** Jimi Hendrix** (1942–70), guitarist

*** Bill Gates** (b. 1955) and *** Paul Allen** (b. 1953) co-founders of Microsoft

*** Apolo Anton Ohno** (b. 1982), Olympic speed skater

Centre: In the middle of the city, totem poles stand watch on Pioneer Square.

Bottom: View over "The Emerald City" from the Space Needle.

After the second such trip, a total of fifty-seven women had been convinced to come to Seattle. The women married the settlers, some would say bringing the first stirrings of civilization to what had been a rather course enclave of lumberjacks.

The lumberjack city. The Northern Pacific Railroad joined Portland to Seattle in 1893, the first time that Seattle was physically connected to the transport system of rest of the United States. This greatly improved the prospects of the local timber business. The economic upswing brought immigrants in its wake, and Seattle's population grew quickly. Even the Great Fire of 1889, in which most of the city was burned to the ground, failed to put a brake on growth. The area around Pioneer Square, formerly composed of fifty rows of wooden houses, was quickly rebuilt in more durable stone and iron. The Yukon Gold Rush gave the local economy an additional push, and Seattle experienced an unparalleled boom.

Symbol of a modern city. The two World Wars made Seattle a stronghold of ship and aeroplane building, but today, the industries most identified with the city are high tech. The computer and Internet industries, including business giants Microsoft and Amazon, were founded in this city. A new, modern Seattle put its best foot forward with the 1962 World's Fair. Many of the symbols of the city were built during that time, such as the Space Needle, Key Arena, the Science Center and the monorail running between the centres of Westlake and Seattle. Smith Tower, the city's earliest landmark structure, had been built fifty years earlier. Dedicated in 1914, at that time it was the highest building west of the Mississippi River.

Over 11,000 coffee shops worldwide. Entirely modern, but livable and lovable, Seattle has always offered an array of cultural and musical offerings. There are galleries and museums, and some kind of festival is taking place nearly every day of the year. The original grunge band "Nirvana" formed in Seattle, and guitarist Jimi Hendrix was born here. Pike Place Market in Seattle still provides a venue for a number of street musicians. It is also where, in 1971, Starbucks Coffee opened the very first of what has exploded into more than 11,000 coffee shops worldwide.

CANADA

Montreal

MONTREAL IS A MARKEDLY EUROPEAN CITY THAT INTEGRATES MANY ELEMENTS OF THE FRENCH OUTLOOK ON LIFE, INCLUDING THE QUÉBECOIS LANGUAGE SPOKEN BY MANY PEOPLE AND A LAISSEZ-FAIRE ATTITUDE.

The severe Canadian winters are fearsome, but people take precautions here in Montreal: there is a second city underground. When it is well below freezing outside, a warm subterranean world awaits. Bars, restaurants, shopping centres and adventure parks are all found in Montreal's immense underground arcades, offering everything the spirit needs to fight off the winter blues.

European settlement of the region began in 1642, when fifty French settlers founded Ville Marie on the bank of the St. Lawrence River. This small colony was known as Montreal from the very beginning, named after the hill of the same name, the highest point in the city. The first European to climb to its 233-metre summit was explorer Jacques Cartier. On reaching the top, he is said to have exclaimed, "*Quel mont royal!*" ("This is one royal hill!"). Today there is a large modern basilica on the summit, St. Joseph's Oratory, with a 97-metre-high dome. Not far away in Mont Royal Park is a free-standing cross that is 31 metres tall. Built in 1924, it glows in different colours at various times of day depending on the angle of the sun. At night, its fibre-optic illumination is visible from miles away.

The historic centre of Montreal reflects the splendour of its golden age in the nineteenth century,

FACTS

* Population of Montreal: *circa* 1.8 million
* Population of the metropolitan area: *circa* 3.6 million
* Places of interest: Biodôme, Botanical Garden, Bell Center, Christ Church Cathedral, Hotel de Ville (City Hall), Lachine Canal National Historic Site, Mont Royal Hill, Old Customs House, Molson Center, Basilica of Notre Dame, Jean Drapeau Park, Olympic Park, Place d'Armes, Saint Joseph's Oratory, Séminaire Saint-Sulpice

FAMOUS CITIZENS

* Oscar Peterson (b. 1925), jazz musician
* Edgar Bronfman, Jr. (b. 1929), businessman (Seagram, Vivendi and Warner Music)
* William Shatner (b. 1931), actor and author
* Leonard Cohen (b. 1934), singer
* Chris Haney (1950-2010) and
* Scott Abbott (b. 1949), inventors of Trivial Pursuit

Notre-Dame de Bonsecours in Montreal's Old City, where the Virgin Mary reaches out her arms from the steeple of the basilica.

when industrialization promoted the city into the economic centre of Canada. Old Montreal was thoroughly renovated and declared a historic district in 1965. The architectural styles found here span three centuries. Chief among these is the Gothic Notre-Dame Basilica (1824–29). Another highlight is the Chapelle de Notre Dame de Bonsecours, the "Little Mariners' Chapel".

The old port. Pointe-à-Callière, the Museum of National History at Old Port, is a must-see for visitors. This neoclassical former customs house is part of a three-building complex and one of the few remaining buildings that testifies to the presence of the British, who conquered Montreal in 1760 in one of the last battles of the Seven Years' War (or French and Indian War). A more than 2-km recreational area runs through the Old Port area.

The modern city centre lies to the south, at the foot of Mont Royal. It is comprised of dozens of skyscrapers, none of which is higher than the peak elevation of the hill, by city ordinance. The heart of Montreal is perhaps best known for its practically endless shopping possibilities, both above ground along Sainte Catherine Street, and in the *Ville Souterraine* (Underground City) below it. The Quartier Latin, with its many bars, street cafés and restaurants is also very much worth visiting. The extensive section from Mont Royal to the Hochelaga-Maisonneuve quarter serves as Montreal's most popular green space. To the east are the expanses of the Montreal's Olympic Park and Stadium, the Botanical Gardens, the Insectarium and the Biodôme, an oasis in the heart of the city where approximately 4,000 animals and 5,000 plants thrive beneath its glass roof. An exploration path leads visitors through environments representing all of the varied regions Canada.

Above: The square in front of city hall bears the name of the explorer Jacques Cartier.

Left: Montreal was the venue for the 1976 Summer Olympic Games.

CANADA

Toronto

TORONTO NEVER SLEEPS. DURING THE DAY, TORONTO IS THE LARGEST FINANCIAL CENTRE IN CANADA, WHILE BY NIGHT THIS COSMOPOLITAN CITY ON LAKE ONTARIO BECOMES A PULSATING CENTRE OF ART AND ENTERTAINMENT.

Festivals, exhibitions, nightclubs and a plethora of restaurants make Toronto the cultural capital of Canada. It is also a centre of the North American film and television industry. Toronto's commercial theatre scene offers an average of fifty different productions per month. In addition, Toronto is clean and safe. "Like New York, but governed by the Swiss", said Sir Peter Ustinov, a citizen of the world and former resident of the city.

From outpost to immigrant stronghold. French trappers were the first Europeans in Ontario, arriving around 1615. They fought their way through the thickly forested Ontario Peninsula for many years without establishing a settlement. In 1720, a small trading post was established where Toronto now stands. The Native Americans from the Huron Nation called the place, which was where their tribes gathered once a year, *Tarantua* ("meeting place"). When the British arrived in 1788, they called the settlement that they founded York. Toronto did not receive its present name until 1834. Immigrants from all over the world flocked to the city in the trail of its English and Scottish founders.

A needle in a haystack. The 553-metre-tall CN Tower has pierced the heavens and dominated the skyline of Toronto since 1976. Other important

Right: The old city hall on Nathan Philipps Square.

Below: The Rogers Centre, or SkyDome, home of the Blue Jays baseball and the Argonauts football teams.

buildings have since joined it. The Rogers Centre, better known as SkyDome Stadium, sits at the foot of the tower. To the east of downtown is the brand new hockey and basketball arena, the Air Canada Centre. Clearly, Toronto is a sports-loving city! Just to the north of the CN Tower are the many skyscrapers that make up Toronto's financial district. Many of these are architectural masterpieces, including the Dominion Centre by architect Mies van der Rohe and the Gallery in BCE Place by the Spanish architect Santiago Calatrava.

Clean and safe, but never dull. Toronto has a very active nightlife scene, giving the lie to the city's reputation for stodginess. The hottest and most popular bars and clubs are found in the heart of the city in the vicinity of King and Queen Streets, just to the west of the business district. No one goes home right after a night at the theatre or after a game. Sports fans in Canada would rather search out a bar to watch ice hockey and baseball live on television, or go out after a game for a snack of fried chicken wings and dark beer. Speaking of ice hockey, Wayne Gretzky's Bar, owned by Canada's most successful professional hockey player ever, is particularly popular. Its walls are full of memorabilia and photographs related to the national pass-time that turn it into an ice-hockey museum.

The Hockey Hall of Fame. One of the grandest buildings in the centre of Toronto is the Hockey Hall of Fame, where the game's top trophy, the Stanley Cup, is on permanent display. The 1847 beaux-arts building was once the Bank of Montreal. In 1993, the National Hockey League decided to relocate its Hall of Fame and museum to this exceptionally accessible location at the corner of Yonge and Front Streets. By far the most popular tourist destination in Toronto, it attracts over a million hockey fans each year from all over the world.

Recreation right outside the front door. The Toronto Islands are located in the harbour directly opposite the city centre. Though they have long been favourite recreation destinations for the city's residents, the islands did not even exist until 1858, when a storm separated what had been a peninsula from the mainland. Since then, the forested isles have been accessible via ferries. The islands are one enormous pedestrian zone: no cars are allowed. The 1803 Gibraltar Point lighthouse, located on Centre Island, is the city's oldest building. Today the islands are an ideal place to relax and enjoy an unparalleled view of the city skyline, reflected in the waters of Lake Ontario.

FACTS

*** Population of Toronto:**
circa 4.77 million

*** Population of the metropolitan area:**
circa 5.2 million

*** Places of interest:**
Algonquin Park, Casa Loma Castle, CN Tower, Eaton Centre, Hockey Hall of Fame, Rogers Centre (SkyDome), Royal Ontario Museum, Toronto Islands, Yonge Street

FAMOUS CITIZENS

*** Frank O. Gehry**
(b. 1929), architect and designer

*** Glenn Gould**
(1932–82), pianist

*** Neil Young**
(b. 1945), rock musician

*** John Candy**
(1950–94), comedian

USA

Boston

ALSO KNOWN AS THE "CRADLE OF LIBERTY", BOSTON IS THE BIRTHPLACE OF AMERICAN FREEDOM AND INDEPENDENCE. THIS CITY SUCCEEDS BETTER THAN MOST IN THE UNITED STATES IN COMBINING OLD-WORLD CHARM WITH MODERN AMERICAN CONVENIENCE.

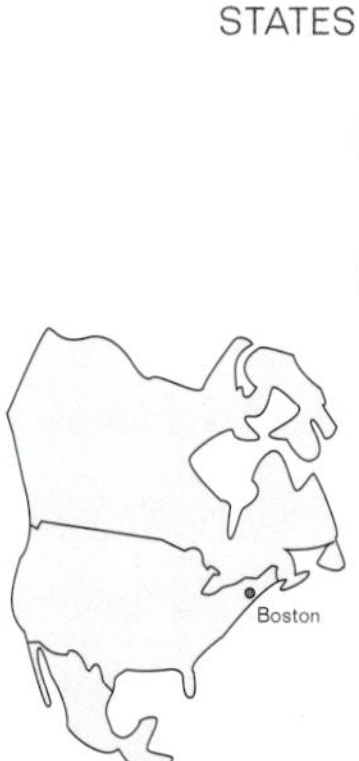

The first wave of urban renewal in the 1950s threatened to change Boston forever, but its citizens protested. As a result, Boston can now boast some of the best-preserved historical buildings and districts in America. In some cases, preservation arguably borders on kitsch. The North End is as clean and orderly as a theatrical stage set, and Faneuil Hall Marketplace can feel like a combination theme park and shopping mall inside a "colonial" building rebuilt from scratch to comply with modern fire-safety laws.

The Pilgrim Fathers. In 1630, Boston was founded by English Puritans on a peninsula along a natural harbour. Originally called "Trimountain" because of three nearby hills, the city received its current name a few years later. Boston was named after the city of the same name in Lincolnshire, England, the birthplace of some of the city's earliest settlers. World-renowned Harvard University, the first institution of higher learning in North America, was founded in 1636, just a few years after the city itself came into being.

The War of Independence. The Boston Tea Party took place on 16 December 1773, setting off a wave of events that would eventually lead to the United States' independence from England. Protests against an increase in the tea tax by the British Crown had

The Massachusetts State House was built according to plans by Boston architect Charles Bullfinch (1763–1844).

FACTS

*** Population of Boston:** *circa* 569,200

*** Population of the metropolitan area:** *circa* 3.8 million

*** Places of interest:** Boston City Hall, Boston Common/Public Gardens, Custom House Tower, John Hancock Tower, Harvard University, Museum of Fine Arts, New England Aquarium, North End, Old South Meeting House, Old State House, Rowes Wharf, Theatre District

FAMOUS CITIZENS

*** Benjamin Franklin** (1706–90), Boston native, statesman, scientist

*** John Quincy Adams** (1767–1848), 6th US president

*** Edgar Allan Poe** (1809–49), writer

*** Susan B. Anthony** (1820–1906), women's rights activist

*** Leonard Nimoy** (b. 1931), actor

led to popular unrest. Boston citizens, dressed as Native Americans, entered the harbour and threw three shiploads of tea into the harbour. In response, the British government closed the harbour and imposed heavy sanctions against the American colonies. The conflict became violent in April 1775 with the Battle of Lexington and Concord. The rest is history. England lost the war, and the United States gained its independence in 1783.

The red line. American history can be experienced all over Boston. A red line on the pavement marks the route of the 4-km-long Freedom Trail, which leads visitors to no fewer than sixteen historic landmarks. Among these is Boston Common, a green space that serves as the starting point for tourists. This is where the first settlers once helped lost souls and witches get back on the straight and narrow path by means of stocks, pillories and gallows. Later on, the Boston militia practised here while cows grazed on the soft green grass; livestock grazed here until 1830. Another worthwhile stopping point on the trail is the Massachusetts State House with its golden dome. Continuing along the trail, visitors pass many more buildings that are rich in history and equally worth seeing. The Old State House at the end of Washington Street deserves special mention. The British governors lived here from 1713 until the end of the colonial period. The British imperial heraldic animals, the lion and the unicorn, still adorn the building.

More modern architecture. The Government Centre, overshadowed by the two towers of the John F. Kennedy Federal Building and city hall opposite it, represents Boston's modern side. Red brick pavements and esplanades soften the impact of the somewhat brutal, strictly functional modern buildings. The 260-metre-high John Hancock Tower is of architectural importance. Resembling a slender prism, this 1972 masterpiece of architect I. M. Pei – the same architect who created the pyramid now in the courtyard of the Louvre in Paris – attracts a great deal of attention. Nineteenth-century Trinity Church is reflected in its blue glass facade. The best view of Boston is from the observation deck on the fiftieth floor of the Prudential Tower. The view extends over the Charles River to Cambridge and, on clear days, all the way to that wonderful seaside recreation area, Cape Cod.

Centre: The reconstructed Beaver II in Boston Harbour is part of the Boston Tea Party Museum.

Bottom: Harvard Business School is famous well beyond Boston city limits.

USA

Detroit

FAMOUS AS AMERICA'S "MOTOR CITY", DETROIT HAS RULED THE NORTH AMERICAN CAR INDUSTRY EVER SINCE HENRY FORD OPENED HIS FIRST ASSEMBLY-LINE FACTORY AT THE START OF THE TWENTIETH CENTURY.

Given the way US cities developed, and the vast spaces between them, America is characterized by a lack of public transport. Owning a car is almost unavoidable, and parking lots and garages are a regular feature of the urban landscape. Despite its reputation as a grimy city of industry, Detroit's economy now depends largely on tourists drawn to the city itself and to the lakes and forests of the surrounding region.

The fort on the lake. The French officer Antoine de la Mothe, the Baron de Cadillac, founded Fort Pontchartrain d'Étroit on 24 July 1701. The fort became an important base in the fight for colonial control of the North American continent. The fort eventually fell into British hands when its French occupants surrendered without a fight on 29 September 1760. The British subsequently lost it to the United States in 1783 after the War of Independence.

Industrial city. Detroit became a booming industrial city in the mid-nineteenth century. It had excellent natural resources at its disposal, if less than outstanding transport connections. Its population grew. It was not only farmers and immigrants making their way west who settled the fertile land around the city; Detroit also attracted workers because of the promise of employment in the new factories and industries.

FACTS

* **Population of Detroit:** *circa* 951,300
* **Population of the metropolitan area:** *circa* 5.89 million
* **Places of interest:** Belle Isle, Charles H. Wright Museum of African - American History, Comerica Park, Detroit Institute of Arts, General Motors Headquarters Towers, General Motors World, Greektown, Grosse Pointe, Henry Ford Museum and Greenfield Village, Historic Fort Wayne, Motown Historical Museum, People Mover, Renaissance Center

FAMOUS CITIZENS

* **William Edward Boeing** (1881–1956), engineer
* **Francis Ford Coppola** (b. 1939), film director
* **Lily Tomlin** (b. 1939), comedian
* **Tom Selleck** (b. 1945), actor
* **Alice Cooper** (b. 1948), rock musician
* **Eminem** (b. 1972), rapper

Greektown is the place to visit in the centre of Detroit, where thriving shops and restaurants line the street.

Before long wealthy investors were happy to invest in the mass production of cars.

Pioneers of auto building. Detroit became the centre of American car production at the beginning of the twentieth century. The "Big Three", Chrysler, Ford and General Motors, made it 'Motor City'. During the 1920s, Detroit prospered and grew on a scale greater than any other industrial city in America. Building after building sprang up in its thriving city centre, where department stores and cinemas lined the streets.

After 1950, Detroit experienced a dramatic exodus. The middle class began to move out of the inner city and downtown area, relocating to the suburbs. As the city centre lost its population, it became less and less desirable from a commercial point of view. The restaurants, department stores and cinemas closed down, never to reopen. Today, about one-third of the city area is empty, full of abandoned buildings or vacant lots where they were torn down. About 4,000 buildings are still abandoned, locked, nailed shut and walled up. Rusty signs hang in the wind, and grass grows in the cracks of the pavements.

Renaissance. There have been many attempts made to revive the city. The 1970s' Detroit Renaissance Center, a steel-and-glass palace in the centre of town, is one of them. Its failure makes it the most conspicuous symbol of the city's decline. In the 1990s, the Greektown district was developed. Occupying just a few downtown blocks around Monroe Street, its restaurants, nightclubs and casinos, all presented with style and class, have been extraordinarily successful. Greektown's success makes it a worthwhile place to visit downtown. Its Greek-themed rows of shops and restaurants are lined up like a string of pearls, each with its own unique items on offer.

Above: Downtown Detroit at night.

Left: Comerica Park is the home of the Detroit Tigers, one of the country's most venerable Major League baseball teams.

USA

Chicago

ON A COLD DAY IN CHICAGO, WHEN BELOW-FREEZING TEMPERATURES AND STRONG, GUSTING WINDS OFF LAKE MICHIGAN MAKE PEOPLE RELUCTANT TO SET FOOT OUTSIDE, THE QUESTION MIGHT ARISE AS TO WHOSE IDEA IT WAS TO BUILD A CITY HERE.

Three million Chicagoans are able to stand up to it, however. They are happy to live here and they have their European, Asian and rural American ancestors to thank for it. This colourful mix built a city with amazing architecture, a unique jazz and blues tradition, universities loaded with Nobel Prize winners, and some of the most fanatical sports fans one can imagine.

"Checaugou" means "where the land smells of onions". As an old Algonquin legend says "the first white man to settle here was a black man". The name of this "black man" was Jean Baptiste Point du Sable. He was the son of a businessman from Québec and an African-American slave mother. In the 1770s, he founded a trading post on the spot where Chicago now stands. When it was connected to the railway system in the nineteenth century, it grew into the most important economic centre of the American Midwest.

The first skyscrapers on Earth. The Great Chicago Fire of October 1871 blazed for more than two days and destroyed almost one-third of the city. Chicago had to be rebuilt in a flash. Famous architects such as Louis Sullivan and Frank Lloyd Wright came to Chicago to work their magic. By the end of the nineteenth century, exploding property prices

Right: Lincoln Park with the two antennae of the John Hancock Center behind it.

Below: The Adler Planetarium on Lake Shore Drive.

forced property owners to build upwards. A few extra floors would not do; new buildings rose up into the sky. Innovations in construction and design made the first "skyscrapers" possible. In 1885, the steel-framed Home Insurance Building, at 39 metres high, was the tallest inhabited structure on Earth. Sadly, it was torn down in 1931.

Al Capone. At the beginning of the twentieth century, Chicago was famous around the world as the epitome of a crime-ridden and politically corrupt metropolis. There were riots, strikes, election frauds and abuses of power. The period following World War I was characterized by social and racial unrest, as well as an increase in organized crime, especially related to alcohol during Prohibition, much of which was under the control of Al Capone. The man known as "Scarface" owes his reputation to a number of screen adaptations based on his career. In the end, he went behind bars, convicted of tax evasion.

This is America. Today, Chicago is still a leader in urban architecture. The only city that has more skyscrapers than Chicago is New York, which is not surprising considering that this is where they began. Two of the most impressive freestanding structures in the world are found in Chicago. The John Hancock Center, at 457 metres, and the Sears Tower, at 527 metres (or 443 metres without its antennae), were each, for a time, the tallest building in the world. Given the number of former and current record holders among its giants, Chicago's skyline is cumulatively taller than that of New York City.

Chicago culture. This Midwestern city has much more to offer than its striking skyline and gritty reputation. The Adler Planetarium and Astronomy Museum are among the city's major attractions. Built in 1930, it is one of the oldest planetariums in North America. It is located on Lake Michigan, right behind the John G. Shedd Aquarium, the largest indoor aquarium in the world. The Field Museum of Natural History is also nearby.

Jazz, blues and soul. There is a long tradition of music in the "Windy City". A great number of important musicians were drawn to Chicago's music scene and played here. The hard-driving Chicago Blues developed out of a combination of urban swing jazz and Louisiana-Delta Blues. While Sixties flower power and the hippie sound became popular in San Francisco, the city on Lake Michigan was the home of Chicago Soul. Stylistically blending urban soul music with southern gospel, Etta James and Jackie Wilson were two of Chicago's most popular recording artists.

FACTS

- **Population of Chicago:** *circa* 2.86 million
- **Population of the metropolitan area:** *circa* 9.29 million
- **Places of interest:** Adler Planetarium, AON Center, Art Institute of Chicago, Brookfield Zoo, Goodman Theater, John Hancock Center, Merle Reskin Theater, Museum of Contemporary Art, Sears Tower, Shedd Aquarium, Fine Arts Building, Millennium Park, Symphony Hall, Lyric Opera

FAMOUS CITIZENS

- **Edgar Rice Burroughs** (1875–1950) and
- **Raymond Chandler** (1888–1959), writers
- **Walt Disney** (1901–66), creator of Mickey Mouse
- **Muddy Waters** (1915–83), Blues musician
- **Harrison Ford** (b. 1942), actor
- **Hillary Rodham Clinton** (b. 1947), politician

USA

New York City

THE FASCINATION GENERATED BY NEW YORK CITY IS HARD TO PUT INTO WORDS. THE SHEER NUMBER OF ATTRACTIONS WITHIN THE LARGEST CITY IN THE USA IS SIMPLY OVERWHELMING. AS MILLIONS OF VISITORS AGREE, NEW YORK CITY HAS IT ALL.

New York, the city of superlatives, is much more than the island of Manhattan. For over a century New York was the gateway to the "Promised Land", to an America of unlimited opportunity. Many people coming to New York today do so for different reasons than immigrants of yore. Tourists come to experience the fast pace of this vast metropolis. Who doesn't want to be part of the crowd in Times Square on New Year's Eve, if only once? Artists and intellectuals flock to New York to partake of the creative energy of city life, stimulated by first-class cultural institutions and events.

Manhattan. When explorer Henry Hudson, for whom the Hudson River is named, sailed into New York Bay in 1609, his enthusiastic description of New York's natural harbour sparked the interest of his Dutch sponsors. In 1624, they founded their first settlement on the island the Algonquin Indians called "Manahatta" ("hilly countryside"). The city of Nieuw Amsterdam was born in 1626 when the Dutch bought the island from the Algonquins for 60 Dutch gulden, or roughly $24. New Amsterdam became a British colony on 24 September 1664 as part of a treaty ending a war between Holland and England. The British victors changed the city's name to honour the Duke of York.

FACTS

✱ Population of New York: *circa* 8 million

✱ Population of the metropolitan area: *circa* 22.3 million

✱ Places of interest: American Museum of Natural History, Brooklyn Bridge, Carnegie Hall, St John the Divine Cathedral, Central Park, Chrysler Building, Ellis Island, Empire State Building, Flatiron Building, Statue of Liberty, Grand Central Station, Ground Zero, Metropolitan Opera, Museum of Modern Art, Riverside Church, Rockefeller Center, St Patrick's Cathedral, Guggenheim Museum, Trinity Church, Woolworth Building

The Statue of Liberty on Liberty Island greets those who arrive in New York by way of the sea. The working model of the original statue (2 m high) can be found in the Luxembourg Gardens in Paris.

The young republic. During the War of American Independence (1776–83), the British occupied New York City for nearly the entire war, and the city burned to the ground twice. Undeterred, New York City grew steadily following American independence. In 1788, New York was named the capital of the United States, a role taken over by Philadelphia two years later. New York developed into the economic centre of the USA instead. The establishment of the stock exchange on Wall Street in 1792 secured the city's reputation as the financial capital of the New World. Its harbours and shipyards took in goods, and hard-working immigrants, from all over the world.

War in the streets. Throughout the nineteenth century, New York was a great construction zone, with new homes and parks erected almost daily. Central Park, laid out in 1858–66, was one of many public-works projects of the time. Beloved by New Yorkers as well as tourists, Central Park is still a popular place to stroll, have a picnic and especially to people-watch. In the nineteenth century, the newer parts of New York were laid out in its characteristic grid system; only Broadway and the older part of the city south of Washington Square lie outside the draughtsboard pattern of streets. As the century proceeded, more and more emigrants from Europe arrived in the fast-growing city. Violence and unrest came with them. Most newcomers had to settle, at least initially, in slums like the infamous Five Points and Bowery. In July 1863, at the height of the American Civil War, the so-called Draft Riots broke out, violent confrontation between long-time New Yorkers and recent immigrants. The bloody street fights led to at least 120 deaths over four days of chaos. Over 100 buildings were destroyed, most of them burned to the ground. The Martin Scorsese movie *Gangs of New York* is a memorable recreation of this unsettled time.

Above: The United Nations Building at United Nations Plaza is an easily recognizable part of the New York skyline.

Left: Central Park was laid out between 1858 and 1866.

The Brooklyn Bridge crossing the East River was completed in 1883.

New York boomed in the 1920s, as did many American cities, riding a wave of enthusiasm based on unrestricted trade on the stock market. Some of the money generated flowed into building the New York skyline. In 1913, the Woolworth building, at 222 metres, was the tallest in the world. Construction of the buildings that would surpass it, the Chrysler and Empire State Buildings, was well under way when the intoxicating binge came to an end. The hangover that followed was brutal. On 24 October 1929, "Black Thursday", it all collapsed like a house of cards. The city sank under the weight of a mountain of debts. Countless people were put out of work, bankrupted and made homeless overnight. The unemployment rate soared above 25 per cent.

Manhattan, city of theatres. Today, New York is once again the centre of international finance. In 1945 it became a centre of international diplomacy when it was chosen as the seat of the United Nations. Despite these distinctions, New York is probably best known as a beacon of culture. There is no other city with as many art galleries, museums and theatres. Living in the cultural and artistic centre of the USA, New Yorkers enjoy an international reputation as trendsetters par excellence. In New York, where there are over forty theatres around Times Square alone, lovers of the stage are confronted with a wealth of options. For music lovers, the Metropolitan Opera, founded in 1883 and known as the "Met", is located in nearby Lincoln Center. From the Empire (opened in 1893) to the Lyceum (opened in 1903), the New York theatre scene offers something for everyone.

There is just so much to see. New York's museums, whether devoted to art, science or history, make internationally famous collections accessible to one and all. The American Museum of Natural History is one of the oldest and largest natural science museums in the world. Its five storeys and over 30 million items on exhibit offer much more than can be experienced in a single day. Art lovers are also richly rewarded. MoMa, the Museum of Modern Art, houses one of the world's most important collections of the twentieth century through contemporary painting, sculpture and design. Its 2002–2004 facelift cost $70 million. While MoMa was under construction, museums around the world were able to exhibit a host of modern masterpieces, all on loan from New York.

A street-level view of Manhattan's Empire State Building – for nearly 40 years it was the tallest building in the world. To its right is the Chrysler Building.

FAMOUS CITIZENS

* **Walt Whitman** (1819–92), poet
* **Louis Comfort Tiffany** (1848–1933), artist
* **Humphrey Bogart** (1899–1957), actor
* **Lou Gehrig** (1903–1941), baseball player
* **Robert Oppenheimer** (1904–67), physicist
* **Arthur Miller** (1915–2005), writer
* **Aaron Copeland** (1900–90) and **Leonard Bernstein** (1918–90), composers
* **Andy Warhol** (1928–87), artist
* **Stanley Kubrick** (1928–1999), director
* **Al Pacino** (b. 1940) and * **Robert de Niro** (b. 1943), actors

Lady Liberty stands tall on her towering pedestal on Liberty Island in Upper New York Bay, greeting all who enter New York Harbor. Gustave Eiffel, who built the Eiffel Tower, fashioned its enormous iron frame, with the statue itself the work of sculptor Frédéric Auguste Bartholdi. France's gift of friendship was dedicated in 1886 after a "short" delay. The statue had been planned for the hundredth anniversary of the USA ten years earlier, but it took longer than expected to raise the funds for its pedestal. Most boat tours to Liberty Island depart from Battery Park at the south end of Manhattan. Some tour boats also head for Ellis Island, once the "Gateway to America". In its great hall and warren of offices, nearly seventeen million emigrants suffered through the formalities of immigration. Today, these buildings house the Ellis Island Immigration Museum.

The Brooklyn Bridge. There is no end of important architecture here, by no means limited to high-rises, although with some 5,500 buildings over twelve storeys high, New York is certainly a city full of towers and skyscrapers. The few remaining colonial-period and many nineteenth-century buildings are of interest, as are the bridges joining Manhattan to the mainland. When it opened in 1883, the Brooklyn Bridge was the longest suspension bridge on Earth. In order to determine its safe working load, the P. T. Barnum Circus, with numerous elephants in tow, crossed the bridge before it was opened to the public.

Greenwich Village is a Manhattan neighbourhood bounded by 14th Street, Houston Street, the Hudson River to the west and Broadway to the east. Home to New York University, "the Village" is a popular residential area. Its claim to fame, however, is as a bohemian district of street artists, cafés and experimental theatre. Artists and musicians from all over the city and the world began their careers here, including Bob Dylan, Andy Warhol, photographer Robert Mapplethorpe and choreographer Martha Graham.

September 11th, 2001. The unimaginable happened on a Tuesday in September 2001 when two airplanes crashed into the Twin Towers of the World Trade Center. Over 3,000 people died. The world held its breath. At Ground Zero, where the Twin Towers once stood, the new Freedom Tower will eventually be built, along with a museum devoted to peace. The empty "footprints" where the original towers stood will remain visible.

Centre: Wall Street with the New York Stock Exchange.

Bottom: View of Times Square from above, the heart of the American theatre world.

USA

Denver

DENVER, THE CAPITAL OF COLORADO, IS ONE OF AMERICA'S YOUNGEST MAJOR CITIES. LOCATED ON A ROCKY MOUNTAIN PLATEAU AT AN ELEVATION NEARLY 1.5 KM ABOVE SEA LEVEL, DENVER IS ONE OF THE FASTEST-GROWING CITIES IN THE AMERICAN WEST.

Denver offers a unique mix of the "Old West" and a cityscape dominated by skyscrapers and modern architecture. With over 200 parks and gardens, Denver also has more green space in proportion to its total area than any other city in the country. Local interest in preservation of the area's historical legacy is reflected in Denver's carefully restored streets and protected natural areas. With an average of 300-plus days of sunshine per year, more than Miami, Denver is also the "brightest" city in North America. **Denver was founded** on the South Platte River in 1858, following the discovery of gold the previous year. The early years were very difficult for the pioneers. The new city had to overcome floods, devastating fires, Indian attacks and even raids by Confederate troops during the American Civil War. Throughout the nineteenth century, repeated discoveries of gold in the Rocky Mountains turned Denver into a boom town. Saloons and casinos opened their doors, making Denver not only an attraction for settlers on the westward trail, but also a hideout for outlaws. As one railway line after another made its way to Denver, the city soon became an important transport hub. By 1870, the Denver Pacific, Kansas Pacific and Colorado Central Railroads all made stops in Denver.

Right: 16th Street runs through the heart of the city.

Below: The Colorado State Capitol was built in 1890.

Bullish trends. At the turn of the twentieth century, surplus profits were invested in the beautification of the city. The first of many parks were laid out, statues were erected, and ordinary streets were transformed into picturesque boulevards. Denver was by far the most elegant city within a radius of a thousand kilometres. Few western cities could compete. While the energy crisis at the end of the 1970s slowed the pace of Denver's rapid growth, by 2005 the city's population had more than doubled since 1960. Today, Denver remains one of the fastest-growing cities in the USA.

No Olympics. Denver was short-listed to host the 1976 Olympic Winter Games, but the governor of Colorado, Richard Lamm, turned down the opportunity because of the high costs associated. No one in Denver or Colorado seems to have taken it amiss. On the contrary, the frugal Lamm was repeatedly re-elected, remaining in office from 1974 to 1987. A decision that would have been politically disastrous in most cities had the opposite effect in Denver. Instead of being voted out of office, Richard Lamm became the longest-serving governor in Colorado state history.

Photography prohibited. The frugal nature of its citizenry aside, Denver is home to one of the two United States Mints. Ten thousand million coins are struck here each year. Denver is also America's second-largest repository for gold bullion, which is stored here on its way to Fort Knox in Kentucky. Visitors are welcome to tour the mint facilities, where admission is free, but care must be taken to follow the rules. Taking photographs, for example, is strictly prohibited!

Where *Dynasty* was filmed. During the energy boom of the 1980s, Denver became associated with luxurious living thanks to the popular television series *Dynasty*, much of which was filmed nearby. The skyscrapers that rise above the south end of the 16th Street Mall formed the backdrop to the opening credits. Open only to pedestrians and a shuttle bus, the 16th Street Mall forms the core of Denver's historic central area. The long boulevard (about 1 km) is lined with decorative trees, flower beds and benches. Numerous boutiques, department stores and cafés beckon to visitors strolling along its spotless pavements. The Cherry Creek shopping district is also close to the city centre. Along its tree-lined streets, visitors can find over 420 department stores, boutiques, art galleries, cafés and restaurants. Needless to say, Alexis Carrington and Crystal Carrington shopped here, too.

FACTS

* **Population of Denver:** *circa* 556,900
* **Population of the metropolitan area:** *circa* 2.6 million
* **Places of interest:** Black American West Museum and Heritage Center, Brown Palace Hotel, Buckhorn Exchange, Buffalo Bill's Grave and Museum, Colorado State Capitol, Confluence Park, Denver Art Museum, Denver Zoo, Four Mile House, Molly Brown House Museum, Red Rocks Park, Richthofen Castle, Pepsi Center, home of the Denver Nuggets

FAMOUS CITIZENS

* **Ruth Handler** (1916–2002), inventor of the Barbie doll
* **Debra Paget** (b. 1933), actress
* **John Kerry** (b. 1943), politician
* **Tim Allen** (b. 1953), actor and comedian

USA

St. Louis

ST. LOUIS LIES JUST SOUTH OF THE CONFLUENCE OF THE MISSISSIPPI AND MISSOURI RIVERS. BIRTHPLACE OF THE GREAT AMERICAN POET T.S. ELIOT, ST. LOUIS BEGAN AS A STARTING PLACE FOR ADVENTURERS, TRAPPERS AND PIONEERS OPENING UP THE WEST.

St. Louis, today a modern business, industrial and culture centre, is still a place where east meets west. This cosmopolitan metropolis has a noticeably European flair. Immigrant Spaniards, French and Germans have all left traces of their legacies behind. Mississippi River culture is also lovingly preserved; Ragtime, Dixieland, Blues and Jazz music can still be heard on the banks of the mighty river. St Louis also produced the wild Rock 'n' Roll of Chuck Berry, one of the city's most famous native sons.

Fifteen million dollars. In 1763, a French trader named Pierre Laclède built a trading post in the area that is now St. Louis. The city, named after King Louis IX of France, was founded one year later on 15 February 1764. It soon fell under Spanish rule, but was returned to France when Napoleon I sold it to the United States in 1803 as part of the Louisiana Purchase. Soon afterwards, President Thomas Jefferson launched an expedition from St. Louis, sending explorers Meriweather Louis and William Clark, among others, out into the vast expanse of newly acquired territories to see just what America had got for its $15 million.

Gateway to the west. As the gateway to the west, St. Louis played a decisive role in the pioneer history of the United States. During the early nineteenth

Beer has been brewed at the Anheuser-Busch Brewery in St. Louis since 1870, an important legacy of St. Louis's German-American citizens.

FACTS

*** Population of St. Louis:** *circa* 348,000

*** Population of the metropolitan area:** *circa* 2.6 million

*** Places of interest:** Forest Park, Gateway Arch, Laclède's Landing, Memorial Plaza, Missouri Botanical Garden, Scott Joplin Museum, Six Flags Over Mid-America, St. Louis Art Museum and Union Station

FAMOUS CITIZENS

*** Mark Twain** (1835–1910), writer

*** T. S. Eliot** (1888–1965), author (Nobel Prize 1945)

*** Charles Lindbergh** (1902–74), aviator

*** Josephine Baker** (1906–75), entertainer

*** Miles Davis** (1926–91), jazz musician

*** Jackie Joyner-Kersee** (b. 1962), Olympic athlete

century, it was the most important departure point for parts unknown, and very much one of the last outposts of familiar civilization. Countless settlers stopped here along the pioneer trail. The Gateway Arch, a 192-metre-high steel arch, commemorates the role the city played. Since its completion in 1965, this impressive, immense piece of sculpture has served as the emblem of St. Louis. A special cable car travels up to the highest point of the arch, where there is an observation deck. Beneath it, replicas of paddle-wheel steamboats depart on river tours up and down the Mississippi and Missouri Rivers.

"Prost"! The influx of settlers from the East Coast of the United States reached a high point once St. Louis was connected to the railways in 1857. A great number of emigrants from Germany came here, and they eventually made up one-third of the city's population. They brought their homeland traditions with them to America, many of which, including Oktoberfest and Badenfest, have been preserved to this day. The immigrants also brought the art of beer brewing to St. Louis. The Anheuser-Busch Brewery, maker of Budweiser beer, is currently one of the largest breweries in the world.

The city's green heart. The year 1904 marked a high point in the history of St. Louis. In that year, both the Olympic Games and the World's Fair took place here. The World's Fair grounds were located west of the city centre in Forest Park. Forest Park is still one of America's most beautiful urban parks. Its woodlands, lakes and splendid buildings occupy a space even larger than New York's Central Park. Recently refurbished for its hundredth anniversary, the park is full of tourist destinations, including the famous St. Louis Art Museum. Built on top of Art Hill, this beaux-arts-style museum is the last surviving structure from the 1904 World's Fair. It houses approximately 30,000 objects, including international works of art from all periods. Its collection of German Expressionist art is considered one of the largest and most important in the world.

Centre: The old St. Louis Courthouse.

Bottom: Steamboats have been a familiar sight on the Mississippi River for nearly 200 years.

USA

Washington, DC

WASHINGTON DC IS NOT A STATE, BUT AS A FEDERAL DISTRICT, IT IS MUCH MORE THAN A CITY. THE DISTRICT OF COLUMBIA WAS ESTABLISHED IN 1790 AS A PLACE WHERE THE US CONGRESS, SENATORS AND PRESIDENT COULD GATHER TO GOVERN THE COUNTRY.

The capital of the United States welcomes some twenty million visitors every year. Many have business at one of the over 140 government agencies. Others visit the city for its many tourist attractions. With the White House, Capitol and so much more, Washington DC is world-famous for its monuments and museums. Founded in a swamp on the Potamac, it has become a cultural and intellectual centre matched by few.

Back to the drawing board. Pierre Charles L'Enfant (1755–1825), a Frenchman who had fought against the British at the side of George Washington, submitted his plans for the new capital in 1792. Construction began that same year with the laying of the cornerstone of the White House at 1600 Pennsylvania Avenue. The land for the new city lay on the banks of the Potomac River, on territory claimed by both Maryland and Virginia. Washington himself is said to have selected the spot. The capital was already called the "City of Washington" as early as 1791, a name it formally assumed after George Washington's death. The government set the first Thursday in December 1800 as the date for completion of the city, a deadline that would prove difficult to meet.

Washington in crisis. After just a few months of construction, L'Enfant had a falling out with the

FACTS

✻ **Population of Washington:** *circa* 553,500

✻ **Population of the metropolitan area (including Baltimore):** *circa* 8 million

✻ **Places of interest:** Jefferson Memorial, John F. Kennedy Center for the Performing Arts, Hirshhorn Museum, Lincoln Memorial, National Gallery of Art, National Museum of the American Indian, Smithsonian Institution, United States Capitol Building, Vietnam Veterans Memorial, Washington Monument, White House and United States Holocaust Memorial Museum

FAMOUS CITIZENS

✻ **John Foster Dulles** (1888–1959), politician

✻ **J. Edgar Hoover** (1895–1972), founder of the FBI

✻ **Marvin Gaye** (1939–84), soul singer

The US House of Representatives and the Senate convene in the Capitol Building.

project engineer, Benjamin Banneker. After sulking for several weeks, he resigned, or perhaps Banneker fired him. Today there is a monument in Washington commemorating L'Enfant and his design. The new capital has certainly had its ups and downs. Washington DC was barely finished and only partially inhabited when British troops captured it in 1814 during the War of 1812. The Capitol Building, sitting unfinished on a small hill at the east end of the Mall, was burned to the ground. For decades, the city languished in a deep economic depression. It was many years before a new Capitol, seat of the House of Representatives and the Senate, could be rebuilt.

John F. Kennedy. In the course of an early twentieth-century beautification plan, a decorative landscaping program was instigated leading to the construction of numerous parks and the refurbishment of the city's many monuments. Nevertheless, Washington had to contend with its image as a provincial town until well into the twentieth century. President John F. Kennedy was the first to promote it as "a city with a blend of Southern charm and Northern efficiency". The Kennedy Centre for the Performing Arts was built as a memorial to JFK, giving this city of bureaucrats a cosmopolitan atmosphere and access to culture that had been sorely lacking.

On September 11th, 2001, Washington DC was targeted by terrorists when a hijacked airliner crashed into the Pentagon. At the same time, two airplanes flew at full speed into the World Trade Center in New York. Ongoing security measures for the most important government buildings remain in place and the damaged sections of the Pentagon have been rebuilt. Tourists are also returning to Washington to enjoy the 4-km-long National Mall with its dense concentration of enticing museums – many of which are free of charge – and monuments.

Above: The Smithsonian Castle is part of the great museum district.

Left: The White House, the official residence of the president of the United States.

USA

San Francisco

SAN FRANCISCO IS A JEWEL OF A CITY. THE GOLDEN GATE BRIDGE, ALCATRAZ AND CABLE CARS RUNNING UP AND DOWN ITS STEEP HILLS ARE JUST A FEW OF THE UNIQUE ATTRACTIONS OF THIS RENOWNED GATHERING PLACE OF UNCONVENTIONAL THINKERS.

San Francisco, long home to romantics, dreamers and creative thinkers, has never stopped attracting visitors from all over the world. San Francisco is truly multicultural, with every European nation represented and Latin American and Asian flavours pervading its atmosphere. Perhaps because the next earthquake, locally referred to as the "The Big One", is a foregone and scientifically proven conclusion, a mood of *carpe diem* (Latin for "seize the day") prevails.

Upswing following the Gold Rush. The Ohlone tribe were the first to settle in the San Francisco Bay area, which they called the "Edge of the World". Europeans first entered San Francisco Bay in 1775. Settlement began in 1776 with the founding of Mission Dolores, the only building in a town the Spanish called San Francisco de Asís (St. Francis of Assisi). The mission buildings have survived until the present day. Not far from the mission, American settlers founded a city named Yerba Buena, located in what is now the bustling centre of San Francisco. San Francisco was the gateway for fur trappers, pioneers and settlers long before it became a destination for those seeking gold. The 1848 California Gold Rush brought wealth, but also vice, with street crime kept under control by lynch-happy local militias.

Right: The former prison of Alcatraz perches on an island in San Francisco Bay.

Below: Cable cars are a familiar part of San Francisco life.

As the Gold Rush waned, San Francisco flourished as a banking centre. Fine hotels, elegant houses and many theatres and restaurants lined its boulevards. **Earthquakes motivate.** Located along the San Andreas fault, San Francisco has always been prone to earthquakes. The city was especially hard hit by "The Big One", an earthquake measuring 8.3 on the Richter scale, on 18 April 1906. The quake set off a series of catastrophic fires that quickly raged out of control, destroying nearly the entire city. Still, San Francisco was up and running again by the 1920s. During the worldwide Great Depression, the Golden Gate Bridge and the Bay Bridge were constructed as part of Franklin D. Roosevelt's New Deal. World War II also benefited the city economically. A large part of the United States Navy Pacific Fleet was assembled and launched from Treasure Island, a military base in the middle of San Francisco Harbor.

The Summer of Love and its painful aftermath. The Sixties belonged to San Francisco dreamers like Scott McKenzie, the singer who drew an entire generation to the city with his song "San Francisco". The city on the bay was in the throes of a social revolution in favour of feminism, gay rights and free speech. Growing political activism and experimentation with drugs fuelled the 1969 "Summer of Love", accompanied by the music of bands including the Grateful Dead and Jefferson Airplane. The Summer of Love collapsed across the country in race riots and confrontations with the police. In San Francisco, gay-rights activists continued to clash with authorities well into the 1970s.

Tourist destination San Francisco. There is much for tourists to see and do in San Francisco. There are churches, including the original Mission Dolores. Museums include the Exploratorium, the Museum of Asian Art, the Cable Car Museum and the San Francisco Museum of Modern Art. Parks such as the Golden Gate, Buena Vista and Yerba Buena provide idyllic views of one of the most beautiful natural urban landscapes in the world. Fisherman's Wharf and Pier 39, famous for their many cafés, bars and restaurants, are must-sees. Although it has been a long time since this area has had anything to do with fishing, fantastic seafood restaurants abound. Finally, one must mention Alcatraz, the erstwhile high-security prison perched on an island in San Francisco Bay and made famous in countless movies and television shows. Its inmates were a cross section of American crime, and even infamous Chicago gang boss Al Capone served a sentence on "The Rock".

FACTS

* **Population of San Francisco:** *circa* 744,000
* **Population of the metropolitan area:** *circa* 4.16 million
* **Places of interest:** Alcatraz, Buena Vista Park, Cable Car Museum, California Academy of Science, Coit Tower, Exploratorium, Fisherman's Wharf, Lombard Street, Grace Cathedral, Mission Dolores, Pier 39, San Francisco Museum of Modern Art, Telegraph Hill.

FAMOUS CITIZENS

* **Jack London** (1876–1916), writer
* **Isadora Duncan** (1877–1927), dancer
* **Clint Eastwood** (b. 1930), actor
* **Dian Fossey** (1932–85), zoologist
* **Bruce Lee** (1940–73), actor and martial artist

USA

Las Vegas

LAS VEGAS IS A MOST IMPROBABLE PLACE. RISING FROM THE DESERT, THE FAMED STRIP GLITTERS WITH THE LIGHTS OF ONE FANTASTIC ESTABLISHMENT AFTER ANOTHER, EACH MORE GRANDIOSE THAN THE LAST. AND YES, THERE ARE A LOT OF WEDDING CHAPELS.

More than thirty-five million people a year are drawn to the gambling metropolis of Las Vegas in the middle of the Nevada desert. Yet there is more than gambling going on here. Only 25 per cent of the city's income comes from gambling-related industries; tourists increasingly come for the shows, boxing matches and glamour that make Las Vegas an unforgettable vacation paradise.

Gambling on success. In 1865, the United States Army built Fort Baker where Las Vegas stands today. Because of water sources in the open tracts of land nearby, the "vegas" that give the city its name, a town grew up around the base. It soon became an important jumping-off point for the exploration of the surrounding country. It would be a long time, however, before the settlement around Fort Baker developed into a city. A population surge in 1905 led to a demand for additional plots of land, leading to the incorporation of the City of Las Vegas on 15th May of that year. The construction of the Hoover Dam on the Colorado River in the 1930s provided the young metropolis with ample electricity. The blue waters of Lake Mead retained by the dam are a startling feature in the middle of the dry desert landscape. Much the same can be said of the bright lights of Las Vegas itself.

An enormous canopy provides shade for the pedestrian path through the Fremont Street experience.

FACTS

✻ **Population of Las Vegas:** *circa* 534,900

✻ **Population of the metropolitan area:** *circa* 1.7 million

✻ **Places of interest:** Bellagio, Caesar's Palace, Death Valley, Excalibur Hotel, Hoover Dam, The Luxor, The Mirage, New York-New York Hotel, Paris Las Vegas, Red Rock Canyon and Treasure Island.

FAMOUS CITIZENS

✻ **Pat Morita** (1932–2005), actress

✻ **Andre Agassi** (b. 1970), tennis player

✻ **Charisma Carpenter** (b. 1970), actress

Las Vegas began to grow rapidly after gambling was legalized in Nevada following the repeal of Prohibition. In the 1940s, gang boss Bugsy Siegel built the first Las Vegas hotel that had its own gambling casino. Others soon followed, triggering a wave of development that still seems to have no end in sight. More recently, the residential areas of the city have expanded far out into the desert, where demands on water and sewage facilities have strained the fragile infrastructure to breaking point.

Casinos are still the main attraction, however. A drive along Las Vegas Boulevard, better known as "The Strip", makes this perfectly clear. In every direction the eye beholds casino hotels in the shape of gigantic pyramids accompanied by the Sphinx, an Eiffel Tower, a knight's castle, a fire-breathing volcano or a miniature New York City. It is all part of a sea of flashing light and neon signs. In addition to casino gambling, stage shows featuring top stars are a big attraction. Las Vegas has always been a place to go for a good show, beginning with the days when Frank Sinatra, Dean Martin and Sammy Davis, Jr were the most popular performers.

Fremont Street. There are shopping opportunities galore on the Strip. Although most hotels and casinos have their very own inclusive shopping centres, the main retail area of Las Vegas is located along Fremont Street. Visitors can stroll through a pedestrian zone shaded by a huge canopy offering protection from the hot desert sun. At night, the approximately 2 million lights strung across the canopy produce a colourful effect.

Day trips in every direction. Not interested in the Hoover Dam? Then how about the Grand Canyon? It is 800 km from Las Vegas, and the drive is a lot of fun. If the Grand Canyon seems too far, visit the much closer Red Rock Canyon National Conservation Area. Countless Hollywood Westerns were shot among its impressive red-rock formations. The beauty of the light reflecting off the canyon walls, especially at sunrise and sunset, is almost impossible to describe. Valley of Fire State Park, 55 km north of Las Vegas, is also famous for its rock formations. Over a period of 150 million years, time, wind and weather have worn away the sandstone blocks into a wide variety of figures and shapes, many of which sport fanciful names. Elephant Rock is one of the best known and grandest of these natural sculptures.

Centre: Caesar's Palace is one of the truly classic Las Vegas experiences.

Bottom: Marriage made easy, as here in the Little White Chapel.

USA

Los Angeles

LOS ANGELES IS CALIFORNIA'S BIGGEST CITY. DOWNTOWN, HOLLYWOOD, THE WESTSIDE AND THE GLAMOROUS SUBURBS OF SANTA MONICA, MALIBU AND VENICE BEACH FORM A CONTINUOUS URBAN WONDERLAND FROM THE HOLLYWOOD HILLS TO THE PACIFIC.

The city's original name was El Pueblo de Nuestra Señora de Reina de los Angeles de Porciuncula, which means "The City of Our Blessed Lady, Queen of the Angels of Porciuncula". Now, it's Los Angeles, or simply LA. Its historical name does have a little in common with today's city: in popular perception, Los Angeles spreads across much of southern California. What we call Los Angeles is not a single municipality, however, but an assemblage of suburbs, independent communities and beach towns. The actual incorporated City of Los Angeles is but a small part.

Let's go to Hollywood. Los Angeles was founded on 4 September 1781, more than 200 years after the Spanish first set foot in California. The city quickly became a melting pot for diverse immigrants and international culture. Americans, Chinese and Spaniards all lived here together before the USA annexed the city in 1850. It was a few more years before the railway finally reached southern California and Los Angeles. Rapid development ensued. Coal mining was already an important part of the economy when oil was discovered in 1892. People started pouring into California from all over the country and the world. Even in the early twentieth century, Los Angeles was still rapidly expanding. A very

FACTS

* Population of Los Angeles: *circa* 3.87 million
* Population of the metropolitan area: *circa* 17.55 million
* Places of interest: The Bradbury Office Building, Dodger Stadium, Disneyland, El Pueblo de Los Angeles State Historic Park, Getty Museum Center, Grauman's Chinese Theater, Griffith Park, Hollywood Bowl, Our Lady of the Angels Cathedral, Library Tower, Ocean Front Walk, Walt Disney Concert Hall

FAMOUS CITIZENS

* Raymond Chandler (1888–1959), writer
* Ayn Rand (1905–82), writer, philospher
* Marilyn Monroe (1926–62), actress
* Frank Gehry (b. 1929), architect
* David Hockney (b. 1937), artist

Many thousands of film and recording artists.

Rodeo Drive in Hollywood is one of the most exclusive shopping addresses in Los Angeles.

young motion-picture industry blossomed as production companies moved from New York to Los Angeles, where the dry, sunny climate meant less filming time would be lost due to bad weather.

Beverly Hills is a world-famous enclave of the rich and beautiful. Anyone able to own a house here has really "made it", but not necessarily in the film industry. Successful people from all walks of life live in super-luxurious mansions. In Beverly Hills, high society rubs shoulders with actors, musicians and star athletes. Scouts, or guides, offer visitors tours that promise a glimpse of Beverly Hills celebrities or, at the very least, a look at the outside of their homes.

The celebrated Hollywood Walk of Fame covers the pavement on both sides of Hollywood Boulevard. At Vine Street, it turns a corner and runs three more blocks between Sunset Boulevard and Yucca Street. More than 2200 prominent film and entertainment industry figures have their names immortalized here, accompanied by an inlaid pink terrazzo star.

When architect Frank O. Gehry memorably enhanced his own little house in Santa Monica by covering it with chicken wire and angular iron bars, his less than appreciative neighbours tried to get him thrown out of town. Today the whole world looks in awe at Gehry's most recent architectural masterpiece in the centre of LA. The shimmering, steel-clad, stylistically daring Walt Disney Concert Hall, home to the Los Angeles Philharmonic, is one of the most admired modern buildings in the city.

Still, many visitors are less interested in architecture than the Pacific beaches. Venice Beach and its most famous drag, Ocean Front Walk, have appeared in countless Hollywood films. Santa Monica is another of California's venerable beach towns. As the many tourists strolling along its sands can attest, surfers and local beauties are still part of the landscape.

Above: The beach at Malibu was one of the sets for the popular television series *Baywatch*.

Left: The Walt Disney Concert Hall opened in 2003.

USA

Dallas

DALLAS, FONDLY CALLED "BIG D" BY ITS RESIDENTS, HOLDS A UNIQUE STATUS IN TEXAS FOR MANY REASONS. THE URBAN CONGLOMERATION KNOWN AS DALLAS–FORT WORTH IS ONE OF THE MOST IMPORTANT BUSINESS AND FINANCE CENTRES IN THE AMERICAN SOUTH-WEST.

Dallas, once a town populated by cowboys and large herds of cattle, is now a modern, teeming business metropolis with soaring high-rise buildings and luxurious commercial development. Its cultural offerings are also impressive. Dallas boasts an arts district of a quality that few other American cities can match. The city's bars, restaurants and entertainment options are rich and varied, complemented, of course, by its outstanding shopping opportunities. In fact, Dallas has more shopping centres than any other US city.

From oil to J.R. Ewing. The first pioneers founded Dallas as a trading post in 1846, and by the end of the nineteenth century Dallas was already the biggest city in Texas. The discovery of oil in 1930 made Dallas a boom town for business and industry. On 22 November 1963, the city gained notoriety in a tragic way when President John F. Kennedy was assassinated while travelling with a motorcade through its streets. Overnight, the city became associated with negative headlines. It would be decades before Dallas recovered from the shock. Then along came the TV series *Dallas*, which ran from 1978 to 1991 and was wildly popular for a time, featuring the villainous figure of J.R. Ewing. Played

Right: The Old Red Courthouse dates to the 19th century.

Below: Old City Park is an open-air museum on nearly 5 hectares in the heart of Dallas.

brilliantly by Larry Hagman, the character met with mixed reviews in the real Dallas. Still, there was no denying that the hit television show revived the city and gave it a new, thoroughly positive image. Even today, the working ranch that served as the model for the fictional Ewing family's Southfork is a popular tourist attraction.

The spirit of JFK. Dallas is also coming to terms with the shadows of its past. The Sixth Floor Museum, which houses collections related to the Kennedy assassination, was dedicated in 1993. It is located in the former Texas School Book Depository, where the assassin fired the fatal shots at the president out of one of its windows. Out of respect for the Kennedy family, the actual window is not accessible to the public. The museum's exhibits highlight Kennedy's life, work and legacy, as well as the impact of his death on the American people and the world. Photographs, films, documents and other artefacts shed light on the social and political climate of the early 1960s, the events of 22 November 1963, and John Fitzgerald Kennedy's abiding influence on American history. John F. Kennedy is also memorialized in the historic district, where a white limestone monument was dedicated to him in 1970. According its architect, Philip Johnson, the open roof symbolizes "the freedom of JFK's spirit". The interior of the monument is empty, except for a simple marble plaque engraved with his name.

Where it all began. Dominated by futuristic skyscrapers, Dallas also has a number of historical attractions. Among them is the Dallas County Historical Plaza, the very place where the settlement of the city began. John Neely Bryan, the colonist from Tennessee who founded Dallas, built a log cabin at this location in 1841, and a reproduction of the original is on display. At the living museum in Old City Park, the history of the Texas pioneers is vividly and realistically recreated. The open-air museum houses, which is spread out over nearly 5 hectares, is a collection of 38 buildings dating from the period between 1840 and 1910, including farm buildings, elegant Victorian houses, a train depot, a general store, a physician's office, a restaurant and also a typical saloon. "Residents" in historical dress lead visitors on an exciting journey back in time to the days of the wild, wild west.

FACTS

* **Population of Dallas:** *circa* 1.2 million
* **Population of the metropolitan area:** *circa* 6 million
* **Places of interest:** American Museum of Miniature Arts, City Hall, Dallas County Historical Plaza, Dallas Museum of Arts (DMA), Dallas Museum of Natural History, Pioneer Plaza, Old City Park, Reunion Tower, Sixth Floor Museum, Conspiracy Museum, Women's Museum

FAMOUS CITIZENS

* **Erykah Badu** (b. 1971), soul singer
* **T-Bone Walker** (1910–75) and
* **Stevie Ray Vaughan** (1954–90) Blues musicians
* **Meat Loaf** (b. 1947), rock singer and actor

USA

San Diego

LIFE IN SAN DIEGO TAKES PLACE MAINLY OUTDOORS. BICYCLES HAVE SURFBOARD RACKS, AND PEOPLE WILL TELL YOU THAT THEY DRIVE A PICKUP TRUCK BECAUSE THEIR SURFBOARD FITS BETTER THAN IT DOES IN A CAR.

Surfing can happen any time of day. People surf in the morning before work, during lunch breaks and at sunset after work. Neoprene suits are as much a part of the San Diego scene as pinstripes and ties in other cities. With its long stretch of beaches, more than 100 km of them, and its endlessly perfect weather, the San Diego lifestyle is special, even by Californian standards.

The Franciscan Mission. San Diego is located on the south coast of California, not far from the Mexican border. The city sits on a large bay, well protected by the surrounding flat peninsulas. It was this ideal natural harbour that led the Spanish missionary Father Junipero Serra to establish the Mission of San Diego de Alcalá here in 1769. A Portuguese explorer in the service of the Spanish, named Juan Cabrillo, had arrived in the region long before (1542), naming the coastline "San Miguel". It only become San Diego in 1602, when Father Serra dedicated his mission to St. James, "San Diego" in Spanish.

Military success. In 1850, annexation by the USA boosted San Diego's development from a mission town to an important port city. When gold was discovered in 1869, the whole region around San Diego boomed. Within a few years, railways had been built connecting this most distant south-western corner of

Old Town San Diego Historic Park transports visitors back to the 19th century.

FACTS

✱ **Population of San Diego:** *circa* 1.28 million

✱ **Population of the metropolitan area:** *circa* 3 million

✱ **Places of interest:** Balboa Park, Eagle Mine, Old Town San Diego Historic Park, La Jolla Playhouse, Miramar Airfield and Museum, Mission Basilica San Diego de Alcalá, Mission Bay, Oceanside Beach, Old Town, Point Loma, San Diego Zoo and SeaWorld San Diego.

FAMOUS CITIZENS

✱ **Gregory Peck** (1916–2003), actor

✱ **Robert Duvall** (b. 1931), actor

✱ **Barbara Hambly** (b. 1951), fantasy writer

✱ **Cameron Diaz** (b. 1972), actress

Centre: San Diego is a paradise for water-sports enthusiasts, especially sailors.

Bottom: SeaWorld San Diego is one of the largest marine parks in the world.

the United States with the rest of the nation. San Diego also profited from completion of the Panama Canal in 1914 and from resident Army, Navy and Marine Corps bases. During World War II, San Diego was the second largest military port in the country, after New York Harbor. After that war, San Diego's population soared when many soldiers and sailors who had been stationed there chose to stay to work in the thriving shipbuilding and construction industries. Since the end of the Cold War, the military is no longer a dominant industry, becoming less important every year. Biotech and telecommunications industries, thriving in San Diego since the 1980s, have taken the shipyard's place, employing hundreds of thousands, including highly skilled immigrants from all over the world. Many new high-tech and research laboratories have made a major contribution to the city's already impressive levels of economic and population diversity.

Sun, sand and sea. The nearly 3 million residents of greater San Diego, as well as its million visitors annually, can count on an average of 300 sunny days per year on the beach. The restful, relaxing atmosphere at Pacific Beach, Mission Beach and Ocean Beach is very different from the hectic pace of the lively beaches of Santa Monica or Venice Beach in Los Angeles. Ocean Beach is especially popular, a dream beach in every sense of the word, with inviting cafés, exclusive boutiques and pulsating discos. It is also the best destination for anyone wanting to try a whole range of water sports. Rental shops offer everything from surfboards and parasails to scuba gear and speedboats, ready to cater to any adventure.

The ocean world. A must for every visitor is Balboa Park. Known locally as San Diego's "green lung", it's the perfect place for a long stroll or pleasant picnic. There are also eighteen museums, three theatres and the famous San Diego Zoo to satisfy anyone's desire for culture and knowledge. The San Diego Zoo is the largest zoo in the world. Its oceanic counterpart, SeaWorld San Diego, is one of the largest marine parks. This Mission Bay facility is dedicated to ocean research, offering a one-of-a-kind glimpse into the world of sharks, dolphins, killer whales and penguins. SeaWorld San Diego's thoroughly entertaining exhibits and shows are but a small part of what this important scientific centre contributes to our knowledge of marine life around the world.

USA

New Orleans

LOCATED ALONG THE MISSISSIPPI RIVER BETWEEN THE TIDAL WATERS OF LAKE PONTCHARTRAIN AND THE GULF OF MEXICO, "THE BIG EASY" HAS LONG BEEN FAMOUS FOR ITS OWN BRAND OF UNIQUELY EXCITING CULTURAL LIFE.

New Orleans was once among the most important economic centres in the southern United States. When Hurricane Katrina hit New Orleans in the summer of 2005, however, it brought the metropolis most famous for its jazz musicians, Mardi Gras and an irrepressible *joie de vivre* to the brink of destruction. Flooding caused the levees protecting the city to break, and within hours, large parts of New Orleans, most of which had been built at an elevation well below sea level, stood under metres of water, and the darkest period in its history began.

The Louisiana Purchase. La Nouvelle Orléans, founded by the French in 1718, has seen three North American colonial powers come and go. Economic ventures in Louisiana failed just as miserably for the French as they did their Spanish predecessors. The British were not interested in taking risks. For them, New Orleans was just a small town on the Mississippi River, best viewed from the sugar plantations on the far shores of Lake Ponchartrain. Investing in New Orleans cost a great deal of money that brought very little in return. The Louisiana Territory, a vast area extending from the Canadian border south to New Orleans, was finally sold to the United States by the French in 1803 as part of Napoleon Bonaparte's plan

Right: Jazz musicians can be heard throughout the French Quarter.

Below: The buildings in the French Quarter testify to New Orlean's French past.

to sell off all French holdings in North America. The total area gained by the young United States was more than 2 million km^2.

By the mid-nineteenth century, New Orleans was the most important harbour on the Mississippi. After 1867, business suffered as a result of the Civil War and Reconstruction, and the city did not recover its former prosperity until the 1930s. While offshore oil drilling and onshore refineries were the main source of income in the region, New Orleans began to focus on tourism in the 1960s. The entire city was spruced up with an eye towards drawing the curious to New Orlean's unique local culture. In the mid-1970s, the gigantic Louisiana Superdome was built, at the time the world's largest fixed-dome structure. In the following years, the business district developed around the sports and convention facilities that followed.

The world famous French Quarter is located just south of the central business district. With architecture influenced by French and Spanish styles, the quarter's narrow streets and old houses with wrought-iron balconies are icons of New Orleans, as are the hundreds of arcades, cafés and bars found there. The grid-pattern street plan common to most North American cities is not in evidence here, where narrow alleys lead off cobblestone streets to secret courtyards and authentic jazz clubs. Basin and Bourbon Streets are the birthplace of New Orleans Jazz, with its brassy sound, masterfully interpreted by the city's most illustrious son, Louis Armstrong. Today, the New Orleans airport bears his name. Other sites abound. The Cathedral of Saint Louis Cathedral is located on Jackson Square in the Old Town. Royal Street, also in the French Quarter and famous for its antique stores, is also a part of New Orlean's picture-postcard image. Near Jackson Square lies the Cabildo, the former Spanish governor's palace. It is now a museum devoted to New Orleans' colourful history.

New Orlean's famous streetcars have defined the image of the city for over a hundred years. Many routes have evocative names: there really is a streetcar "named" Desire, one that terminates in the neighbourhood of that name. The Riverfront Line, fondly dubbed "Ladies in Red" because of their colour, leads into the French Quarter. The green cars of the St. Charles Line travel through the old colonial residential quarter to the Garden District, Zoological Gardens and Tulane University. It will also take you to Lafayette Cemetery No 1, site of New Orlean's most visited grave, that of voodoo queen Marie Laveau. Shrouded in an atmosphere of mystery, her final resting place is easily recognizable.

FACTS

* **Population of New Orleans:** *circa* 490,000
* **Population of the metropolitan area:** *circa* 1.3 million
* **Places of interest:** Aquarium of the Americas, Beauregard-Keyes Home, Lafayette Cemetery No 1, City Park, Confederate Memorial Hall Museum, Fort Pike State, French Quarter, Jazzland Theme Park, Louisiana State Museum, Superdome, New Orleans Historic Voodoo Museum, Preservation Hall, Storyville District

FAMOUS CITIZENS

* **Louis Armstrong** (1901–71), * **Mahalia Jackson** (1901–72) and * **Fats Domino** (b. 1928), musicians
* **Lillian Hellman** (1905–84), playwright
* **Truman Capote** (1924–84), writer
* **Randy Newman** (b. 1943), composer

USA

Miami

MIAMI SOMETIMES FEELS LIKE A HUGE HOLLYWOOD SET. THE CLICHÉS ABOUT THE CITY AND ITS ILLUSTRIOUS BEACH COMMUNITY, MIAMI BEACH – NEARLY ALL OF WHICH ARE BASED IN FACT – ARE BUT A SMALL PART OF MIAMI'S COLOURFUL MOSAIC.

International financial deals are not the only thing happening in Miami. The city's concerts, theatre performances, gallery exhibits, ballet companies and museums offer plentiful cultural stimulation and world-class entertainment. Located in picturesque south Florida, Miami is a popular location for television and movie crews. Fashion photographers from glossy magazines pose their models against the backdrop of the turquoise waters of the Gulf of Mexico or the deep blue Atlantic Ocean. Looking at Miami's striking skyline, home to corporate headquarters of hundreds of international financial institutions, it is hard to image that until recently southern Florida was a landscape dominated by mosquito-infested swamps. The first Spanish explorers of the region, arriving in 1513 with Ponce de León, declared it completely uninhabitable.

The real history of the city, which was founded on 28 July 1896, began with the advent of the railway. Freezing Canadians and New Yorkers climbed aboard to escape to beautiful, sunny Miami. In the 1920s, during the days of Prohibition, Miami was known as a city with legalized gambling and less than serious efforts to enforce the ban on alcohol. The result was a building boom. Little by little, starting with hotels and apartments, the Miami skyline began to rise.

FACTS

*** Name in the local language:** In the language of the local Seminole Native Americans, Mayaimi means "Big Water"

*** Population of Miami:** *circa* 379,700

*** Population of the metropolitan area:** *circa* 2.2 million

*** Places of interest:** Art Deco Historic District and Ocean Drive, Bal Harbour, Coral Gables, Everglades National Park, Key Biscayne, Little Havana, Miami Seaquarium, Miami Museum of Science, Miami Museum of Contemporary Art.

FAMOUS CITIZENS

*** Sidney Poitier** (b. 1924), actor

*** Deborah Harry** (b. 1945), pop singer

*** Patricia Cornwell** (b. 1956) and *** Carl Hiaasen** (b.1953), writers

*** Eva Mendes** (b. 1974), actress

Art Deco hotels lined up along the world-famous Ocean Drive.

Melting pot for Latin Americans. After Fidel Castro seized power in Cuba in 1959, a stream of refugees poured into south Florida. The impact was enormous. Hoards of Cuban refugees arrived in Miami, settling in the neighbourhood called "Little Havana". There, salsa music resounds in the streets, men play dominoes and chess in the parks, and the air is thick with the aroma of coffee and cigar smoke.
A trip along the palm-tree-lined Ocean Drive, Miami Beach's famous boulevard in the heart of its famous Art Deco district, offers breathtaking views of the Atlantic Ocean, the beach and, of course, the rich and famous. With its uniquely "Miami Style" Art Deco architecture, the entire district is under historic protection today. Rich with pastel colours and full of eclectic details, there is no other cityscape like it on Earth. Unfortunately, the building boom of the 1920s also caused considerable damage to the natural environment. Over 120 hectares of the unique Everglades wetlands were drained to provide Miami with water and sewage facilities and dry land on which to build. Even today, south Florida draws millions of litres of water from the Everglades. Interrupting the water cycle that supplies this magnificent natural landscape with moisture and nutrients diminishes the vitality of the biosphere. At present, national parks and wildlife preserves protect barely 20 per cent of the Everglades watershed. The unique flora and fauna of the Everglades were added to the UNESCO List of World Natural Heritage Sites in 1979. Still, the environment was classified as endangered in 1993.
No stay in Miami would be complete without a short trip to Coral Gables, one of the first planned communities in the country. Distinguished by its beautiful Spanish colonial-style villas, Coral Gables also boasts elegant country clubs, world-class art galleries and the University of Miami.

Above: In the area surrounding Miami, the Everglades are a unique wildlife preserve.

Left: The Venetian Pool in Coral Gables is the largest hotel pool in the continental USA.

The major cities of Australia and New Zealand all have colonial origins, skyscrapers and, of course, sunny beaches – with one exception, the inland city of Canberra. Australian beaches have white sands and palm trees, while many in New Zealand are adventure destinations with cliffs, volcanic sands, wind and waves. Each has its own unique character, yet all are "so very British".

OCEANIA

AUSTRALIA

Sydney

ON 28 JANUARY 1788, CAPTAIN ARTHUR PHILLIP'S CREW HOISTED THE UNION JACK AT SYDNEY COVE. THE MEN ON BOARD THE FIRST FLEET, INCLUDING THE 800 PRISONERS AMONG THEM, WERE THE FIRST EUROPEAN SETTLERS ON THE NEW CONTINENT.

Despite a number of initial difficulties, including despotic military governors, hunger and rebellion, by the mid-nineteenth century Sydney was eastern Australia's centre of commerce. This was in part due to the Gold Rush of 1851, which brought many immigrants to Australia's eastern shores. European and Asian immigrants have always made up a significant proportion of Sydney's population, giving the city a distinctly cosmopolitan flair.

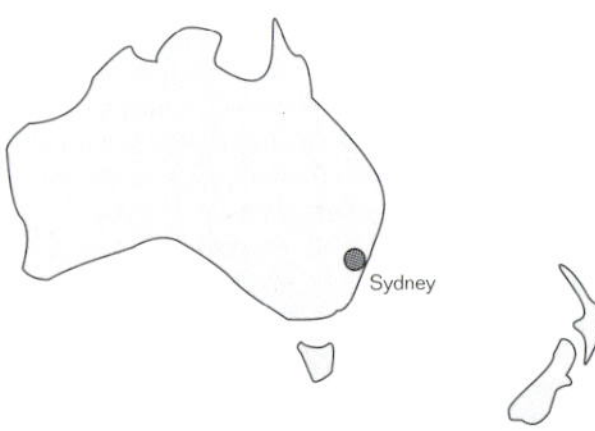

Captain James Cook's "discovery". When Cook returned to England after his 1770 voyage of discovery, he told the British authorities that the region around Botany Bay, some 29 km from the site of Sydney today, was, for all intents and purposes, uninhabited. This was far from true. The indigenous Aboriginal peoples had lived there for thousands of years. As was the case in America, the settlement of cities and the appropriation of land involved the worst sort of roguery. Thousands of Aborigines were ousted overnight, and many thousand more died of smallpox carried by the Europeans.

The lead and zinc rushes. After the dissolution of the Botany Bay penal colony in 1841, Sydney's stature improved. Its burgeoning mercantile harbour provided a boost to the local economy, and the 1851

Right: The Royal Botanic Gardens are a green oasis in front of Sydney's skyline.

Below: The Sydney Harbour Bridge connects north and south Sydney.

Gold Rush provided the immigrant labour needed to keep things running. Sydney's biggest economic boom came in the 1880s, when the largest deposits of lead, zinc and silver in the world were discovered nearby at Broken Hill. The wealth and prosperity they brought to the city led to the construction of many splendid buildings, including the Great Hall of the prestigious University of Sydney. Many lovely homes in the parishes of Paddington and Stanmore were also built during the "silver" era. Woollahra district, a bastion of the traditional, conservative and prosperous citizens of Sydney, was also developed during this period. As the city continued to upgrade its infrastructure over the course of the nineteenth century, it enlarged its harbour fortification system as well. Fort Dennison on Rock Island still stands today and is one of Sydney's most popular attractions. As part of the city's 100th anniversary festivities in 1888, Centennial Parklands was dedicated with great pomp and circumstance. It remains one of Sydney's most popular and genuinely beautiful recreation areas, conveniently located very near the city.

Federation style and the Great Depression. The beginning of the twentieth century brought a new architectural style to Australia. Federation style means large, climate-appropriate houses built primarily of local materials and set on large, landscaped lots. Land was by no means scarce at that time, and these elegant houses were built on the grandest scale possible. In 1929, everything changed. Australia and Sydney were hit by the world financial crisis brought on by the stock market crash. In the early 1930s, a few public works projects were begun to lessen the economic effects. One of these projects, which were similar to the WPA programs in the USA, led to the construction of the magnificent Sydney Harbour Bridge. Australia recovered from the crash sooner than many other parts of the world, and by 1932, things were again looking up.

Australian dream. Of all the Australian cities, Sydney is the one that most uniquely reflects the special characteristics of the people "down under". In addition to its vibrant urban lifestyle, historical buildings and sparkling nightlife, Sydney is just a stone's throw from some of Australia's most pristine natural areas. The contrast between civilized urban culture and the untamed, mysterious wilderness just beyond is all part of the Australian dream. The landmark Sydney Opera House, located in the middle of the harbour, has become the symbol of that dream for many. Immigrants still come to Sydney in droves, and the city continues to prosper and grow.

FACTS

*** Population of Sydney:**
circa 3.77 million

*** Population of the metropolitan area:**
circa 4.4 million

*** Places of interest:**
Blue Mountains, Bondi Beach, Chinatown, Harbour Bridge, Manly Beach, Sydney Aquarium, Sydney Cove, Sydney Olympic Park, Sydney Opera House, Sydney Tower, Sydney Zoo, State Theatre, The Rocks, Three Sisters

FAMOUS CITIZENS

*** Edmund Barton**
(1849–1920), politician, first prime minister of Australia

*** William McMahon**
(1908–1988), politician

*** James Clavell**
(1924–1974), writer

*** Michael Hutchence**
(1960–1997), rock singer

AUSTRALIA

Canberra

CANBERRA IS AUSTRALIA'S CAPITAL CITY. UNLIKE SYDNEY AND MELBOURNE, IT IS A PLANNED CITY, DRAWN UP QUITE RECENTLY, AT THE BEGINNING OF THE TWENTIETH CENTURY, AS THE SOLUTION TO A PROTRACTED ARGUMENT.

Both Sydney and Melbourne wanted to be Australia's capital, a dispute impossible to resolve. The solution was to create the Independent Australian Capital Territory between them, and to hold a contest for the plan of its major city, Canberra. The Australian Capital Territory is controlled by the federal government and belongs to no state of the Commonwealth. Canberra is its beautiful city, a modern metropolis with fine art galleries, impressive museums, outstanding restaurants and lots of tourist attractions. The region's national parks and wildlife refuges have paths for bush hiking, allowing people to observe animals and plants in the wild, up close.

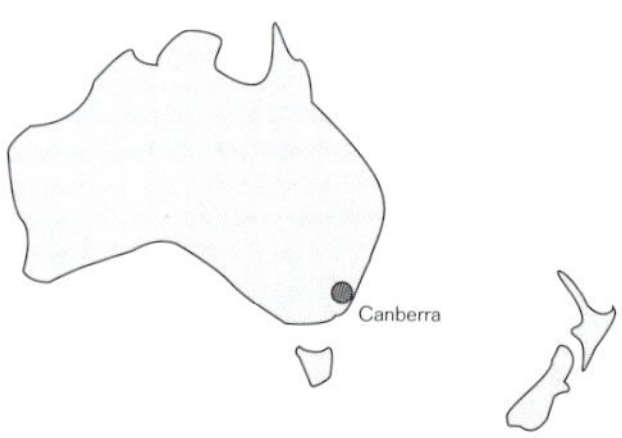

Distinct seasons. Founded on 12 March 1913, Canberra lies nestled in the natural amphitheatre formed by Mount Ainslee, Red Hill, Mount Pleasant and Black Mountain. The region is geographically known as the limestone plains, an upland plateau at an altitude of 600 metres. In contrast to the coastal cities, Canberra, with its inland location and high altitude, has four distinct seasons. In the winter, temperatures can fall below freezing point. The mountain ridges to the west and south of Canberra, as high as 1,900 metres above sea level, are covered with snow all winter, making it a skier's paradise.

FACTS

* Population of Canberra:** *circa* 320,000

✻ Places of interest: All Saints Church, Australian National Gallery, Namadgi National Park, National Aquarium and Wildlife Park, National Botanic Gardens, National Capital Exhibition, National Film and Sound Archive, National Museum of Australia, National War Museum, New Parliament House, Old Parliament House, Pine Island, Telstra Tower, Tidbinbilla Nature Reserve, War Memorial

FAMOUS CITIZENS

✻ Ross Stretton (1952–2005), ballet dancer and choreographer

✻ Richard Tognetti (b. 1965), violinist

✻ Michael Milton (b. 1973), skier

✻ Imogen Bailey (b. 1977), model

The Old Parliament House with the Australian War Memorial lies to the north of Anzac Parade.

Canberra got its name from the very first European settlement in the area, a farm station called "Canberry" founded by Joshua Moore in 1824. Canberry is a version of the area's Aboriginal name, Kamberra, which means "a gathering place". The city's architect was Walter Burley Griffin (1876–1937), a Yankee from Illinois who won the international design competition for the city in 1912. His plans involved the creation of an extensive garden city, and his intentions are still evident in the cityscape. Canberra's squares, government and administrative buildings, and numerous parks are all regularly aligned and perfectly spaced, a drawing-board city. Bureaucratic delays and the advent of World War I meant that the federal government was not able to move officially from Melbourne into the "Old" Parliament House until 1927. At that time, the city and region had just about 5,000 inhabitants. Canberra's population only began to increase significantly in the 1950s.

Nice place to live. Many Australians think of Canberra as boring, presumably because so many politicians and civil servants live there. While Canberrra cannot compete with the thrill of the world's great metropolises, it offers many other advantages. Residents appreciate the pleasant climate and proximity to nature. In summer, lakes provide great swimming, and in the winter, the snowy mountains are close enough for one-day ski trips. The city shows off its best side each spring at its annual Floriade, a massive flower show and gardening festival.

The best view of Canberra, including the New Parliament House with the artificially constructed Lake Burley Griffin in front of it, is from Mount Ainslie. Museums, galleries and many other places of interest can be found around the lake, including the National Gallery, the court building, the National Library and many smaller museums.

Above: The National War Museum resembles Islamic architecture

Left: Parliament Square, designed by native Aborigines.

AUSTRALIA

Melbourne

AS SO OFTEN IN AUSTRALIA'S HISTORY, MELBOURNE WAS FOUNDED THROUGH FRAUD WHEN ADVENTURER JOHN BATMAN, AN AUSTRALIAN FLUENT IN SEVERAL ABORIGINAL LANGUAGES, MADE A "DEAL" WITH ABORIGINES TO LEASE LAND ON BEHALF OF SPECULATORS.

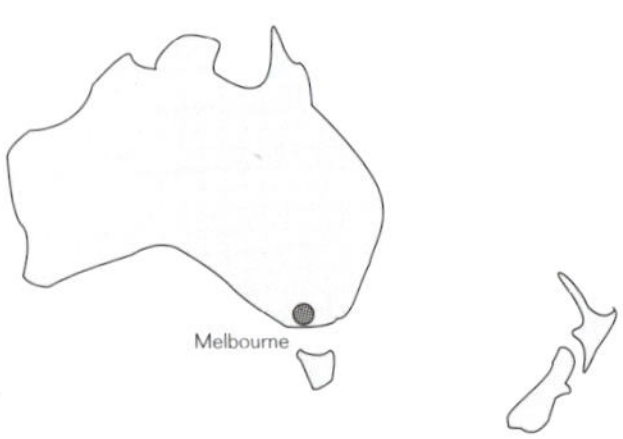

While offering the Aborigines any compensation at all was progressive in a colonial culture that preferred to simply run them off the land, the fact that the native people had little understanding of rents, leases or, indeed, the concept that land was something to be bought, sold and leased at all, made his arrangements no less exploitative. In return for a long-term lease of 240,000 hectares of the finest grazing land in Australia, Batman gave the Aborigines axes, salt, flour, blankets and jewellery. The total value of the goods was £200. Colonial administrators later declared his leases invalid, claiming that the government, not the Aborigines, were the true owners of the land. After paying Batman compensation, they took over the territory and founded a settlement as the seat of regional government. The settlement became the city of Melbourne in 1837, named after Viscount Melbourne, the British prime minister at the time.

A strict grid plan. Melbourne's location was its strongest suit. While the "acquired" farmland was of excellent quality, the city's location on the banks of the Yarra River and well-protected Port Phillip Bay contributed to its rapid commercial development. The influx of energetic immigrants and eager investors from England were factors in the economic

The Victoria Arts Centre includes the National Gallery, a splendid concert hall and a theatre complex.

FACTS

*** Population of Melbourne:** *circa* 3.38 million

*** Population of the metropolitan area:** *circa* 3.73 million

*** Places of interest:** Fitzroy Gardens (including Cook House), Flinders Street Station, Melbourne Aquarium, Melbourne Museum, National Gallery of Victoria, National Museum of Victoria, 1 Freshwater Place, Royal Exhibition Buildings, St. Patrick's Cathedral, State Parliament House

FAMOUS CITIZENS

*** Stanley Bruce** (1883–1967), politician

*** Rupert Murdoch** (b. 1931), media tycoon

*** Germaine Greer** (b. 1939), feminist writer

*** Kylie Minogue** (b. 1968), singer and actress

*** Cate Blanchett** (b. 1969), actress

development of the young city. Once the city had 5,000 residents, city planners intervened and imposed a strict grid plan to check chaotic growth in every direction. Melbourne's planners decreed that every main street would be exactly 30 metres wide, with perpendicular side streets one-third that width. The strict grid plan has been in place ever since.

Melbourne became the capital of the new Victoria Colony in 1851. As luck would have it, miners in the outback came upon a rich seam of gold just four days later. Melbourne prospered like no other city on the continent, even after the gold rush waned. A second boom was sparked by industrial development and immigration after World War II. Melbourne's population more than tripled, and the plains around the Yarra River gradually grew crowded as 3 million people from 140 nations arrived to claim their piece of the Australian dream. City planners again stepped in, authorizing the construction and development of suburbs and satellite towns. In the downtown commercial districts, Melbourne began building upwards and skyscrapers appeared on the horizon.

A rather unassuming city, Melbourne's grand sights are few in comparison to stylish Sydney. Of course, there is still a great deal to see, much of it no less interesting than the prized attractions of her arch-rival, including the Melbourne Museum, the State Parliament, the royal exhibition buildings, the Stock Market, majestic St. Patrick's Cathedral and Flinders Street Station. No 1 Freshwater Place is a luxury residential complex, with a striking, elegant design that makes it Australia's thinnest building as well as one of its tallest.

Melbourne is renowned for sports. The annual Melbourne Formula 1 Grand Prix held at the Albert Park Circuit is famous around the world, but there are many more sporting highlights to experience. The professional tennis season starts here with the Australian Open, drawing the best players in the world to compete in the first of four major tournaments. Local sports attract an even greater following. When the Magpies, Bombers and Kangaroos take the field, life is put on hold. Melbourne's football players have always been their sports heroes, but cricket and rugby are also popular. The Grand Final of the Australian Football League (AFL) takes place each year at the Melbourne Cricket Ground. One of the eight Melbourne teams usually participates.

Centre: Flinders Street Station is the most famous railway station in Australia.

Bottom: The striking Shot Tower stands in central Melbourne.

NEW ZEALAND

Auckland

IF YOU ASK AUCKLAND "TOWNIES", WHO ARE A THIRD OF ALL NEW ZEALANDERS, IT IS UNANIMOUS: AUCKLAND IS THE TRUE CAPITAL OF NEW ZEALAND. AUCKLAND RESIDENTS SIMPLY TURN A DEAF EAR TO ANY MENTION OF THE OFFICIAL CAPITAL IN WELLINGTON.

Even if it is not the official capital, Auckland is by far the largest and most important city in New Zealand. It is the first place most tourists visit, and the very heart of this green island nation. Located on New Zealand's North Island, there are holiday resorts all around Auckland. There are sandy bays with surf that invites surfing, as well as national parks with thermal hot springs and sputtering geysers. The Earth boils and bubbles here, with hot water and mud shooting up into the air. The North Island is also the home of New Zealand's most famous delicacy the kiwi fruit.

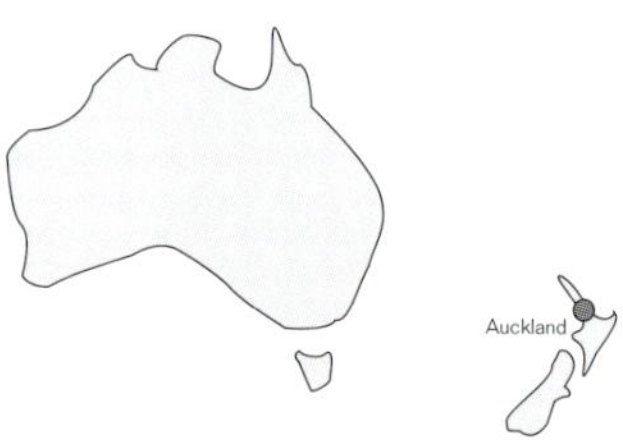

The legend of Hawaiiki. Auckland is called Tamaki Makaurau ("City of 100 Lovers") by the Maori people, because so very many people desired to settle in this fertile and sheltered location. In Maori legend and history, the site of Auckland was not an easy place to hold on to. There were always rivals ready to fight to win her back.

Where the first Maori people came from originally is still not entirely clear. According to their own legends, they migrated here from a land they call Hawaiki, presumably a group of Polynesian islands in the South Pacific. The first European to explore the region was Samuel Marsden, who mapped the North Island in 1820. The first settlement on the site of

Right: View of the skyline and Hauraki Gulf from Mount Eden.

Below: Dawn over Waitemata Harbour and the Auckland skyline.

Auckland along the Mahurangi River followed within a decade. In 1840, over fifty Maori chiefs met in Auckland to sign the Treaty of Waitangi, generally considered to mark the founding of New Zealand as a nation. From the British point of view, it gave the crown colonial rights over both islands. From the Maori point of view, it gave them special privileges in return, most of which have yet to be fulfilled. Auckland was the seat of colonial administration until 1865. From the mid- to late nineteenth century, the city grew rapidly as countless adventurers and immigrants from all over the world arrived to seek gold or harvest the valuable, amber-like resin of the Kauri tree. Many came from California, China and India. Auckland also welcomed a large contingent of Croatian immigrants. After World War II, there was a wave of immigration from the Netherlands.

Well before the turn of the twentieth century, Auckland's ethnic diversity was exceptional. Almost two-thirds of the present population can trace their origins to Europe, with the remaining third made up of Maori, Pacific Islanders and Asians. This melting pot of cultures is particularly evident in Auckland's exquisite Pacific Rim cuisine, much of which incorporates seafood from its rich fishing industry. As might be expected in a country where there are twenty-five sheep for every New Zealander, Auckland's lamb dishes and cheese specialties are also a treat. Croatian immigrants grow grapes and make wines that have won international acclaim. The oldest and best wineries in New Zealand lie just outside Auckland's city gates.

City of sails. The countryside around the city has a total of 48 volcanoes, which are inactive. Auckland is built on the slope of one of them. Parks turn the city into a green oasis, with picturesque bays framing the lush scenery. Anyone gazing out over Waitemata Harbour understands how Auckland acquired the epithet "City of Sails". Many racing yachts that have won the America's Cup call Auckland their homeport. Auckland's city centre extends right up to Waitemata Harbour. From the water, the city's entire skyline is in view.

Hauraki Maritime Park is one of the most visited destinations in the Auckland region. Founded in 1967, it extends over a huge area along the North Island's east coast, encompassing 47 islands. Among these is dreamy Waiheke Island, where New Zealand's best red wines are produced, and Motuihe Island, a favourite picnic spot. On Rakino, the summer sunshine famously bathes the exotic Pohutukawa trees in a red glow, right around Christmas time.

FACTS

* **Population of Auckland:** *circa* 417,900
* **Population of the metropolitan area:** *circa* 1.23 million
* **Places of interest:** Aotea Centre, Auckland City Gallery, Auckland War Memorial Museum, Auckland Zoo, Ferry Building, Kelly Tarlton's Antarctic Encounter and Underwater World, Mount Eden, One Tree Hill, Park Auckland Domain, Sky Tower, Town Hall, Viaduct Basin

FAMOUS CITIZENS

* **Sir Edmund Hillary** (b. 1919-2008), mountaineer
* **Sir Peter Blake** (1948–2001), America's Cup yachtsman
* **Julian Bethwaite** (b. 1957), Australian builder of sailing boats
* **Andrew Adamson** (b. 1966), director

NEW ZEALAND

Wellington

WELLINGTON, SITUATED ON THE SOUTHERN TIP OF NEW ZEALAND'S NORTHERN ISLAND, IS THE SOUTHERNMOST CAPITAL CITY IN THE WORLD. THE HEFTY WINDS THAT BLOW PERSISTENTLY OFF COOK STRAIT HAVE EARNED IT THE EPITHET "WINDY CITY".

Wedged between steep hills, Wellington's limited space for expansion has forced the city to build high in order to accommodate increased demand for commercial and residential space. Victorian structures fell victim to new construction and modernization, giving Wellington the most modern skyline in the country.

The Maori people called the area around Wellington Te Upoko o te Ika a Maui ("the Head of Maui's fish"), a reference to an incident in the Polynesian Maui Cycle when the hero, Maui, fought his brothers over a great fish, leading to the land being cut up both by the fish's thrashing tail and by their knives. When James Cook made a side trip here in 1773, the rough landscape of the bay was densely settled. Maori tribes fought one another constantly for the best coastal locations. This, along with the strong, unfavourable winds, may explain why Cook did not drop anchor and go ashore. European settlement began with the landing of the warship *Tory* on 20 September 1839. In January of the following year, William Wakefield, commander of the first expedition of the New Zealand Company, "bought" the area from the Maoris for one hundred muskets. Wakefield thus became the founder of Wellington. The city was named in honour of Arthur Wellesley, the first Duke

FACTS

✻ **Population of Wellington:** *circa* 183,900

✻ **Population of the metropolitan area:** *circa* 370,000

✻ **Places of interest:** Wellington Botanic Garden, Cable Car, Colonial Cottage Museum, Dowse Art Museum, Maritime Museum, Mount Bruce National Wildlife Centre, Mount Victoria, Museum of New Zealand Te Papa Tongarewa, National Library, Old Government Building, Old St. Paul's, Parliament House, Rimutaka Forest Park, Waterfront, Wellington Zoo, W. F. Massey Memorial

FAMOUS CITIZENS

✻ **Katherine Mansfield** (1888–1923), writer

✻ **Jane Campion** (b.1954), film director

✻ **Russell Crowe** (b. 1964), actor

✻ **James Napier** (b. 1982), actor

The cable tramway climbs up Kelburn Hill towards Wellington Botanic Gardens.

of Wellington and England's national hero in the Napoleonic Wars. Wellington was named New Zealand's capital on 26 July 1865.

Wellington is more than the political centre of the country; it has also made a name for itself as a city of culture. Wellington is the home of Te Papa, New Zealand's pioneering, interactive national museum, as well as to the New Zealand Symphony Orchestra and such national treasures as the original Treaty of Waitangi. New Zealand's most famous writer, Katherine Mansfield, was born in Wellington and published her first short stories in a local literary magazine. New Zealand's capital is remarkably diverse topographically, with mountains and hills embracing the compact city and its prodigious harbour. At the summit of Mount Victoria, which can be reached by a cable tramway built in 1902, visitors can enjoy the beauties of Kelburn Hill and the Botanic Gardens. The gardens, established in 1869, now cover 26 hectares.

Watch out for penguins! Wellington is almost certainly the only capital city in the world where penguins freely roam the streets. This encourages visitors to walk alongside them; the city centre is best experienced on foot. Visitors (and penguins) can wander through its shopping arcades, lovely cafés and, less happily, constant traffic. Nowhere else in the country is urban life lived as intensely as in Wellington.

Unique adventure tours are available along the Kapiti coast and hiking trails run all along the craggy coastline. Just off the coast, the world famous bird sanctuary of Kapiti Island attracts visitors from afar. The environs of Wellington are known for their luxurious country lifestyle. Many great estates lie inland, just over the hills. Directly north of Wellington is Hutt Valley, where visitors can arrange bush and coastal hikes, SUV trips, golfing, mountain biking and fishing.

Above: Katherine Mansfield's home is now a museum.

Left: Wellingtonians have affectionately dubbed their Parliament building "The Beehive".

Picture Credits

© Corbis: 199 b.; Bruce Adams 85 t.; Paul Almasy 8 b. 2nd fr. l., 21 t. l., 63 t. r., 142, 149 b. l.; Atlantide Phototravel 105 b. r., 113 b., 141 b.; Ricardo Azoury 33 b. l., 179 b. l., 181 t. l.; David Ball 69 t. r., 148; Peter Beck 31 t.; Bettmann 10; Bibliotheca Alexandrina 17 c.; Kristi J. Black 29 t. r., 29 b.; James P. Blair 213 b. l.; Tibor Bognár 8/9, 31 b., 70, 120, 127 b., 145 b., 167 t.; Bohemian Nomad Picturemakers 53 b. l.; B.S.P.I. 228 b. 2nd fr. l.; Luc Buerman 121 b.; Joao Luiz Bulcao 181 t. r.; Bruce Burkhardt 127 t. l.; Jan Butchofsky-Houser 175 t., 211 t.; Michelle Chaplow 233 t.; L. Clarke 221 t. l.; W. Cody 200, 201 b. r.; Stephanie Colasanti 60; Dean Conger 123 t. l.; Jerry Cooke 49 t.; Marco Cristofori 104; Richard Cummins 201 b. l., 216; Fridmar Damm 22, 97 c., 131 b. r., 196, 183 c., 169 b., 177 t. r.; Gillian Darley 157 b. l.; James Davis 15 t. r., 21 t. r.; Bennett Dean 57 t. r.; Dennis Degnan 187 b. r., 179 t.; Abbie Enock 19 b. l.; Ric Ergenbright 12; Macduff Everton 71 t., 86, 99 b. r., 155 b., 181 b., 185 b.; Eye Ubiquitous 158, 159 t. r.; Randy Faris 167 b. l.; Sandy Felsenthal 203 t. l.; Kevin Fleming 199 c.; Rufus F. Folkks 110, 219 b. l.; Owen Franken 128, 174; Free Agents Limited 35 t. r., 76 b. 2nd fr. l., 77 b. 4th fr. l., 87 t. l., 63 b., 121 c., 159 b., 207 c., 234; Franz Marc Frei 64, 89 b. l., 95 t. l., 95 b., 135 t. l., 152, 227 b. r.; Yves Gellie 43 b. l.; Audrey Gibson 212; Xavi Gomes 155 c.; Larry Dale Gordon 180, 183 b.; Philip Gould 224; Annie Griffiths Belt 51 t. l., 51 b., 211 b., 188/189 b. 3rd fr. l.; Darrel Gulin 17 b.; Rainer Hackenberg 141 t. r.; Robert Harding 69 b., 151 t. r., 189 b. 5th fr. l., 213 b. r., 215 b., 217 b., 225 t. l., 225 b.; Blaine Harrington III 65 b. r., 209 b., 217 c.; Brownie Harris 197 t. l.; Thomas Hartwell 16; Martin Harvey 9 b. 4th fr. l.; Jason Hawkes 116; Dallas and John Heaton 75 b.; Lindsay Hebberd 27 b. 5th fr. l.; Chris Hellier 147 b.; Jon Hicks 23 t. r., 55 c., 55 b., 71 b. l., 89 t., 89 b. r., 101 t. l., 101 t. r., 101 b., 109 t., 109 b., 136; David Higgs 112; So Hing-Keung 59 t.; Andrew Holbrooke 219 b. r.; Robert Holmes 18, 203 t. r., 223 b., 239 b. r.; Angelo Hornak 117 t. r.; Jeremy Horner 56, 57 b., 117 t. l., 164, 173 b.; Dave G. Houser 20, 83 b. r., 129 b. l., 159 t. l., 209 t. r., 227 b. l.; K. Imamura 77 b. 5th fr. l., 127 t. r.; Hanan Isachar 29 t. l., 51 t. r.; Harald A. Jahn 131 b. l.; Ladislav Janicek 93 t. l., 105 t., 133 t., 160; Andrea Jemolo 93 t. r.; Wolfgang Kaehler 74, 75 t. l., 161 t., 133 b., 237 t. r.; Catherine Karnow 68, 79 c.; Ed Kashi 40, 41 b., 42, 143 b. l.; Layne Kennedy 78, 201 t.; Michael John Kielty 109 c.; Karl Kinne 214; Kit Kittle 195 b. l.; Richard Klune 80, 81 t. r., 85 c., 97 b., 102, 103 t., 103 c., 103 b., 145 t., 139 b., 217 t., 221 t. r., 228/229, 229 b. 5th fr. l., 231 t. r., 235 t., 239 b. l.; Wilfried Krecichwost 228/229 b. 3th fr. l., 237 t. l.; Bob Krist 5 t., 6/7, 59 b. l., 73 c., 79 t., 150, 153 b. l.; Otto Lang 143 t.; Danny Lehman 28, 83 b. l., 140, 166, 169 t. r.; Charles & Josette Lenars 177 t. l., 229 b. 4th fr. l.; Chris Lisle 33 t., 57 t. l., 61 c., 61 b., 67 t., 69 t. l., 88, 91 t., 91 b.; Liu Liqun 31 c.; Xiaoyang Liu 46, 47 t., 47 c.; Yang Liu 26/27; Robert Landau 219 t.; London Aerial Library 119 t. r.; Benjamin Lowry 44; Araldo de Luca 4; Frank Lukasseck 27 b. 4th fr. l.; Ludovic Maisant 113 t. l.; William Manning 125 b. r.; Buddy Mays 129 b. r., 185 t. l.; Gunter Marx 191 b.; Gideon Mendel 23 t. l.; Samer Mohdad 41 c.; Gail Mooney 145 c.; Momatiuk-Eastcott 9 b. 5th fr. l.,115 t.; Sally A. Morgen 191 t. l.; Francoise de Mulder 11 t. r., 11 b.; Colin McPherson 99 t.; Mike McQueen 58; Lance Nelson 76/77, 119 b. l.; Clive Newton 45 t. r.; Michael Nicholson 161 c., 132, 133 c.; Richard T. Nowitz 25 c., 79 b., 93 b., 94, 95 t. r., 107 t. l., 119 b. r., 178, 179 b. r., 190, 221 b.; Charles O'Rear 8/9 b. 3rd fr. l., 24, 25 b., 122; Diego Lezama Orezzoli 182; Christine Osborne 14; Karlheinz Oster 5 b., 157 b. r., 238; Parrot Pascal 11 t. l.; P. Pet 8 b. far l., 19 t.; Sergio Pitamitz 26 b. far fr. l., 38, 39 t., 125 b. l., 141 t. l., 144, 171 b., 163 b. 4th fr. l., 187 t.; Ann Purcell 173 t.; Carl & Ann Purcell 21 b.; Louie Psihoyos 53 t., 126; Jose Fuste Raga 13 c., 23 b., 25 t., 32, 33 b. r., 34, 36, 37 t. l., 37 t. r., 37 b., 47 b., 52, 55 t., 62, 65 b. l., 71 b. r., 72, 73 t., 87 t. r., 92, 114, 125 t., 138, 151 b., 154, 162 b. far l., 183 t., 186, 218, 236, 239 t.; Steve Raymer 82, 84, 85 b., 96, 90; Vittoriano Rastelli 30; Carmen Redondo 19 b. r., 43 t., 115 b. r.; Roger Ressmeyer 215 t. r.; Connie Ricca 211 c.; Joel W. Rogers 162/163 b. 3rd fr. l.; Galen Rowell 81 t. l.; Bill Ross 198, 208, 209 t. l., 223 c.; Guenter Rossenbach 13 b., 15 t. l., 135 b.; Rachel Royse 137 t.; Thomas Rubbert 139 c.; Anders Ryman 15 b.; David Sailors 73 b., 188 b. 2nd fr. l., 213 t.; Santos 134; Christian Sarramon 107 t. r.; Alan Schein 188 b. far l., 226; Michel Setboun 146, 147 t. r.; ML Sinibaldi 26/27 b. 3rd fr. l., 65 t., 76/77 b. 3rd fr. l., 124, 151 t. l.; Skyscan 172; Greg Smith 176; Rainer Schmitz 111 t. r.; Schmitz-Söhnigen 111 t. l., 111 b.; Lee Snider 203 b.; Joseph Sohm 199 t., 202, 210, 220, 222; Paul A. Souders 49 b., 63 t. l., 81 b., 161 b., 189 b. 4th fr. l., 192, 193 c., 195 t., 232; Herbert Spichtinger 91 c., 131 t.; Hubert Stadler 177 b., 184, 185 t. r., 187 b. l., 194; Mark L. Stephenson 53 b. r.; Kurt Stier 83 t., 87 b.; Vince Streano 153 b. r.; Eberhard Streichan 147 t. l.; Keren Su 48, 49 c., 100, 107 b.; Rudy Sulgan 195 b. r., 197 b., 204, 205 b. l., 205 b. r., 206; Svenja-Foto 115 b. l., 169 t. l.; Murat Taner 35 b., 108, 117 b., 137 b. l., 137 b. r.; Liba Taylor 123 t. r.; Arthur Thévenart 39 b. r., 54; Paul Thompson 97 t.; Thierry Tronnel 121 t.; Turbo 205 t.; Peter Turnley 59 b. r.; Penny Tweedie 233 b. l., 233 b. r.; Sandro Vannini 98, 105 b. l., 139 t., 149 t., 149 b. r., 153 t.; Pablo Corral Vega 163 b. 5th fr. l., 165 b., 170, 171 t. l., 171 t. r., 175 b. l., 175 b. r.; Francesco Venturi 165 c.; Brian A. Vikander 39 b. l., 67 c.; Patrick Ward 76 b. far l., 106, 155 t., 156, 157 t., 227 t.; David H. Wells 26 b. 2nd fr. l., 50; Nik Wheeler 13 t., 75 t. r., 123 b., 165 t., 167 b. r., 168, 197 t. r., 223 t.; WildCountry 118; Peter c. Wilson 17 t., 162 b. 2nd fr. l., 191 t. r.; Adam Woolfitt 135 t. r., 143 b. r., 173 c.; Alison Wright 41 t., 43 b. r., 61 t.; Michael S. Yamashita 35 t. l., 45 t. l., 45 b., 66, 237 b.; Bo Zaunders 99 b. l.; David Zimmerman 188/189, 207 b.; Daniel Zheng 67 b.; Jim Zuckerman 130, 162/163

© Gerhard Klimmer: 113 t. r., 193 t., 193 b., 231 b., 235 c., 235 b.

© MEV: 215 t. l., 225 t. r.

© Thomas Uhlig: 207 t., 129 t., 228 b. far l., 230, 231 t. l.

© Getty Images: Jerry Alexander 122